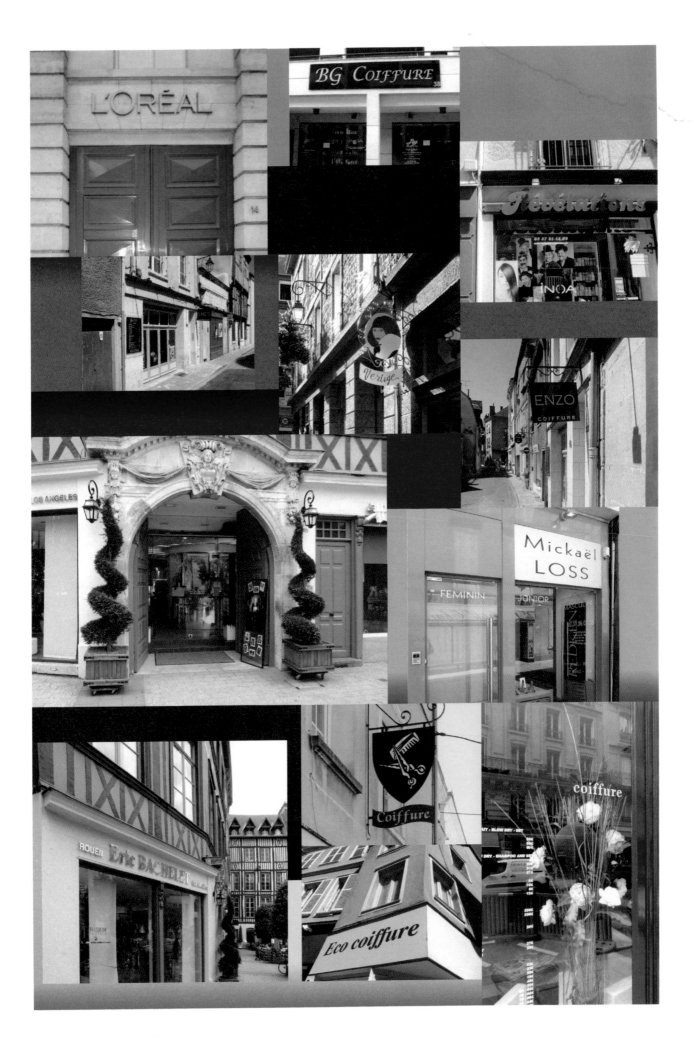

The most valuable asset of a salon is data. We are moving into a new world, a world where you have a generation of new stylists and clientele growing up never knowing anything but the internet. They are a living challenge to all of us to change the way we do business. So think big, think new, but most importantly think quick, your design of your salon today will be different tomorrow. Because if there is one thing I can tell you with absolute certainty, it is this. "The future is now."

Yesterday the world changed, now it's your turn! Jeff and Eric with their new Salon Bible will give you a look of what's happening today in the salons design, equipment and layouts around the world. With fresh ideas, most current equipment and money making design tips. You will have to wait for the next book for tomorrows ideas. One day at a time!

The Salon Building Bible

Five-Point Salon Design System
Construction Costs
Furniture & Equipment Costs
Salon Floor Plans

By Jeff Grissler & Eric Ryant

2013 Edition

"Many salon owners open their businesses without a true understanding of the importance of salon design or a solid floor plan. Typically, they don't get the upfront guidance needed to create the salon of their dreams—one built for function and profit and within their budget. The book series by Ready, Set, Go Publishing have established themselves as educational guides to salon and barbershop owners in the beauty industry. Authors and beauty industry leaders Jeff Grissler and Eric Ryant broke the mold with these books. Their philosophy is to share what they know and what they have learned from owners so that you don't have to make the same mistakes. Why wouldn't you want to learn from others and their mistakes? Avoiding expensive mistakes is a smarter way to start your business. Their book series guide you through the entire process of opening, remodeling, and managing a salon or barbershop business. This new book, "The Salon Building Bible," which gives you everything you need to design a salon (including a numerous floor plans and tons of advice) is the first of its kind and is exactly what the salon industry needs. My hope is that new and seasoned salon and barbershop owners invest in a copy of this book. Not only will they end up building the salon of their dreams, but they will save money while designing and building a highly functional and profitable salon. This is an opportunity to shape their future, but also create the lifestyle that they deserve to lead as business owners."

—Patrick T. Parenty, President of L'Oreal USA,
Professional Products Division

Books by Jeff Grissler and Eric Ryant

Ready Set Go Publishing, LLC

Ready, Set, Go! THE SALON BUILDING BIBLE

Five-Point Salon Design System • Salon Floor Plans • Furniture & Equipment Costs • Construction Costs
Find other Ready Set Go series books on www.salonresourceguide.com

© 2013 Jeff Grissler and Eric Ryant. All Rights Reserved.

First edition.

Published in the U.S. by Ready Set Go Publishing, LLC

1697 Mapleton Avenue, Boulder, Colorado 80304

Printed in the United States of America

ISBN 978-0-9855802-4-7 (p)

ISBN 978-0-9855802-6-1 (e)

About the Authors

Jeff Grissler has been where you are and understands the inner workings of the hair industry and what leads to success as a salon or barbershop owner. As a business owner himself, he knows the business landscape and what owners can expect and guides them to success. Jeff is a partner of and the National Sales Manager for Quest Resources—one of the hair industry's leading financing companies for furniture and equipment. His career in finance actually began on Wall Street and he has been involved in the multimillion dollar hair and beauty industry for over 20 years. Jeff has financed over 15,000 salons and barbershops to help them open their doors or complete their remodeling project through creative financing strategies.

Published in many hair and beauty trade magazines, Jeff is setting a new business standard in the hair industry as we see it today. Jeff has a portfolio of over 600 million dollars in salon and barbershop financing and a network of over 150 manufacturers, distributors, and vendors. A gifted businessman and consultant, Jeff prides himself on his networking ability to bring people together to share new ideas and explore partnerships and marketing techniques. Through his skilled negotiations, he has convinced the banking industry to lift restrictions from the hair and beauty industry. He has also negotiated

contracts and leases with salon/barbershop owners, spa owners, distributors, manufacturers, and banking management.

Jeff was born in New York City before moving to the Jersey Shore. He was a New York City fireman for 15+ years and served during 911. Jeff now resides in Wilmington, NC with his wife, Coleen, and their three children—Kaytlyn, JT, and Julianna Rose.

Jeff offers consulting services to current salon/barbershop owners and to those who have ownership of a salon, barbering, nail, or spa business in their near-term or future career plans. To reach Jeff, you can contact him directly at jeffgrissler@gmail.com.

Eric Ryant is a beauty industry entrepreneur with over 30 years of experience in space planning and design for salons and barbershops. No stranger to the hair and beauty industry, Eric spent many years developing new designs and space plans, getting involved in every facet of the industry. Since the 1980s, Eric has imported salon and barbering furniture from many countries, such as Italy, Germany, Holland, and China, bringing in the latest trends and styles for the U.S. market. Prior to writing this book, Eric owned several successful businesses, all involved in the hair and beauty industry, from a small chain of beauty stores to a cabinet manufacturing facility. He has also collaborated with companies such as Sally Beauty Supply, L'Oreal and The Nailco Group.

Eric's vision is to help business owners to create their dreams with a cost-effective business model and ensure that they stay within budget for the long haul. As part of his successful career, he now teaches and consults with other organizations on how to achieve the same success. Eric can be reached at ericryant@gmail.com.

Acknowledgements

"I never perfected an invention that I did not think about in terms of the service it might give others . . . I find out what the world needs, then I proceed to invent."

—Thomas Edison

It is our hope that the Ready, Set, Go book series will inspire, energize, and lead you to the successful business of your dreams.

Jeff Grissler

You never really understand how important your friends and family are until you take on a large project. The Ready, Set, Go! book series has opened my eyes to how educational books can help so many people. The response from around the country from stylists and future and current salon owners has given me the energy to continue with the book series. The amount of effort that goes into these books is overwhelming. The positive responses from our readers, encouragement from industry friends and supporters, and the motivation from my family and friends keeps me going and thinking about new ways to help my colleagues in the beauty industry. Thank you for believing in me and the RSG Books.

Eric Ryant

This book has been a fascinating project. I would like to acknowledge my brother Marc who, through the years, has designed many salons and is still involved in the industry. I also want to send my love to my three children, Chase, Kendall, and Sloane, who have always been by my side through thick and thin. I am truly blessed to have three wonderful children. They were surprised when I wrote the first book. Now, after finishing the fifth book, they see that anything is possible if you put your mind to it. It is a great feeling to not only inspire my beauty industry colleagues, but also my children.

INTRODUCTION

Congratulations on your first step to creating your dream salon. By buying this book, you've proven that you are serious about your salon business and your future as a salon owner. You probably understand that design and space planning are distinct from other aspects of a salon business. Designing the space of a brand new salon can be one of the most challenging, yet rewarding, aspects of the business.

Although there are specific building codes and requirements that you must meet, you can still use your creativity while incorporating the exact needs and specifications of your business plan and site. This book can help you navigate through the process of:

- Designing your own salon.

- Choosing your salon equipment.

- Understanding of the labor and material costs to build out a new salon or remodel your existing salon.

Whether you are hiring a designer or doing the majority of the design/build yourself, this book gives you everything you need to get started, including floor plans, pricing sheets, and more. With the information provided in this book, you will be able to make an accurate assessment of the total cost for the build-out or remodel of your salon. Plus, you'll be able to make heads or tails of proposals from salon furniture/equipment suppliers, architects, and contractors.

The design and space planning of your business can make a difference in the success or failure of your salon. A well-designed salon maximizes income generating potential. Creating the right design sets you on the path for:

- An optimized work space which results in a harmonious and productive work environment for your staff.

- An atmosphere that encourages loyal patronage and satisfaction.

So how do we achieve this? Our exclusive Five-Point Salon Design System looks intensely at the five major areas of every salon.

★ **POINT #1:** The Entrance (Doorway/Front Desk/Waiting Area)

★ **POINT #2:** The Store Inside Your Salon (Retail Area)

★ **POINT #3:** Your Bread & Butter (Service Area)

★ **POINT #4:** Let Your Color Shine (Color/Dispensary Area)

★ **POINT #5:** Behind the Scenes (Utility Area)

Keeping focused on the function and productivity of these areas will lead to an efficient and profitable salon. We'll teach you how to look critically at these five areas, showing you how to assess each one. By guiding you through the design process area-by-area, you'll be able to think through the various aspects of designing a salon that you may not have considered. Even better, you'll save money and time with the ready-to-use floor plans that we provide in this book and also through the facts, tips and checklists that we've included.

With 13 ready-to-use floor plans, we are certain that you'll find one that meets your needs or that can be adjusted slightly to incorporate your desired design features. Plus, each floor plan comes with a cost breakdown. Half of the challenge is getting a handle on what to really expect to pay for the build out of your new salon. Many new salon prospects sign a lease on a property without having a true understanding of the costs associated with opening a business. We break down each of the floor plans with labor and material costs and three different levels of furniture/equipment costs for budget, medium, and high-end salons. This allows you to eliminate any costly mistakes and puts you on the fast-track to success. Why go into a new business over budget and without any operating money to startup because you spent it on designs, construction overruns, and equipment you couldn't afford.

At the end of the book, you'll also find one chapter that helps you to reassess after a year, three years and five years to determine whether the design used in your salon still serves to make your business sustainable and profitable. When it is time to refresh your salon, you'll find another chapter that is full of ideas for how to schedule in remodels for an operating salon and how to make some budget-friendly updates.

Ready, Set, Go!

TABLE OF CONTENTS

PART I

DESIGN BASICS &
THE FIVE-POINT SALON DESIGN SYSTEM

CHAPTER 1

The Tale of Three Salon Designs

"The salon is your dream, your dream can become a reality. Just manifest it."

—Eric Ryant

Follow along with me in this hypothetical story about your life in the beauty industry.

Early on in your career, you worked as hard as you could to save for your future. You climbed your way up and became a superstar stylist. Then, you got married and bought your first home. You started a family. You moved to a different home to accommodate your growing family. You continued working hard as a stylist in a salon and changed salons once or twice to advance your career. Your children went from babies in daycare, to young children in elementary, and are now in their teenage years. Life is always moving forward.

You've found that there is always something motivating you to work and support the lifestyle that you have chosen for you and your family. You are at the point in your career when opening and running a salon is the next logical step for your own aspirations and advancement. But, you have to do it right and within budget. College expenses are knocking at your door in the near future.

Most new salon owners test the waters with a smaller salon in the beginning to see if they can handle the demands of salon ownership and the responsibility of running a business. So, you too decided to follow suit and started out small. As your business matured, you changed it to meet your personal needs, the needs of your clients, and the needs of your new salon family—your employees.

You found that your salon business really took off, even better than what you hoped and anticipated. A few years in, you realized that it was the right time to scale up. You took advantage of some additional retail space next to your salon and remodeled to expand the

1

services offered and the retail area to increase sales, revenue, and profit. Thankfully, you didn't have to move your salon in order to get the space that you needed.

Sounds like the same issues you dealt with when your family was expanding and growing, right? Sometimes, you "grow out" of what you have. With hard work and determination, you manage to make enough or save enough to remodel your home or move to a bigger house with more bedrooms and a bigger yard. The same is true with your salon; when the time is right, you need to rethink your business and your offerings. In order to keep your customers and beat the competition, remodeling, expanding, or moving your salon are strategic decisions for the health and success of your business.

Now, continuing with the story, let's say that 15 more years have passed. You still own the salon, but your needs are different and your clients expectations have changed. Your kids are done with college and have gotten married. You and your spouse feel that it is time to work less so that you can take more time off to travel, care for your parents, and be available to help care for your soon-to-arrive first grandbaby. Plus, you've taken a good look at the surrounding area of your salon and things are not quite what they used to be.

To put this in perspective, think about your first home and the neighborhood that you moved into. When you first bought your house, the homes were beautiful with well-manicured lawns and you loved the neighborhood and surrounding area. Over time, things began to change. Your friends moved away. Traffic doubled and maybe crime became an issue. This may have been a factor when you moved your family to your next, bigger home. The point is that neighborhoods, that were once up and coming, can change into undesirable areas.

That's no different than when you first opened your salon. Things change, neighborhoods change, strip malls get old, traffic patterns change. And, guess what? Your customers and their needs change too. All of these things are part of growing up. As I said before, life continues; it never stops. Houses get old and need repair or updates. Neighborhoods turn for the worse. And, businesses and their locations are no different.

So, with all of the changes in the area of your salon, you decide that it's time for some adjustments. First, you will need to hire a manager for the times when you are away from the salon. Second, you need to downscale. To make this work, you must:

- Retain your current customers.
- Keep it profitable.
- Attract new clients.
- Maintain a retail focus.

You decide that you need to move your salon to a new area that is "buzzing" with activity, but is close enough and convenient for your loyal client base. You realize that the three extra treatment rooms for services that were hot 15 years ago are no longer in demand and not needed which means you don't need as much space. The reduced square footage means fewer services, but more focused offerings and a big savings in your rent and utilities. Your salon will be in a new part of town—which was earmarked for a well-funded and marketed development program. Rent is still affordable to attract new businesses. There are no other salons in this newly developed part of town which is a major bonus. The area has a ton of foot traffic and media attention. You close on the lease and now you are ready to design your new space! And, life continues . . .

The journey you just read may be similar to yours or you may be just embarking on your career or starting up your very first salon. I can say for certain that the designs, floor plans, equipment, lighting, accents, and branding that you decide on today will change at some point. Change is a must if you want to be successful in this industry and with your business. The following stories will give you a firsthand look at why it's necessary to adapt, change your business philosophies, and do things differently for continued business success.

As you read each one of the stories, you may find that you identify with one of these salon owners and the designs that they picked. We are telling you the tale of these three salon designs for a few reasons.

1. Each salon owner is at a different place in their business and life.
2. The square footage of the salon doesn't matter; it's all in the design and the details and the needs of each salon owner.
3. Budget is the most important thing when it comes to deciding on a location, followed by design, construction, and equipment/furniture.

You can build the salon of your dreams that is within your budget. By using the advice and resources in this book, you'll be ahead of the game (rather than behind the eight ball) because you did not overspend on design, construction, and salon equipment—which are common, costly mistakes made by first time-salon owners.

This book is the first of its kind, allowing you to use one of our 13 designs (see Ready-to-Use Floor Plans & Pricing Models). These are floor plans that you can take away and even alter if need be. Each design includes almost down to the penny what it should cost to build exactly what you want, giving you the information you need to make decisions and determine your budget for construction, furniture, equipment, paint, walls, flooring, ceilings, lighting, accessories, and more.

Salon	About the Salon Owner	How They Took Their Dream and Made It a Reality
A Cut Above	I have worked in the industry for 10 years. I knew from day one of graduating cosmetology school I would own my own salon. I love color and fashion so that was how I envisioned my salon design with both in mind. To this day I have people tell me I have the coolest, fashionable salon in the area.	I knew opening my salon would not be cheap. I worked hard and saved as much as possible. I then went to my parents and asked for help. The amount I needed wasn't crazy. So, they were willing to lend me the difference to get me started. I found a great location and designer. My brother was the contractor. The pieces all came together wonderfully. I couldn't have asked for more. I was blessed with a great family that enabled me to open the salon of my dreams.
Signature Strip Mall Salon	I worked in this salon for eight years. I had the opportunity to buy the existing business. It was in a strip mall, but the salon itself needed a total makeover. I loved the clientele; so, I didn't want to move the location. Plus, it was close to home. We have two major anchors in the strip mall. So, regular traffic creates great walk-in business and it's close to everything.	The salon owner came to me first because I had worked for her the longest. She saw an opportunity in me and realized that I was the only one in the salon that could take over her business and help her with her retirement. My husband is a police officer with a good, steady income. We went to our local bank with a business plan. They approved us for a business loan. We remodeled. Business has grown. I couldn't be happier. My daughter is now in cosmetology school and will be joining the business next year. Love it!
Cutting Edge Salon	I owned a salon before and sold it. I have been cutting hair for over 20 years. After swearing I would never do it again, I knew exactly what I wanted: more efficiency, retail-oriented, and close to my home and family. This design and location reflects everything that I want in my salon business this time around.	I had raised my children and knew it was time to open a salon again. This time I would be more focused. With my other salon, I had small children who needed more of my attention. I didn't have enough money saved to open the salon I really wanted. I have been building a "new salon fund" for a very long time. I have saved and saved for this project. I had a budget in mind, but needed the right location. When I found exactly what I wanted, I jumped on it. I immediately hired a designer and ordered the furniture and equipment that I wanted. I was ready to go!

"A Cut Above" (750 sq. feet)

The most exciting feature about this salon design is the shampoo/color area. They have allotted a large amount of square footage for this area to create a dramatic affect. The storage behind the shampoo bowls double as the back bar and (2) separate color mixing counters and displays. With the wall mounted processors flanking each side, the look is very clean and modern.

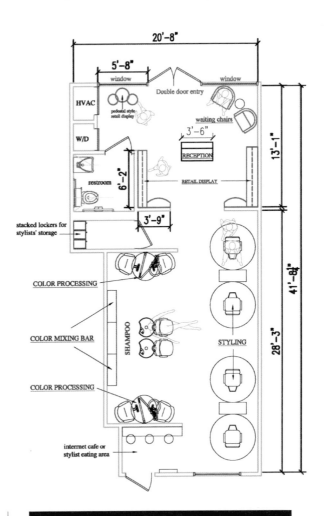

Point #1 (Doorway/Front Desk/Waiting Area)

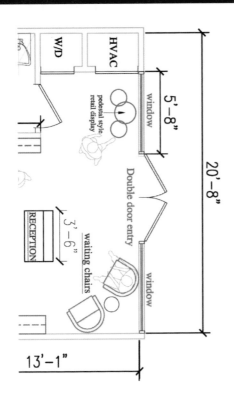

Point #2 (Retail Area)

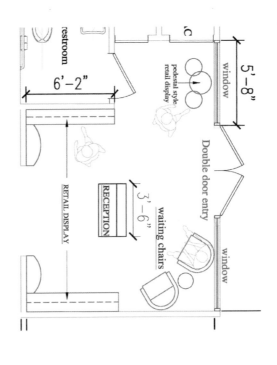

Point #3 (Service Area)

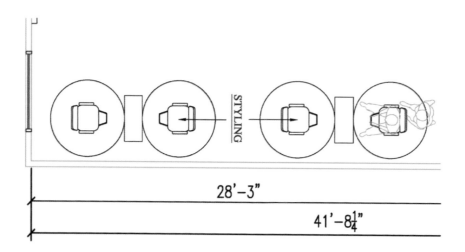

28'-3"

41'-8¼"

Point #4 (Color/Dispensary)

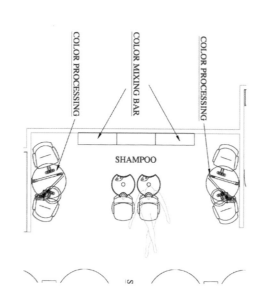

COLOR PROCESSING

COLOR MIXING BAR

COLOR PROCESSING

SHAMPOO

Point #5 (Utility)

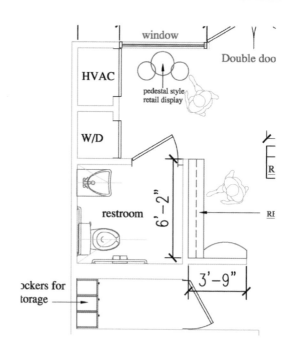

window

Double doo

HVAC

pedestal style
retail display

W/D

6'-2"

restroom

3'-9"

ckers for
torage

"Signature Strip Mall Salon" (1380 sq. feet)

This floor plan has many interesting features. The best element is definitely the exposed color bar. Many salon owners tend to put the color areas closer to the back of the space for client privacy. However, this owner chose to make the color bar more of a focal point within the salon with visibility from the retail, styling, and drying areas.

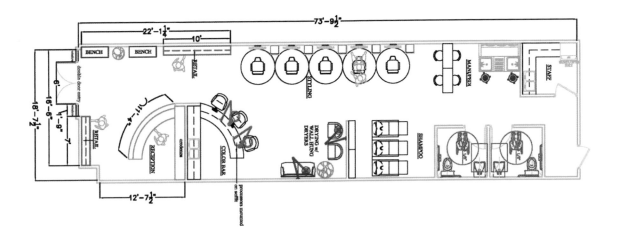

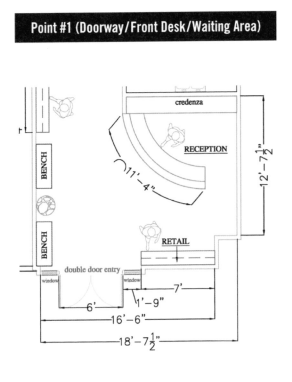

Point #1 (Doorway/Front Desk/Waiting Area)

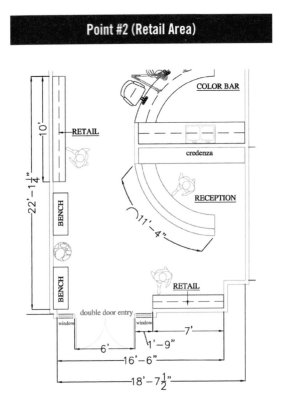

Point #2 (Retail Area)

Point #3 (Service Area)

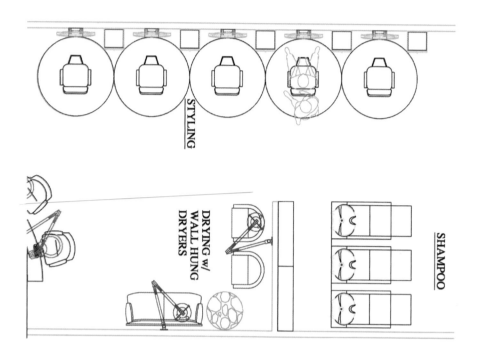

STYLING

DRYING w/
WALL HUNG
DRYERS

SHAMPOO

Point #4 (Color/Dispensary)

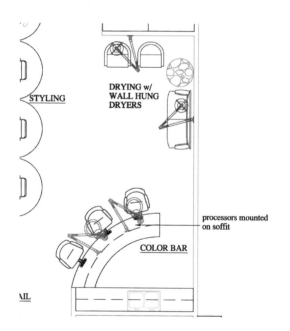

STYLING

DRYING w/
WALL HUNG
DRYERS

processors mounted
on soffit

COLOR BAR

Point #5 (Utility)

WASHER/DRYER STACK

STAFF

"Cutting Edge Salon"
(3500 sq. feet)

The best feature of this layout is the overall traffic flow and open feeling of the salon area. All service areas are easily accessible to each other, which cuts down the travel time back and forth. Maintaining a good work flow is hard to accomplish in large salon settings!

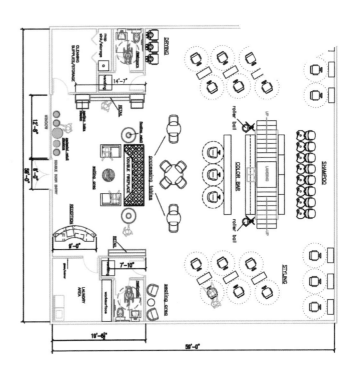

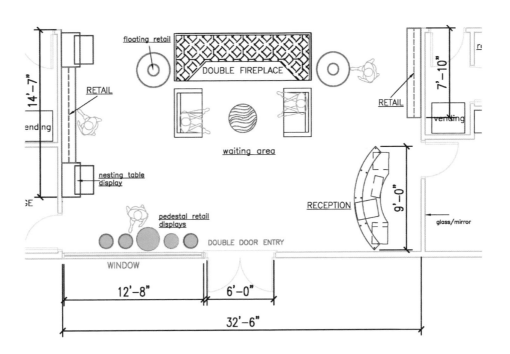

Point #1 (Doorway/Front Desk/Waiting Area) & Point #2 (Retail Area)

Point #3 (Service Area)

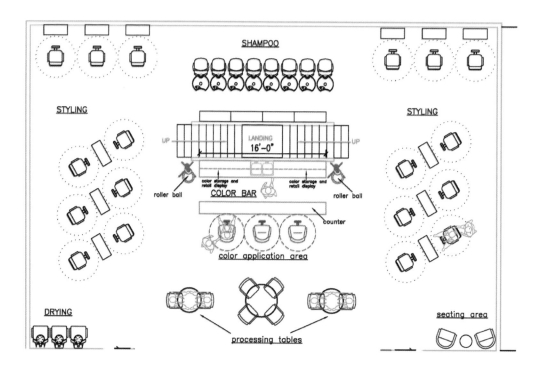

Point #4 (Color/Dispensary)

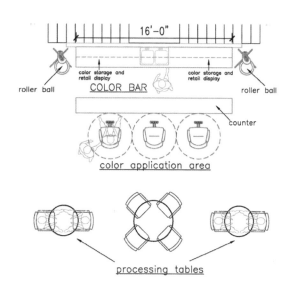

Point #5 (Utility)

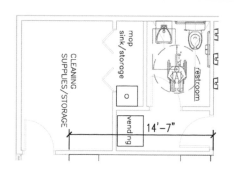

Note: There are two utility areas. One on each side of the salon.

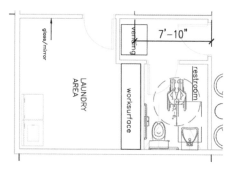

CHAPTER 2

The Five-Point Salon Design System

"Everything is designed. Few things are designed well."

—Brian Reed

As you can imagine, designing a salon is more than just choosing the color for the walls and deciding how many work stations and sinks to install. There is serious work and planning that goes into designing. You have to consider not only what you want, but also the needs of your future employees and/or booth renters and your clients. Plus, there are government requirements and regulations, building codes, and environmental compliance issues that you must meet and properly address in order to operate your business.

The design you choose is something you will have to live with for a long time. The salon furniture you purchase will most likely be built to fit into specific areas of your salon. Change does not come easy and modifications could get expensive. So, make sure that you are happy with the design you choose. It is better to make design changes on paper rather than down the road—once your salon is built out and already open for business.

Many salon owners will establish their business in an existing space, which means making your vision fit the space you have chosen. This is not always an easy task.

If you decide on an older location, the salon you may have always envisioned could come at a much higher construction expense than you initially thought. It's almost always true that older buildings mean older plumbing, electric, air conditioning, and flooring. The list of updates may go on forever, unless the building has undergone some recent modifications. To get an older building up to par and ready as a trendy, fashionable salon could be quite expensive.

Fortunately, many newer storefronts (whether on city streets, strip malls or boutique shopping villages) have the basic layouts: a "sales" floor, checkout/reception counter, storage room, at least one restroom, and an employee area of some sort.

Often, the spaces that are available for rent or lease in a strip mall are rectangular. In most shopping centers, you'll find spaces with following standard dimensions:

- 20'x60' or 1200 square feet
- 20'x70' or 1400 square feet
- 30'x80' or 2400 square feet

These standard dimensions allow you to cost-effectively transform it from what it was in a former life into your own space.

Within your salon, you'll have designated square footage for each of the areas and departments for the operation of your salon. Your exact square footage must be optimized for the success of your salon. The space, structural elements, functional areas, flow patterns, electricity, and plumbing all need to figure into the design, as well as the aesthetics. The square footage needed for each area is both practical and psychological. Each of these areas or departments has specific and unique needs for:

- Efficient operation
- Electricity and plumbing
- Flooring, lighting, storage, and display

Overall, you don't want too much or too little space or the salon will look either empty or cramped. Traffic flow and sightlines are also influenced by the design. You don't want employees or clients bumping into each other or impeding their movement around the salon. You don't want a wall of retail that blocks the view of other retail products or feels oppressive or limiting to the client.

Remember, the larger, modern salons often double as spas, offering waxing, massage, facials, or new treatments such as aromatherapy. Do you plan to have these types of extended services? If so, you may need to plan for private rooms that are separate from the rest of the spa. Don't forget that each extended service that you provide also means additional opportunities for retail and the need for retail display.

Through the Five-Point Salon Design System, the design is broken down into five major areas with all the facets and features for each area (described in the table that follows).

★ Five-Point Salon Design System ★

POINT #1: The Entrance (Doorway/Front Desk/Waiting Area)

Start with the idea of welcoming and opulence. Move your front desk deeper into the salon. It's called the front desk, but it doesn't have to be right in the front. It should be visible from the front door; but, it could be placed quite a ways back or to the side of the entrance. If you put it deeper into the salon, you encourage clients to become aware of and explore the salon's retail zone before walking straight to the desk.

POINT #2: The Store Inside Your Salon (Retail Area)

Encourage browsing with a grocery store design. Grocery stores encourage you to visit every area of the store by spreading out essentials—vegetables, deli, bread, eggs, butter and milk—across the floor, leading you from one to the other, showing you other items for sale along the way. Design your retail area in a similar way. Space out top-selling products to give your clients the chance to see other products for sale.

POINT #3: Your Bread & Butter (Service Area)

This area includes all your services: hair styling, manicure/pedicure, makeup/skin care, massage, etc. These are hard-working areas so they should be laid out in such a way as to minimize the movements necessary by your stylists and technicians, while giving them enough room for full access. Lots of accessible storage and shelving is important. There should be a balance of privacy and community feeling in these areas. Obviously a massage area needs to have visual privacy. A pedicure area might be best separated from the rest of the salon, but with a view to it. Styling areas need to make the client feel special and attended to while not separating them from interaction with other clients.

POINT #4: Let Your Color Shine (Color & Dispensary Area)

The color area has become the new focal point in salons around the country. Gone are the old Formica cabinets with the sinks attached to the wall. Many salons use the color/ wash area as a gathering spot instead of hiding this behind a full or half wall. Salons look to this area as a new means of making money by offering paraffin washes and shampoo massages or condition plus shampoos. The color dispensary is no longer in the back room. They are front and center, a place where it is not uncommon to have a color consult with your client as she watches you miss the magic formula that will make her hair beautiful. These areas are the new hot spots in the salon that can easily separate your place of business from a competitor around the corner.

Five-Point Salon Design System (cont'd)

POINT #5: Behind the Scenes (Utility Area)

There are certain areas in the salon that we cannot forget about that are critical in the functionality of any busy salon. Let's not overlook the importance of a break room for your staff. We all need a place to rest are feet and eat lunch or make a quick phone call, without a break room your staff will eat lunch and make calls from their cell phones while at their station. That's a critical design flaw. If you have the room, then you should incorporate a break room into your salon plan.

Don't forget about a utility room. If you are fortunate to have the space, your break room can house your washer/dryer, utility sink, a refrigerator, storage cabinets, and a small table for your staff. For some, the utility room may also need to hold the furnace. Many times, the break room/utility room also acts as a dispensary room if you don't have the space in the salon area. In many cases, this area becomes the all-purpose room. A lot goes on in this area so it's important not to overlook this area in the scope of your design.

You'll also need to plan out how many restrooms and changing rooms that you'll need or if you'll design your restrooms so that they can double as a changing room. There may also be building code requirements for the number of bathrooms that you have in your salon. Before planning these areas, you should know the types of services that you will offer and how many service providers you will have. Most importantly, don't forget to make sure that your restrooms meet all building code requirements for handicap accessibility.

An important concept in building design is layout. A lot of thought needs to go into how each area of the salon flows into the next area. Each area is critically important to the success of the business as each area is dependent on the others. A successful retail salon can communicate with clients that they are beauty experts by laying out their salon in such a way that showcases the products that they carry. The flow of traffic through your salon should make sense. The arrangement of retail displays and products encourages interactions and sales. The aesthetics and general atmosphere communicates your brand, message—affordable luxury, edgy, posh, community, etc.

Good design, including thoughtful planning for each of the areas in your salon will help you create the atmosphere and experience that you have envisioned for your salon. The upcoming chapters will dive into the details of each of the five areas and give you tips on:

- How to design each area to be efficient and esthetically pleasing
- How to take advantage of space for retail sales
- How to layout your floor plan to encourage clients to book more services
- How to use furniture and equipment as design elements

But, before you move on, think about the following:

- What are your thoughts around how you would like to set up the flow of your salon?
- What is the brand message that you want to convey for your salon?
- What is the atmosphere that you want to create … for both your employees and your clients? Is it exclusive? Is it chic? Is it homey? Is it ultra-trendy?

Salon Owners Talk About . . . the Good, the Bad, and the Ugly

For a recent salon, Rita Hazan of Rita Hazan Salon, said, "I took an empty, 8,000 square foot space and built it out exactly the way I wanted. Each outlet, each station, the floors – and this time, every single aspect was considered based on wear and tear and chosen to look beautiful and glamorous…and to last."

Ready, Set, Go! Expert Advice!

The fresh appeal of open salon layouts is taking root with startups. Studies have shown that employees like to congregate for official and social purposes. Open spaces enhance collaboration and cooperation among workers. Greater productivity is achieved when employees are given the opportunity to contribute to a common goal in a supportive environment that encourages teamwork and cohesiveness.

CHAPTER 3

Point #1 - The Entrance
(Doorway/Front Desk/Waiting Area)

"An entry is like a great party invitation: it sets the tone for what's to come."

—Tobi Fairley

First impressions are everything! You do not get a second chance to make a first impression. When walking into your salon, the most important thing is the client's first impression or the "WOW" factor. The experience from the moment they walk into your salon will set the tone in your client's mind about your salon. It is very important to give an excellent "first impression."

So, where does the first impression begin from a "design" perspective? You guessed it! Your first chance to create a first impression is from your salon's exterior. This is how you welcome your clients and attract clients who are walking or driving by your salon. When clients come through your doorway, they continue building their impression, quickly assessing whether your establishment feels safe, trustworthy, and professional. So, it's important to not only look at the interior floor plans, but what you want to do with the exterior that will tie everything together.

For just a moment, imagine yourself in the shoes of a first-time client. If it helps, think about a new store that you visited recently and the entryway of that business.

- What did you see?
- How did you feel?
- Did you feel like it was inviting? If so, what made it feel that way to you?
- Did you understand what type of business you were stepping into? If not, what confusing messages were sent from the exterior?
- Did you feel excited about entering this doorway? Did you feel like you couldn't wait to get in? If not, what simple changes flashed through your mind that could have made the exterior more exciting?

Doorway to Wealth

The front door is **OPPORTUNITY**. Every time a client walks through those doors, another opportunity arises. We all know that opportunities bring greater wealth, new clients, happier employees, and the potential for increased sales, which makes for a healthy, profitable business.

> **Salon Owners Talk About . . .**
> **the Good, the Bad, and the Ugly**
>
> "Your doorway and entrance, they have to appeal to all five of your senses. You have one shot and that's it; make it a good one."
>
> —Jill Krahn, Hair Success Salon and Spas, Fargo, ND

As you can imagine, an untidy, drab, or obscure entrance deters clients. Therefore, the front entrance plays a special role in the energy that flows through your place of business. Our experience in the industry has given us some special insight into creating an inviting entrance to salons. Following, you'll find a few ideas that can draw in new clients, create sales, and boost your bottom line.

Establish a Sense of Safety—The entrance to your salon is the first impression of your business. Aside from your services and your style, it should be approachable from the outside. Clients will be repelled by an entry that is dirty or dimly lit. They will be afraid to enter a dark hallway or turn unknown corners. Be sure the entryway is wide, bright, and clean.

Create an Identity—The entrance gives the first clues of what lies beyond the door, it is important to create a clearly defined, professional identity. You can do this by using items that convey the personality and uniqueness of what your business has to offer. Colors, shapes, images, and lighting choices all work together to form an impression on the potential client. A well-planned salon is as unique as the clients who walk through the door. Be creative; but, be mindful of the result that your design will have. Always ask yourself, "Is this going to attract or repel my targeted client demographic?" Take a moment to think about the type of client that would be attracted to these two different entryways:

- Homey feel with warm colors, soft lights, and images of nature.
- High tech, with exposed pipes, high contrast colors, industrial or abstract art, and stark lighting.

Channel Clients into the Salon—Use hip-height items (such as: furnishings, rails, partial walls) around the entryway, which provide a subtle, supportive energy, both physically and emotionally. Entryways that have the feeling of support are less stressful to cross and encourage shoppers to relax and diffuse any discomfort that they may have. Large, bare entryways may scare people off and often intimidate the first-time client because they feel vulnerable. Keeping fixtures below eye level in the entry area also allows more sightlines into the salon.

Keep It Clean—Clean the storefront daily. Remove clutter and dirt top to bottom. Clean the door handle and make sure if you have a glass door it is cleaned before you open for business. Just by sweeping the sidewalks and cleaning the door and windows daily, you demonstrate the pride you take in your business—one element leading to consumer confidence.

Promote Your Brand—In addition to your sign, use storefront banners. Make the most of your entrance by promoting your brand and the retail products your store sells. Your sign, banners, and window displays should not overwhelm your clients and should be easy to read.

Put Out the Welcome Mat—Place a welcome mat in front of your entry door. This mat symbolizes that the owner is welcoming you into his place of business. It's a small touch that can also help a salon stay clean. Make sure to quickly replace worn out mats.

Install an Awning—Awnings provide aesthetics and function. It's also another prominent location for your salon's name and logo. By using color and design, you'll offer a hint of the style to expect inside the salon. With an attractive and practical awning, people are protected from the elements such as wind and rain. Passersby are much more likely to stop, look at window displays, peek inside, and even enter if you can pique their curiosity. The awning may also allow a retail business the ability to display their merchandise outside to draw in clients regardless of the weather.

> ### Salon Owners Talk About . . .
> ### the Good, the Bad, and the Ugly
>
> "My outside is brick with beautiful awnings painted black with white trim. We have many walk-in customers because of the cool, slick vibe the building gives off."
>
> —Marybeth Fiore, Hair Trendz, Storrs, CT

Light the Way—Lighting an awning gives good light and makes your entrance glow at night. If you don't have an awning (or if you can't add one due to building/code constraints), consider adding new lights to the exterior of your salon. Place them right above your door and outside your windows. If that's not possible, then make sure to keep your windows clear from clutter so that you can light up the outside from the inside of your salon.

Doorway to Wealth Checklist

Did you follow these tips to make your storefront inviting?

○ Give clients and passers by an idea of what to expect inside by what you show outside. This can be done with window treatments, awnings, signage, and logo design.

○ Make sure your name is front and center. Clients should be able to easily see your name and identify who you are and what you do.

○ All signage should be tasteful with clear, legible lettering.

○ Contrasting colors and textures create interest. Use the colors that are associated with your brand.

○ Make sure your front door is well lit and your clients feel safe when entering.

○ Keep it simple. A cluttered front door and window is an instant turnoff to clients.

○ Place a welcome mat in front of your door.

○ Keep your front entrance clean, neat, and inviting. Clean your front door at the start of each day.

○ Create a funnel into your store. Channel the client into the salon with low, supportive entryway fixtures and long sightlines. Remember, wide, bare entryways can be intimidating.

○ Make your merchandise your focal point. They should sell beauty, the services your clients want and the lifestyles they want to lead.

○ Make your windows tell your story.

　- Windows are a perfect display for featured, new or specialty products. Your windows should sell the products your clients want and the feelings they want to feel.

　- Windows displays should change with the seasons, new products, etc. Less is more when it comes to decorating your windows and entrance. Be tasteful, but not cluttered.

Front Desk

When the client initially walks into the front door, it is important that their eyes have a focal point and a person to go to for immediate direction. That person, a receptionist or greeter, must be ready to welcome and direct this client from the helm of the entryway—The Front Desk! So, it's critical to have the front desk visible and in control of entrance to the service area of the salon. Additionally, the front desk should be pleasing to the eye, because that's one of the things your client first sees. The front desk must look clean, organized, and professional.

Here is a typical design for the front of a salon:

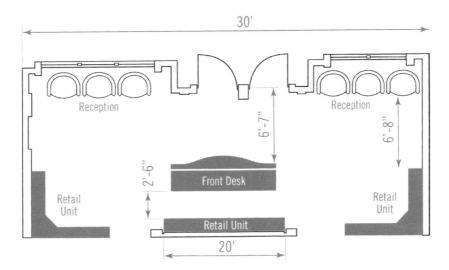

We recommend that you direct the flow of traffic in your salon through the placement of your front desk(s). For instance, if the desk is centrally located, have the stylist take them in along one side of the desk and bring them through the other opposite side of the desk when their service is complete. You may even want to draw arrows on a copy of your floor plan to show the flow through your salon. New and returning clients will quickly learn the traffic flow pattern which will make it easier on busy days when your entryway and waiting area may be full of clients who are checking in, checking out, waiting, and shopping in your retail area.

The actual size of the front desk varies and is dependent on the size of the salon and the amount of staff. In a large salon, you might have a "check-in desk" for arriving clients and a separate "checkout desk" for making service payments, purchasing products, and scheduling future appointments. Every salon location and setup is different. However, most front desks are large enough to accommodate a computer, keyboard, printer, and writing shelf for the client. When designing your front desk, make the size big enough to manage your operation properly by keeping these front desk functions in mind:

- Booking appointments
- Answering the phone
- Greeting clients

- Collecting payment for services rendered
- Paying and managing bills (if the salon doesn't have room for an office)
- Selling services and products
- Displaying product and salon promotions
- Getting the client's email address or phone number for appointment reminders
- Updating client information
- Processing incoming and outgoing mail
- Storing/handling tips for service providers

Front Desk Checklist

○ Is the front desk visible from and in control of entrance to the service area of the salon?

○ Is the front desk functional and pleasing to the eye?

○ Is the front desk clean, organized, and professional?

○ What is the directional flow of traffic through your salon? Are you using the front desk to help establish this flow?

○ Is the size of the desk suitable for all functions? For the front desk staff? For the client? Product and salon promotions?

○ Does all of the equipment fit at the front desk? Phone system? Computer? Printer? Credit card machines?

○ Do you need two front desks? One for checking clients in and one for checking clients out?

Waiting (Reception Seating)

For a standard-sized salon that is 1200 to 2400 square feet, the retail/reception area should be 200 to 300 square feet, but no more than 500 square feet for a larger salon. So, if a salon is 20 feet wide, then your retail/reception area is 10 to 15 feet deep. Keep in mind, the size that you designate for retail may be limited by the space layout and design for your services. If the intent of your business is to incorporate retail as a big part of your business, then you may have to give up space on your styling floor or for your break room or shampoo area. There is no set rule to follow when it comes to designing adequate space for selling retail. Each salon is different. It all comes down to your budget and square footage. Setting aside this amount of space at the front of your store provides enough space for seating in the "waiting" area; and it also gives ample space for the front desk and the main retail area.

As far as actual seating goes, don't go overboard. With an efficiently managed front desk and timely service providers, people should not be sitting and waiting. Fewer seats will actually encourage your clients to browse your retail area if they have the need to wait for a couple of minutes.

For an eight to 10-station salon, we recommend four to six waiting chairs. It is a must to get individual chairs with arms. Steer away from couches, benches, or other options where clients are required to sit right next to one another without any separation or barriers. Because of personal space issues, it becomes an uncomfortable situation when your client is next to a "stranger" waiting for their appointment. When choosing seating, keep in mind that most guests do not like:

• Sitting on the same chair or coach with someone they don't know.

• Sitting directly across for each other.

Although many salons currently are using sleek couches that vary in color there is no real rule of thumb when it comes to reception seating. Bench seats have become very popular. They do come in many colors and are reasonably priced. Whatever you end up choosing, you want the client to feel at ease while they are waiting; having an individual chair for someone is the best approach for making them feel safe and relaxed.

Waiting (Reception) Checklist

○ Have you kept your waiting/reception area between the recommended 200 and 300 square feet or 500 square feet if you are building out a larger salon?

○ Have you kept your seating in the waiting/reception area to four to six chairs for an eight to 10-station salon?

○ What style seating have you selected? Individual chairs with arms? Couches? Benches?

Ready, Set, Go! Expert Advice!

Ergonomic furniture can be beneficial for employees who spend long hours in the same position. Your front desk help or manicurist or pedicurist may find that a cheaper chair doesn't give them the comfort of an Ergonomic chair. In the same manner, customers who are provided comfortable seating are less likely to mind the wait than those who find themselves waiting in uncomfortable chairs. The importance of your waiting area design and chairs is an area that can't be overlooked when designing and purchasing equipment. Don't forget about those guests who are patiently waiting to get services in your salon. Their comfort while waiting is as important as the service they will receive. Make their wait an experience, not a nuisance.

CHAPTER 4

Point #2 - The Store Inside Your Salon
(Retail Area)

"Buying is a profound pleasure."

—Simone de Beauvoir

"**C**onsumers spend 7 billion dollars a year on hair-care products globally," say analysts at Goldman Sachs; but, 80% are purchased outside the salon! According to Hairdressing World Forum, 15 to 30 percent of the income of a salon can come from retail sales. Far too many salons overlook one of the easiest avenues for increased revenue … RETAIL. Selling retail products helps put a salon on solid financial footing by bringing in increased profits for both owners and employees and making a name for the salon in the community.

When you think about it, the opportunity for clients to learn about and make retail purchase decisions will occur three-to-four times while they are at your salon:

- When they check in
- When seated in the waiting area
- During their service
- When they check out

Let's look at the shape, size, and structure of a salon retail area. Notice in the design that follows that we recommend dedicating at least five feet of wall space to either side of the reception desk, as well as the area behind the reception desk.

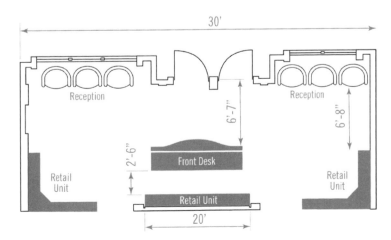

Retail by Design

Many salon designers will tell you that every salon needs dedicated retail space in their reception area. They're right! The reception area is a place where clients congregate before seeing stylists and a place they pause to pay and schedule their next appointment. It only makes sense for retail and reception to blend into one another and even occupy the same space.

> **Salon Owners Talk About . . .**
> **the Good, the Bad, and the Ugly**
>
> "You must hit the retail area first. Our guests love the fact that they walk into a store then a salon."
>
> —Marybeth Fiore, Hair Trendz, Storrs, CT

Unfortunately, most salon owners do not make retail a priority when designing and laying out their salon. This early design consideration has the most upside potential to create a steady retail revenue stream. Clients will become more loyal when they rely on you and your salon for their beauty needs—including not only the high-quality salon treatments, but also the salon-quality products. So, don't disregard the revenue generating possibilities from selling products that are associated with the main functions of the salon, such as: shampoo and conditioner, styling gel, hair spray, hair accessories, makeup, manicure and pedicure supplies, and even massage oil and candles.

> **Salon Owners Talk About . . .**
> **the Good, the Bad, and the Ugly**
>
> Ted Gibson of Ted Gibson Salons embraced retail and the impact it has had on his business is staggering.
>
> *"[I] can only do so many haircuts and colors in a day, but selling retail enables [me] to offer benefits, amenities, and extras in the salon. I didn't take that into account when I opened my first salon, but since then I have made drastic changes. We focus on retail and have built a business that grew 45% in the past year."*

The designs we included in this book are retail-oriented and all provide a centralized retail area in the salon with a lot of space for merchandise. Each design, included later in the book, has retail as the focal point of their business, but also accounts for other retail displays throughout the salon and showcases that the service areas of the salon are the main areas for generating profits. We have created this as a separate point and chapter in this book because the most effective retail areas are those that are designed into the floor plan and along with the conception of the business. Designing the retail area has some specific considerations:

- Layout for flow and interest
- Allowance for passive and active selling
- Visibility and accessibility of retail displays

Remember, clients can also make purchase decisions during their service. Therefore, retail space can and should be incorporated throughout the salon or wherever services occur. It is very important to take advantage of these opportunities and have retail displays nearby when service providers are educating their clients about the products that they are using during the service. With that in mind, have you considered the following areas?

- Windows
- The service floor
- The service stations
- The spa area
- Shampoo and color stations

Devoting Space to Retail

Determining how much space is devoted to retail can be difficult. Depending on the layout of your salon, whether you own, rent, or are building a new structure, and a dozen other factors, you may have more or less space to devote to retail. But, let's be clear on one thing: a successful salon must integrate retail sales into their strategy in order to maximize profit opportunities and provide clients with a one-stop-shop for their beauty needs.

So, how much space are we talking about?

- For a salon with up to 10 stations, we recommend 200 to 300 square feet for the central retail space at the front of the salon. That is the right amount of square footage to create a cozy, but not cramped feel, when you include four to six waiting chairs, the front desk, and space for retail.

- For larger salons, or for those interested in becoming the authority on the products that support their services, more retail space may be necessary. But, you should not dedicate more than 500 square feet of retail space in your salon because anything larger begins to feel overwhelming.

NOTE

As stated earlier, there is no magic number when it comes to deciding on how much square footage to allocate to your retail area. It really depends on many things. If you really want to have a retail focus, you should emphasize this in your planning stages and discuss with your salon designer or architect (if you are using one).

When considering retail opportunities in other areas throughout the salon, it depends largely on your layout, overall square footage, and traffic flow. For additional retail display throughout the salon, we would recommend using tables or open or two-sided shelving units as dividers between sections or departments of the salon. This keeps the styling floor separate from the shampoo area, while allowing the shelving units or tables to function as a retail center. Space for these outlying retail areas can run from one to 20 square feet, and can take the shape of everything from floating wall shelves to distributor-provided floor displays.

Choosing Retail Displays

The beauty of owning your own salon is that you establish the tone and décor. When it comes to retail display, the sky's the limit. You are only limited by creativity, budget, and space. While cost may be a concern when it comes to selecting your retail display units, keep two things in mind:

1. Retail is a money-making center for the salon.
2. You can find chic displays on any budget.

Types of Units

Retail display units come in all shapes and sizes, but they are broken down into two general categories: wall and floor units. We will get into the placement of these in more detail later. For now, think about how a combination of the right wall and floor units can work for your salon.

- **Wall Units**—From standard retail shelving to floating shelves to glass shelves to specialized units designed to display specific products, they all have one thing in common: they are attached to or sit against the wall. They also come in a variety of sizes and shapes. Wall units are available from almost anywhere, from a local craftsman to Ikea to an antique store or vintage shop. What you get and how you put it together depends on the salon experience you are creating. You should account for 10 to 15 feet of wall space for retail displays.

- **Floor Units**—Floor units, called freestanding units by some, are any arrangement of shelves, tables or displays designed to stand on the floor without being anchored to a wall and allow clients to view products from any side. These include tables, pedestals, and towers that are square, rectangular, or circular in shape. Pedestals come in all shapes and sizes (tall to short, small to large, slim to bulky) and we recommend using a variety of pedestals to add interest to your retail areas.

> ### Ready, Set, Go! Expert Advice!
>
> If you are having a hard time picturing the layout of your retail area or other part of your salon, then head over to the nearest liquor store for some boxes. You can use them to create a 3-D model of your floor plan for the retail area. Try to get boxes that are approximately the same size. Simply stack the boxes on top of one another and approximate the shape and size of the furniture, displays and other features that you are having a tough time visualizing. You can move them around until you get the layout just how you like it. You might want to invite some friends and family over to fill up the space with people to see how it would look on a busy day. You can eliminate a lot of regret down the road by going through this exercise.

Where to Find Retail Display Units

Depending on the style of your salon, you have several choices for where to look for and purchase retail display units. As a starting point, we have provided a list of different places that may have what you want for your space. Remember, the process of finding the right display units should be fun and creative. Keep an open mind and consider ways to repurpose unusual pieces for your purpose.

- **Product Distributors.** Call your local product distributor representative to find out what type of retail units come with the product you will be stocking and selling in your salon. Wall units from distributors will have light boxes or display windows built in, or will incorporate the product line name or company logo on the unit. These kinds of units often look very sleek, chic, and cutting edge; however, they may not go with your salon's vibe or décor.

- **Antique & Thrift Stores.** Perfect for finding antique apothecary cases, freestanding bookshelves, chifforobes/armoires, medicine cabinets, medical and retail display units and other furniture and décor items.

- **Restaurant Supply Stores.** Restaurant supply stores carry a variety of furniture pieces designed for professional kitchen and pantry storage. Depending on your salon's look, the industrial feel of these units may work well. You will find wire-framed shelving, metal and wood-topped butcher blocks, and steel tables that could be just the piece you need. Also, don't overlook the potential in pot racks and overhead storage systems.

- **Local Craftsmen.** For a custom look or size, enlist the services of a local craftsman. These cabinetmakers and furniture makers can often produce and install shelving units quickly and cost effectively.

- **Ikea.** Many urban areas have an Ikea—the Swedish furniture and home goods giant—which is the perfect store for low-cost, easy-to-assemble retail display options. They carry standard items like furniture items and bookcases—as well as custom retail solutions and specialized storage, display, and decoration pieces—which will fit almost any salon. Plus, the free online planner tools will help you see all your choices in a virtual, 3-D setting.

- **Hardware Stores.** At a hardware store, you can get anything from materials to build your own cabinet, to unfinished cabinets, to stock or custom kitchen cabinets and storage shelving, to brackets and boards to build your own shelves. Prices vary by unit or board foot (for shelving).

Retail by Design Checklist

○ Have you designed in adequate retail space for your salon based on your total square feet and number of stations and service providers?

○ Have you considered all locations for retail display in your salon?

    - Windows?

    - Service floor and in between service stations/departments?

    - Manicure/pedicure/spa area?

    - Shampoo and color stations?

○ In the design, are retail displays visible and accessible?

○ Does your layout encourage browsing and conversation with salon professionals about products?

○ Does your layout draw clients deeper into the retail area?

○ Has your design been laid out on paper?

○ Have you created a 3-D model of your design in your salon space using cardboard boxes to physically see what you are building out before finalizing the design?

○ Have you determine how many wall and floor display units you will purchase?

○ Have you determined how you will acquire your retail display units?

> **Salon Owners Talk About . . .**
> **the Good, the Bad, and the Ugly**

"Owners tend to over-develop the styling area. They don't realize the importance of the design of their retail area. You're either in retail or you're not. If you're not, you're not in the game of beauty."

—David Osgood, R.G. Shakour, Master Salon Designer Nashua, NH

"The retail area has to be designed with easy access to exit the salon. Buying on the way out the door is a must. I make the guest walk through a maze of retail to reach the checkout counter."

—Jill Krahn, Hair Success Salon and Spas, Fargo, ND

★ Five-Point Salon Design System ★

How do you plan to use each area of the salon to support retail display and sales?

POINT #1: The Entrance (Doorway/Front Desk/Waiting Area)

POINT #2: The Store Inside Your Salon (Retail Area)

POINT #3: Your Bread & Butter (Service Area)

POINT #4: Let Your Color Shine (Color & Dispensary Area)

POINT #5: Behind the Scenes (Utility Area)

Ready, Set, Go! Expert Advice!

Retail spaces must be designed to draw people into the space to shop. The storefront must act as a billboard for the store, often employing large display windows that allow shoppers to see into the space and the product inside.

CHAPTER 5

Point #3 - Your Bread & Butter
(Service Area)

"Cater to your customers' lifestyles. It will create instant rapport and a lasting sense of, 'I belong here.'"

—Marilyn Suttle

More than likely, you decided to become a salon owner because of your talents "behind the chair." Without a doubt, the service area is the bread and butter of your salon business. It's the reason why you have clients and the reason why you decided to own a salon. Your clients are coming to your salon for their beauty treatments. Of course, that can include a new hair style, color, a manicure or pedicure, a facial, a massage, or any combination of services. Why not make it an experience that is worthy of telling their friends, family, and coworkers all about you, your salon, and your story.

Setting up the experience of a lifetime for your clients starts with the design of this main stage area. Your service area is the "main stage" because you and your staff are on stage daily creating your own masterpieces. Call it what you will, but this area has to be designed correctly and set up with high-volume in mind. Why not design and build this area to be the most glamorous stage in your area—like the Academy Awards stage.

Think about how much goes on when watching the Academy Awards as the movie stars get their awards—there is singing, dancing, cameras, lights, and plenty of action. The salons main stage must be designed and built with plenty of glitz and glamour—with the pretense that there will be plenty of action constantly going on. You may not have dancing, but you'll probably have music and the energy of your clients and staff buzzing about in this area. They need to be comfortable and have the ability to get up and around without the feeling of being in the way of each other. This area is where the magic happens. So, it has to be perfect and much thought has to go into the design, furniture, and layout; and, it has to:

- Be comfortable for clients and staff
- Convey your brand
- Showcase your salon's services and retail products
- Be memorable
- Efficiently use available space
- Provide ample space for productivity

Let's take a look at each of the departments within the service area.

The Styling Department

Feeling comfortable in this space is very important to clients—they want relaxation, maybe a little luxury, roominess, and a place for their belongings. With those considerations in mind, let's look at the different types of stations and equipment needs for the styling area.

Wall Stations

The minimum space for a wall station, from center-to-center, is 4 feet and 6 inches. It gives ample space for each stylist to work and does not waste any space. Salon owners have used as much as 6 feet for each station because of the station design. But, when considering revenue potential, adding another foot and a half to each station means that you miss out on being able to add two more stations, which is missed revenue opportunity. We recommend the biggest spread from center-to-center be no more than 5 feet. Any more than that is wasted space.

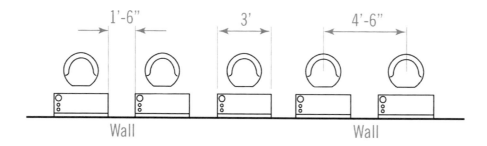

Freestanding Stations

They should be no wider than 36 inches and as narrow as possible. Most of the storage space needs to be located on the sides of the units with a small shelf in front, where the mirror is located. The dimensions for most units are 36 inches wide and 30 to 36 inches deep. If you add chairs on each side, the unit takes up 12 feet of depth.

One thing that needs to be considered when discussing a freestanding unit is the walkway space around the unit where the stylist is working. This is usually a main traffic area. So, it is recommended that another 3 feet is added to each side for traffic flow. The overall depth of the station, including traffic, is 18 feet. It can change by the way you might angle the station, but you won't know until you space-plan the complete salon.

Be aware that you need to hook electrical to the freestanding station, which will either come from the floor or the ceiling. Either one can be expensive and must be researched while designing.

Potential added expenses and design challenges for freestanding stations:

- If you have a concrete floor and no basement, you will need to cut the concrete to run wiring.
- Exposed wires from the ceiling are unattractive and may not get proper electrical approval from the town's or city's building inspector.
- You may have to upgrade your electrical panel.
- Freestanding stations have to be bolted to the floor. They do have the tendency to tip over so if you've a concrete slab the installation may be a little more difficult. Drilling into concrete is not easy and takes a little bit more time.
- You may need more lights to give proper lighting to each freestanding station because there is not as much "borrowed" lighting as you would get from wall-mounted stations.

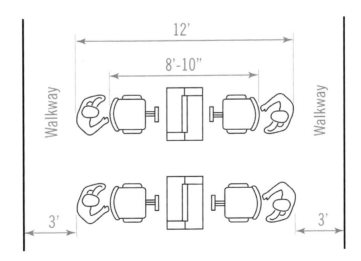

Styling Chairs

Different chair styles:

1. **Chair containing round or 5-star bottom base:** The overall dimensions are 24 inches by 24 inches around. Weight varies from chair to chair. A good quality chair usually has a weight of 60 pounds or more.

   a. Round base: more stability, with weight and diameter a factor. For cleaning, it is recommended that it be moveable because a ring develops from hair buildup around the base bottom.

   b. 5-star base: less stability and easier for a client to tip it over when putting weight on the footrest. Easier to clean by taking a hair blower and blowing out all the hair underneath the chair.

2. **Chair containing a U-shaped or T-shaped footrest:**

   a. U-shaped: this footrest is shaped like a U and has been in the industry for many years. Clients tend to trip over it when getting off the chair.

   b. T-shaped: this footrest was developed about 30 years ago, originally in Europe. A much better design for clients.

3. **Styling chair with no footrest:**

   Most of the time, you will see this chair in Europe or Asia, and they typically have a floor-mounted footrest for the client. They do not work for the U.S. market because in America the stylists like to turn the chairs to different positions, whereas in Europe, the stylist works around the chair. We do not recommend going with this style.

Shampoo Sinks

One change up from traditional salon designs or floor plans is that the shampoo sinks are no longer stuck in the back. This part of the salon is now considered a profit center for the salon, showcasing products that the clients can buy. With freestanding shampoo units, you can give your salon a dramatic look and make it attractive and visible. Use the number of stations to determine the quantity of sinks (shown in the following chart).

Sink Guideline

# of stations	# of sinks
1	1
2-5	2
6-9	3
10-13	4
14-18	5

Note: *These guidelines do not include the sinks for a separate color department. You should use the same formula for calculating the amount of sinks if you have a separate color department. Larger salons may have a separate wash area just for color. There is no rule of thumb in this case for how many sinks or shuttles that are required. It really depends on the volume of the salon.*

Freestanding Backwash Shampoo Sinks

When space-planning for freestanding backwash sink units, the size is approximately two feet wide by four feet long, without a footrest. Following are a couple of layouts which also feature a cabinet behind the sinks for shampoos, conditioners, and towels.

These units are usually spaced 30 inches apart from the center of each drain. Doing so gives a six-inch space between sinks. There are many ways to design how these sinks are situated, but you always need at least 30 inches of clearance behind them for the shampoo person to wash the client.

The rule of thumb is that freestanding units are placed at least 54 inches from the wall. You can also design the shampoo units to have a gap in between for shampooing from the side. In this case, the plumbing needs to be 48 inches or four feet on center.

NOTE

When purchasing freestanding units, be aware of the type of fittings that are supplied for hookup. Many of the fixtures are metric and do not fit easily to American pipe fittings. You will have to get adapters and it will be a time-consuming, aggravating project.

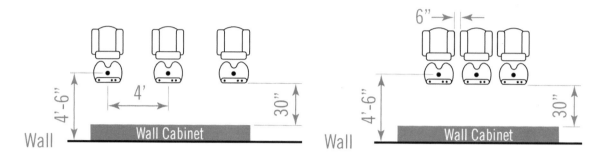

Washing from behind the sink AND from the side   *Washing from behind the sink only*

To install freestanding sinks, the floor will usually need to be cut for waste and waterline installation, which can be expensive. If you have a location with a basement, then floor cutting is not an issue and it is very easy to move pipes and put the sinks where you desire. However, we recommend that you insulate the hot water lines in the basement. Usually, they are exposed and may be too far away from the hot water heater to maintain desirable water temperatures.

Wall-Mounted Shampoo Sinks

Generally, each wall-mounted sink takes up 4 feet of space. So, if you have three sinks, it will take up 12 feet of wall space. You can go a little smaller, but you should be very careful with spacing for wall-mounted sinks. You need to account for two feet for the sink itself, plus another two feet in between each sink. Anything less than will make it difficult to get in between the shampoo sinks without bumping into the next sink over when shampooing a client. For most wall-mounted sinks, the waste and waterlines can be installed in the wall, which can be a cost savings. Whenever possible, your wall-mounted sinks should share a wall with your utility area which will keep the water heater in close proximity to the sinks.

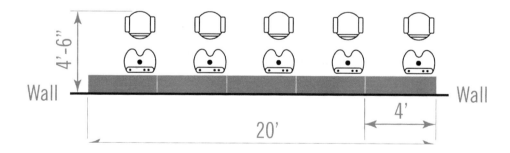

Each location is different. Review these options with your designer and architect for the design option that is best for your design features, budget, and space.

Hair Dryers with Chairs

The size of a typical dryer chair is 24 inches wide by 36 inches long. The weight is approximately 60 pounds with the dryer included. Each dryer draws 9.8 amps at maximum use; we recommend you have access to a 20 amp plug. A four-dryer area needs 10 feet of space and about 48 inches of depth, not including walk-by traffic. Please make sure that you have ample electrical outlets for power. The amount of dryers that you should carry is based on the clientele and services you supply.

A dr... be use... They ran... from $18... ...00 dollars and easily store in a closet or an out of the way place in the salon.

- Surrounded by retirement communities: recommend 1 dryer per 2 styling chairs
- Progressive coloring salon: recommend 1 dryer per 4 styling chairs

Manicure/Pedicure Department

Our suggestion is that you rent the manicure/pedicure area out and let them buy their own supplies. If you compare the numbers, you will make more money renting this department out with a lot fewer headaches. Following, you'll find specific design considerations and furniture/equipment choices for both departments.

Pedicure Department

Now, it's time to talk about the pedicure department. Can you believe over 40 companies manufacture all the different types of pedicure units? It can be very confusing. So, we will break down each style unit for you to decide.

Option 1: Chair with a Separate Footbath

It is the most basic style and the footbath ranges from $30–$100, depending on the functions. The water must be filled and emptied by the pedicurist for each service. No plumbing is required and the "plastic" footbath needs to be sanitized after each use.

Option 2: Chair with a Separate Footbath that Has a Built-in Pump

This unit is portable and can be put into a closet and taken out for a single use. After use, the unit needs to be brought (on wheels) over to a sink or toilet to discharge the dirty water, which is done by the pump in the unit. The price range for this type of unit is $775–$1100.

Option 3: Pedicure Unit Built Like a "Shoeshine" Bench

These do look very good and have a nice, cozy appeal. They can be built three different ways:

a. Least expensive: unit with a portable footbath (described in #1). These types of units are now starting to become popular. With everyone concerned about germs, they are a very efficient and safe way of offering a pedicure. Plastic inserts are used, which fit in the tray. Just throw away the plastic pan when finished with the client's service. The benefit is nothing to clean and you are on to the next client. The downside is you have to walk to the sink to fill a new plastic bowl in between each service. If not planned and designed well, that could be a nightmare.

b. Unit with a regular sink (kitchen style) which gives the pedicurist water for filling and draining. It is built into the unit, flush mounted.

c. Unit with a whirlpool sink which looks like a kitchen sink, but contains the whirlpool capability with pumps built underneath the unit.

All of these built-in units look great and usually match the rest of the salon in the exact color. But, they all have the same common problem—the unit has no height adjustments.

The benches are designed to sit at a certain height. Many companies design the bench for an average person 5'6" tall. Let's say you have a male client that is 6'4" tall. When they sit in the unit, their knees are up to their chest! A woman who is 4'11" will need to slide down just to reach the bowl. Usually, pillows need to be propped for that person and the pedicure becomes an uncomfortable experience.

Some of these units come with nice options. The bottom line is that if they have no height adjustment, they will not work well for all of your clients. Another possible issue is that these units are made of wood (mostly plywood) and laminate. If water splashes on the surface and it's not sealed properly, then the wood will swell and cause delamination. The price range for these units start at $800 for the base model and can go up to $4000 for all the bells and whistles.

Option 4: Pedicure Unit with a Piped Whirlpool System

This type unit has been in the industry for a long time. What we mean by "piped" is that tubes are running inside the unit and water gets pushed through the pipes by a motor. Then, the water is blown through jets that create a whirlpool action.

Over the last ten years, states have outlawed this type of unit. The reason is that after you use the unit, a small amount of water is left in the tubes inside of the unit. There is no way to sanitize the unit completely by flushing the system. If the unit is not used, the water—even though it's a small amount—builds bacteria, a natural process. Once the unit gets used again, bacteria may affect the client and create a rash or open sores. There are documented cases of this and we do not recommend this style unit. If you do buy this system, carry good insurance! The unit ranges from $1300–$2000.

Option 5: Pedicure Unit with a "Pipeless" Whirlpool System.

A "pipeless" pedicure unit has all the same functions as the "piped" unit except it has no pipe. It contains a motor that is built behind a fan and it is mounted inside the tub that is covered by a plate. The plate protects you from any injury. The motor turns the fan, which creates a whirlpool, and after use, you take the cover off and sanitize it so there is no issue of bacteria. There are many types of units and the price range begins at $1800 and goes up to $12,000. My recommendation is that you buy this item from an established dealer. With a lot of these units, you have problems, regardless of how expensive. You want to choose a reputable company so that you can count on them to still be in business when a problem requires you to replace parts or a motor.

Following is a typical pedicure layout.

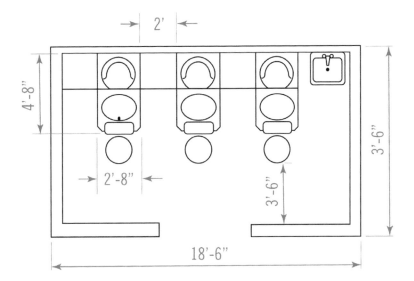

Manicure Department

Now that we have finished the pedicure area, we should talk about the manicure or nail department. What we have found in our experience is that most commissioned "nail techs" make, on average, about 70 percent commission. Once you buy supplies and handle all of the appointments, you are lucky to make 10 percent. Salons have manicurists as a service for their clients so that they come to their salon for more services, stay at their salon longer, and create more loyalty and another opportunity to sell retail.

The normal size of a table is 48 inches long by 18 inches wide. The height of the table should be 30 inches. We suggest that manicure tables be positioned against a wall and spaced

6 feet apart. That gives enough room for the client and nail tech to be comfortable.

Putting in nail tables and pedicure units is not cheap. In the long run and for the expense involved, it may not make financial sense. It may make sense to rent out manicure and pedicure areas. Really think through your plan and the return on investment and earning potential. If you are a nail technician and you are looking to specialize in nails at your salon, then go for it! Plus, the more services your clients get at your salon the more loyal they will become.

Following is typical spacing for manicure tables.

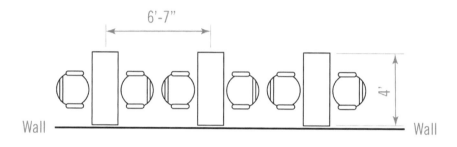

Facial/Massage Department

The last department to talk about is the facial/massage rooms you might put into your salon. Following is a typical design for a three-room design. Two of the rooms are for facials and the other is for massage. A shower can be added; but, considering the cost involved, it would be like adding another bathroom.

> **NOTE**
>
> Treatment rooms may also have a small cabinet with overhead cupboards for essentials, such as towels, oils, ointments, and other waxing/treatment related products. Additionally, you may want to install a small sink for technicians and clients.

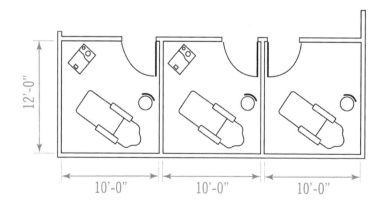

According to SpaTrade.com, "the minimum dimensions for a massage room are 10 feet by 12 feet. This will give you almost 4 feet (45 inches) on each side of the table." If you have the room, we would definitely recommend making the rooms this size. This size room will allow the technician and the client to have enough room to be comfortable if giving a massage and or facial. The standard table size of a facial bed or massage table is 73 to 77 inches long; add another 10 to 12 inches if you include a head rest. If the room is any smaller, the technician will not be able to get behind the client's head for any treatments.

Service Area Checklist

Stylist Department

○ Stations must have enough space to house all tools for the stylists.

○ Stylists must have enough room to work on each customer; overcrowding is not conducive in the styling area.

○ Roller carts are an effective way to add storage for stylists in their work area. Must remember in your design plan to leave a place to park them to eliminate disruption to the flow of the work area.

○ Make sure the shampoo area is not too far from the styling area.

Pedicure Department

○ Pedicure area should be placed away from the styling area. The pedicure units tend to be loud and noisy.

○ When designing leave enough room for the pedicurist to safely navigate around the area when she is working off her cart on a guest.

○ Design in your floor plan with a sink in the area of the pedicure area for washing and sanitizing pedicure tools.

○ Storage in the area of the pedicurist is important for towels and products.

Service Area Checklist

Manicure Department

○ Putting in an air vent system in this are to take out all smells and any toxins is a good feature to put in the design element of this area. Many states and cities are making this a requirement for all salons that offer manicure and pedicure services.

○ Storage is important in this area.

○ Garbage or towel cabinet for disposal able towels and waste is a good idea to incorporate into your design in this area.

Facial/Massage Department

○ Small cabinet for this area for products or towels is important for treatment rooms.

○ Roller carts are a great way to house products for different treatments. They can be moved from room to room for different types of treatments without being in the way.

Ready, Set, Go! Expert Advice!

Temperature becomes a battle ground among employees. Ensure that thermostats are set at the suitable temperature for the season, keeping the comfort of your clients and employees in mind. We suggest a programmable thermostat with a locking mechanism. Set the thermostat to adjust based on your business hours and to keep the temperature at comfort settings while the salon is open.

The design of your salon is important when trying to maintain temperature settings in your salon. Choppy layouts and too many walls used as room dividers will cut down air flow in the salon setting. This makes it tough to regulate temperatures in the salon when it is busy. Keep this in mind when laying out the salon design. Being too hot or cold in the salon is not a good thing when trying to keep everyone happy.

CHAPTER 6

Point #4 - Let Your Color Shine
(Color/Dispensary Area)

"Beauty without colour seems somehow to belong to another world."
—Murasaki Shikibu

The color department is where you "show me the money!" It is the most profitable department in a salon. Visible color labs or color bars give stylists an opportunity to engage with their clients throughout their entire salon experience. And, guess what? This latest design feature makes your clients feel like part of the process and not left alone. Some clients might enjoy the moments when they can dig into a good magazine article, but most enjoy the social aspect of coming to the salon and visiting with their stylists and other guests. Let's face it; your most successful stylists are conversationalists. They enjoy being around people, talking to people, sharing news and stories—and even acting as the stand-in therapist for clients going through troubling times. Why is a color lab or color bar a smart move for your salon?

1. Creates a more "at-home" environment for clients.

2. Gives clients an opportunity to see other service areas in your salon.

3. Clients will be sitting around a table or at a bar with other salon clients, which could lead to conversations about their favorite salon services, products, and promotions.

4. Stylists will have constant face-time with their clients, which they will enjoy. Plus, it gives stylists more opportunities to offer add-on services, educate them about retail products, and tell them about salon promotions.

5. Keeps stylists in a client-focused mode. When your dispensary and color station is "in the back room," there is a tendency to switch off of "client-mode" and get caught up "me-mode." When in "me-mode," a stylist could get stuck in salon drama, decide it's a good time to make quick personal calls, socialize with their colleagues a little too much, or text with friends outside of the salon.

6. It's important for the client to understand that mixing color is not as simple as going to the store and buying it in a box. When you engage your client with the actual collaboration of creating the specific color used, it gives the client the feeling that the mixture was exclusively made for them. Thus, the client perceives the overall value of the services on a whole different level.

Designing Your Color Department

If you want to go with this latest trend, then you have a couple of options. One is to use a dining-room style table or a bar-height counter top that ranges from four to 12 feet in length. Hydraulic styling chairs are based around the table or bar and the colorist just brings a trolley over to work on the client. Some design ideas include:

- Using stainless steel for countertops

- Incorporating upper cabinets built with slots for color tube separation and display

- Including a sink for water capability

- Providing ample storage for all bowls, brushes, foils, etc.

- Outlets for clients to plug in devices such as cell phones and laptops

- Room for a coffee service

- Overhead mirrors that the stylist can positioned over the clients chair

In Chapter 18, you'll find that we have included salon designs with a color lab or bar. However, we understand that it's not suitable for all salons and that it might not work within the square footage that you have available. If you can make it happen, it definitely has its value and payoffs.

Color/Dispensary Area Checklist

When designing your color lab, remember to:

○ Add enough space for color storage.

○ Keep shelving at reachable levels so that your stylists can easily retrieve the tubes of color.

○ Incorporate a sink or wash down area for all brushes, bowls, etc.

○ Use stainless steel for the counters. Most laminates used may stain or tend to delaminate due to excessive water use.

○ Install heavy-duty hardware on the cabinet drawers. This area will be used frequently. Most cabinets have "standard glides," which will not withstand the level of constant, daily use that a dispensary demands.

○ Choose flooring that is water, stain, and slip resistant in this area.

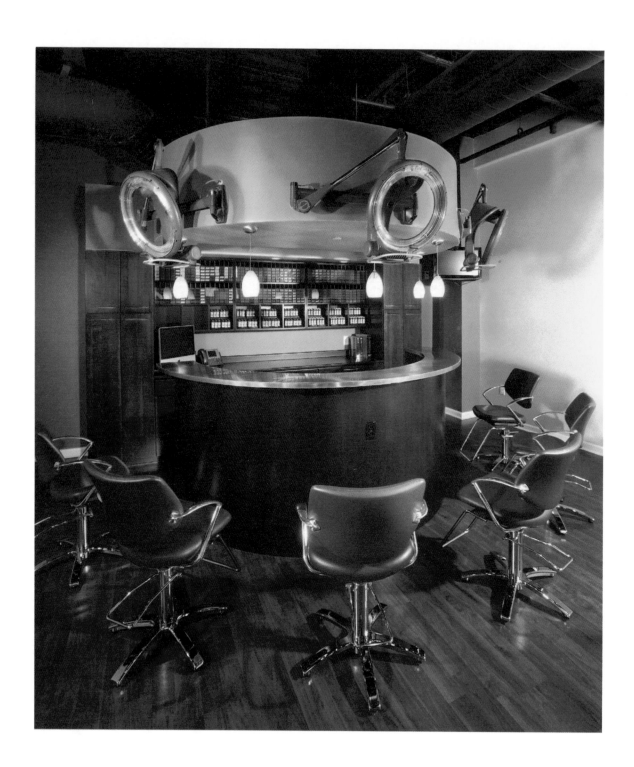

CHAPTER 7

Point #5 - Behind the Scenes
(Utility Area)

"The salons laundry/utility room is self-cleaning, you need to do it yourSELF!"

—Anonymous

Most of us look at this area and figure why spend any money there. It is what it is. These areas are difficult to envision as anything except for a utility room, but they can be so much more. It is one of the most commonly used areas of a salon, but also one of the most poorly designed areas. When you sign your lease, you pay for every square inch that you are renting, including your much needed laundry/utility area.

Good design and efficient organization saves time and effort. You don't necessarily need to have this area decorated like the client-facing areas, but it must be functional and help you deliver services efficiently. Remember, the most important thing in the salon environment is time. You can only cut, style, and color so many people in a given day. Time efficiency is an intricate part of space planning your salon. Little things, such as an overlooked utility/laundry room can mean a loss of time and money.

In fact, this area is much broader than just a "utility room" in the Five-Point Salon Design System. Let's look at the "utility" or "behind the scenes" area. As we define it, this area includes the following:

- A "traditional" utility items, such as a hot water heater, washer, dryer, and laundry tub (and possibly a furnace)
- Furnace/Air Conditioning
- Staff break area
- Restrooms
- Changing rooms
- Storage
- Dispensary (for smaller salons or for those that are not showcasing their color services with service-floor dispensary)

When designing the utility area, think about flow and how to set it up for efficiency:

- It's usually near an exit to the outside parking area, which makes it easily accessible for deliveries instead of bringing in boxes through the front of the salon.

- It's an excellent storage area.

- It's a heavy traffic area for your staff needing to launder towels, store their belongings, eat, make quick phone calls, etc.

The diagram that follows illustrates a typical salon utility room with washer, dryer, hot water heater, sink, refrigerator, storage space for your staff's personal items, and an eating area for their breaks. The following diagram does not include the heating system. Many times, this is located on the roof or in the basement; but, it can also be in the utility room.

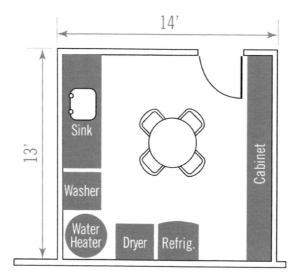

Each salon design is different and some cannot support such a spacious utility area as the one above.

Hot Water Heaters

Another common plumbing issue is the size of the hot water heater. Usually, it is too small for a salon. A salon needs a minimum of an 80-gallon, double-element water heater. Anything less will create a hot water shortage in your salon. The cost is around $500 for an electric water heater. If you have the potential of using a natural gas water heater, this will be more efficient.

Remember, your hot water heater is usually located in the utility area. If your shampoo area is far away from that, you have the potential of losing "hot water" and you will be washing your clients with "cold water." It may be solved by insulating the water lines OR designing the layout of your salon so that the shampoo area is close to the utility area. Just remember, it will cost you more money in the long run if there is too much distance between these two areas.

Washer/Dryer

You will need a washer (and a dryer) for towels. You will want to make sure that your space can accommodate this addition. Consult with your electrician regarding power and amperage requirements for your washer, dryer, and hot water heater, which typically require a 220-volt electrical outlet.

The key to saving energy is buying energy-efficient appliances. When purchasing a washer and dryer for your towels and capes, spend the few dollars more for an energy-efficient machine. Look for Energy Star labeled products. It may cost more when you make the purchase, but it will save you up to 4 percent a month on your electric bill.

- **Washer**—When using your washer, make sure it is full. Do not wash towels on the hot setting. Use the cool setting; this will save you money. It only works if you let your staff know how you want things done. Put directions right on the washer.

- **Dryer**—Drying your salon's towels and capes is essential; it is also one of the primary sources of wasted energy. Install a dryer vent seal to save energy. This will eliminate any drafts from entering the salon when the dryer is not in use and could easily reduce the salon's heating costs. Don't overload the dryer. Overloading the dryer means it takes as much as three times longer to dry. You must have room in the dryer for items to tumble. Towels will never dry if there is no room to tumble. It will also reduce the life of the dryer. That could result in a heavy repair bill or replacement.

Furnace/Air Conditioning

Your clients and staff must be comfortable when working or coming into your salon for services. Most salons today, those that are in strip malls, have the air and heat on the roof of the structure. So, you may not have too much to plan for when it comes to heating and air conditioning. However, older buildings may have the furnace and hot water heater in the basement or in a dedicated utility room or closet. This also will not have much of an effect when it comes to the design and layout of the salon. Many newer buildings will have the furnace and hot water heater in the same area of the space you are renting, which will be in the back of the space usually next to an exit door. You will have to incorporate this into your design plan. This may be a good area for your utility room.

Restrooms

Having the right number of restrooms to meet state requirements is the biggest issue. If you have six stylists or more, most states/counties require two restrooms. It usually costs about $5000 to put in a restroom. You are best off following the requirements of the state or county. Besides, the second restroom can double as a changing room. If you look at an 8-station salon, you can have as many as 25 people in the salon at any given time. One restroom is inadequate.

Many times, existing restrooms do not meet the latest handicap accessibility codes:

- The county may ask you to make it bigger, change the toilet, and/or put in a sink that works for wheelchairs.

- You may have to install handicap rails if they are not there already.

- Your county may also ask you to install a ramp for access to the restrooms if your salon has any kind of elevation.

- The latest codes are for the door to be 36 inches wide and to open out with a lever handle only.

- The inside must have a 44 inch clearance for a wheelchair to completely turn around in the restroom.

- The pipes underneath the sink must have heat-resistant covers to protect a handicapped person's legs when they are underneath the sink.

Changing Rooms

For a spa treatment area, you may also want to include a set of changing rooms. Changing rooms will need to provide privacy and include a chair or a bench, a mirror, hooks to hang robes, and hangers or lockers for clients' clothing.

Ready, Set, Go! Expert Advice!

The default location for laundry rooms used to be in the back of the salon. There are still good reasons to place it in the back (e.g., noise, humidity, water overflow, and deliveries). But, your perfect spot might be next to the pedicure or shampoo area. A suite of salons close to the center of your building could mean that the laundry room would be in the middle of the building. If you choose a location near an area that you are offering massage, waxing or facials, shop for products with UL approval. These units should have extra insulation and improved performance that promise quiet operation and reduced vibration. If the dryer doesn't list a decibel (db) rating, it's probably too noisy to place near the salon or spa treatment area. The same logic might apply to washing machines with high-speed spin cycles (more than 1,000 rpm); they might vibrate too much to be located near these areas as well.

Utility Checklist

Did you remember to plan for the following . . .

○ Cabinet space for storage of products, cleaning supplies, and towels?

○ Lockers for staff to keep personal belongings?

○ Shelf space to fold clothes or to sit and eat lunch?

○ Slop sink that is sized right for mops?

○ Storage for toxic products so clients do not have access?

○ Ceramic tile on the floor for easy cleanup?

○ Keeping this room close to plumbing and electrical panels? (Remember, cutting floors to put in plumbing can be very expensive if the space does not have a basement.)

○ Adequate lighting?

○ Ventilation to the outside of the building to:

  - Circulate fresh air?

  - Release humidity generated by the washer and dryer?

  - Release chemical fumes from dispensing color?

○ Proper insulation in the walls and ceiling? (This eliminates the rest of the salon from hearing what is going on in this room which may include opening and closing of cabinet doors, the sound of the washer and dryer, the sound of the furnace, staff arriving/leaving work, staff on break, etc.)

CHAPTER 8

Universal Design

"Universal Design is not a trend, but an enduring design approach that assumes that the range of human ability is ordinary, not 'special.'"

—Elaine Ostroff

"Ronald L. Mace was a nationally and internationally recognized architect, product designer, and educator whose design philosophy provided a design foundation for a more usable world. He coined the term 'universal design' to describe the concept of designing products and the built environment to serve the needs of people regardless of their age, ability, or status in life." (SOURCE: Ronald L. Mace Universal Design Institute, udinstitute.org)

When designing a salon, you must always remember that your salon needs to meet the needs of your clients. No matter what your niche, your clients will be different ages, have different abilities, and be in different life stages. Universal design (also called accessible or barrier-free design) is geared toward making the salon accessible for everyone. It is "inclusive" in nature—meaning that accommodations and features should be transparent and subtle while remaining visually pleasing and offering safety, comfort, and convenience for all people.

One thing is for certain, everyone has beauty needs! By meeting the needs of many and being accepting of all people, you will encourage individuals and families of all types to become patrons of your salon.

Think for a moment of the individuals in your family, your friends, and their families, and those in your community. Within the network of people that your salon will touch, you will know of someone (directly or indirectly) who either has some form of disability (from birth, from an accident, through an illness, or through the aging process) or is caring for someone who is disabled. You probably also have a few friends who may be expecting a new baby or will bring their new baby to your salon during their appointment.

Now, with these people in mind, think about these questions:

• How would you feel if your salon was not accessible to them?

• What if they couldn't even make it to your front door?

• What if they couldn't move around freely inside your salon?

• What if they couldn't use your salon because it was just too difficult and there were too many barriers that made it unsafe, uncomfortable, or inconvenient?

It would be a sad moment to realize that you did not account for making your salon accessible after you finished construction and opened for business. The expense to making changes after the fact is incredibly high, not to mention the interruption to your business to make any necessary alterations. Our advice is to take the time upfront to consider as many situations and clients as possible.

To avoid these concerns, work with your designer and your architect to plan for an inclusive, accessible salon. Here are some examples to get you thinking about the universal design aspects for your salon:

• Entryways and Hallways: Wider entryways and hallways for wheel chairs, walkers, and baby strollers

• Counters: Higher counters for the older clientele, plus the inclusion of a lower counter at check in/check out for clients in wheel chairs or of shorter stature

• No steps or ramps: Step-less porch or entrance that will increase access and convenience without compromising aesthetics of the salon entrance

• Restrooms: Wider restroom doors and handles or grab bars inside the restrooms (most restrooms will have to be handicap accessible)

• Door handles: Lever handles for doors versus knobs that require twisting

• Light switches: Rocker panels versus the small toggle switches

• Lighting: Lots of light; inside and outside

• Signage: Light-on-dark for visual contrast; large, clear-type faces, bold block lettering

• Flooring: Stable, firm, and slip resistant

Utility Checklist

Did you remember to plan for the following . . .

○ Make entryways and hallways wider for wheel chairs, walkers, and baby strollers.

○ Install counters at heights comfortable for older clientele and for those in wheel chairs or of shorter stature.

○ Look for a location with a step-less porch or entrance (or build one out).

○ Replace narrow doors with those that are wider (no less than 36 inches).

Utility Checklist

○ Install handles or grab bars inside the restrooms (most restrooms will have to be handicap accessible).

○ Replace door knobs that require twisting with lever handles.

○ Replace small toggle light switches with rocker panels (or motion detector light switches, which also serves as a great energy saver).

○ Invest in lighting both inside and outside.

○ Use clear, large type faces and light-on-dark for visual contrast for signage.

○ Choose stable, firm, and slip-resistant flooring.

★ Five-Point Salon Design System ★
(Point-by-Point Assessment)
What universal design features do you have planned for each area of your salon?

POINT #1: The Entrance (Doorway/Front Desk/Waiting Area)

POINT #2: The Store Inside Your Salon (Retail Area)

POINT #3: Your Bread & Butter (Service Area)

POINT #4: Let Your Color Shine (Color & Dispensary Area)

POINT #5: Behind the Scenes (Utility Area)

Ready, Set, Go! Expert Advice!

Universal design refers to broad-spectrum ideas meant to produce buildings, products, and environments that are inherently accessible to both people without disabilities and people with disabilities. Your salon will have many people that walk through the front door daily. The Universal design theory is a must to keep all happy. Listed below are some key components to think about in your layout and design of the salon:

- Smooth, ground level entrances without stairs
- Surfaces that are stable, firm, and slip resistant
- Wide interior doors, hallways, and alcoves with 60" × 60" turning space at doors and dead-ends
- Functional clearances for approach and use of elements and components; important in the styling and retail area
- Lever handles for opening doors rather than twisting knobs (Bathrooms and treatment rooms)
- Single-hand operation with closed fist for operable components including fire alarm pull stations
- Components that do not require tight grasping, pinching or twisting of the wrist
- Light switches with large flat panels rather than small toggle switches
- Buttons and other controls that can be distinguished by touch
- Bright and appropriate lighting, particularly task lighting
- Auditory output redundant with information on visual displays
- Bathroom doors that are at least 36 inches
- Handles and handrails in the bathrooms

CHAPTER 9

Design Trends & Tips

"The way to get good ideas is to get lots of ideas, and throw the bad ones away."

—Linus Pauling

This chapter is all about ideas and the future of salons and how they are transforming to meet the needs of salon consumers. The salon industry constantly changes and evolves. As a norm, high-end salons of the future will have social media mirrors and touch-screen entertainment. Salon services and entertainment will be intrinsically linked. Over the next ten years, consumer attitudes and behaviors are likely to change in unprecedented ways. Retailers and service providers, including the beauty industry, will have to consider a number of questions to maximize viability:

- What will consumers value?
- What will consumers need and want?
- Given what consumers have faced in recent years, how will their attitudes and behaviors continue to change in the coming decade?
- Will the salon equipment and tools evolve so radically that it will also change the design and layout of salons?

To unravel the mystery of what to expect, Jeff Grissler and Eric Ryant have asked leading salon designers of the world about their predictions. Therefore, the trends presented in this chapter come from designers and specialists who work firsthand with salon owners to create new salons day in and day out. The tips in this chapter will help you with the flow and layout of your salon and equipment choices—all of which will improve operations. Lastly, you will get a list of common (and often painful) mistakes that others have made. Avoiding those same mistakes saves you time and money.

Design Trends

After polling our designers and specialists, we've come up with this list of the top design and equipment trends in the beauty industry today.

Color & Accents	
White/Stainless	**Sean Curly**, Regional Furnishings Professionals, SalonCentric "I am currently working on two salons with a white front desk and styling stations. It really gives the 'Wow!' effect when you walk into the salon."
Earth Tones & Metal/Glass	**Mac McAlister**, Salon Furnishing Professional, SalonCentric "In my recent salon designs, I'm seeing more earth tones rather than dark colors. The earth tones that people are using include browns, tans, warm grays, greens, oranges, whites, and some reds, and some blues. The look is finished nicely with a combination of metal and glass." **David Osgood**, Vice President of Sales and Marketing, Interiors by R.G. Shakour "More and more salons in the U.S. are using earth tones. Plums, oranges, and yellows are popular in Europe; these colors are slowly making their way to the U.S. I just finished a salon with white cabinets and a bright blue floor. The vibrant colors make the entire salon pop as soon as you walk through the door."

Features / Services	
Color Bars & Dry Bars	**Sean Curly**, Regional Furnishings Professionals, SalonCentric "I am seeing open color bar concepts and salons getting away from traditional sinks on the wall to a shampoo bar that promotes the feeling of involvement." **Mac McAlister**, Salon Furnishing Professional, SalonCentric "I am seeing an increase in blow dry bars in the Metropolis areas. Consumers like the idea of having their hair styled—whether it is for a special occasion or just because." **David Osgood**, Vice President of Sales and Marketing, Interiors by R.G. Shakour "Color is where the money is. Many salons are still putting in color bars. This is a trend that will continue for the next decade. Dry bars are hot! Customers love the cheap price for a quick blow out. Nice way for a salon to make quick money by utilizing space in the salon just for blowouts."

Recycling / Repurposing / Green Materials	
Antique Accents	**Sean Curly**, Regional Furnishings Professionals, SalonCentric "Outside of antique accents, I haven't seen any recycling of furniture."

Recycling / Repurposing / Green Materials	
Green Materials	Examples: bamboo flooring, porcelain tiles, and environmentally friendly fabrics **Sean Curly**, Regional Furnishings Professionals, SalonCentric "I have used Continuum Footspas as an eco-friendly pedicure unit. Continuum uses recycled material to build their pedicure units." **Mac McAlister**, Salon Furnishing Professional, SalonCentric "I have used Maletti, which is an Italian furniture line that accommodates any salon that wants eco-friendly salon furniture."
Walls	
Stainless Steel & Traditional Drywall	**Sean Curly**, Regional Furnishings Professionals, SalonCentric "I have used stainless steel on the walls. Traditional drywall is still the most common for salon build outs."
Natural Stone & Tile	**David Osgood**, Vice President of Sales and Marketing, Interiors by R.G. Shakour "Salons are using different types of natural stone and tile on walls (and floors). I just finished a salon that used a sandy, earth-tone finish on the walls. They varnished over it for a gloss effect. Very different application, but it gave the salon a cool slick look."
Lighting	
Adding lights around station mirrors	**Mac McAlister**, Salon Furnishing Professional, SalonCentric "I have witnessed many salon remodels that include additional lighting around the styling station mirror. This gives illumination in front of the client and takes away the harsh shadowing effect from overhead lighting."
LED Lighting	**David Osgood**, Vice President of Sales and Marketing, Interiors by R.G. Shakour "Current LED lights are perfect for color processing in salons and give accurate light for stylists and customers without throwing off heat. The good news is that they are energy efficient with no maintenance. Frequently changing lightbulbs is a thing of the past if your use LED in your salon."

SalonCentric

Peter M. Hornig, *Director of Equipment*

"One of the biggest trends I see these days is the request to build for "double-shifting" at the stations. Remodel requests for expanding each chair's ability to support two stylists is increasing as well. Owners are looking to earn more income per station while capitalizing on the increase in available stylists on the street. The savvy salon designer is finding economical and innovative ways to satisfy this demand."

SalonCentric

Joni Fastnacht, *Furnishings Professional*

"I see the concept of rental suites or rooms becoming even more popular around the country to meet the market demand for independent stylists who want to go into business for themselves. Having a salon suite enables them to build a salon within a salon usually a 10x10 room with all the comforts of a full-service salon at an affordable weekly rent. Another trend is the Dry Bar concept which is starting to sprout up in several areas. Of course, I see a lot more salons putting in color bars also. As far as colors, earth tone colors seem to be the color palette of choice."

Photos: Sopra Salon, Prairie Village, KS (2012)

SalonCentric

Dave Golichowski, *Furnishings Professional*

"Open Styling areas and a major focus on Color Bars, Retail, and their clients comfort. The openness of the salon is what I see in the future. People aren't sheltering the color area or the wash areas for shampooing. Everyone wants to see what is going on in the salon. They want to feel like they are part of something. It's no longer an embarrassment to get your hair colored. Why sit your clients off in a dark room by themselves when they can be mingling with other guests who are getting treatments just like them! This is what I see as focus areas."

Photos: Fran Coy Salon and Spa in Ann Arbor, MI (2013)

SalonCentric

Leslie Groves, *Furnishings Professional*

"In the past few years, the trend that I have seen explode is the Color Bar. An exposed Color Bar will not only create a stunning visual effect, it creates excitement! Any size of salon can benefit from increased color service revenue and improved inventory control."

Photos: Salon Foushee, Denver, CO; Salon Owner: Kara Forshay

SalonCentric

Richard G. Winkleman, *Furnishings Professional*

"A few observations for trends:

- *Warm palettes will always remain popular, but trending more than ever are the cooler palettes, materials, and effects.*

- *Boutique interiors/design will continue to grow as it defines a new, younger generation of stylist/hairdresser. No detail is too small to capture the look.*

- *Correct lighting is finally becoming mandatory, trumping the budgets for expensive flooring, etc. Footage/space allowance must define the salon ambiance in such a way as to insure the guest of a pleasurable, yet professional experience."*

Photos: Salon Meritage, Seal Beach, CA

Design Tips

We recommend that your layout and design follow these tried-and-true methods and considerations for a functional, well-planned design.

- **Codes & Ordinances:** Make sure your location meets all required handicap codes and safety guidelines according to local ordinances.

- **Create the Feeling of More Space:** Clients associate a larger floor area with opulence, which they then associate with success and desirability. If your salon is small, there are ways to make it look bigger:

  - Rearrange your aisles, putting more space between them.

  - Adjust the shelves on the walls to be one or two stops higher.

  - Any shelves in the middle of the floor should not limit the sight lines.

  - Flood the area with natural light.

- **Flow:** The flow of movement is very important to running an efficient salon. Clients need to be able to move to different areas of the business without being confused, interfering with employee traffic, or bumping into displays or other clients.

- **Communication:** Ease of communication among staff members and clients makes for a better environment and a positive atmosphere.

- **Product Placement:** Maximize the appearance of retail by giving it prominent placement in your salon. Employee product handling is another important factor. Having the color bar next to the color department is critical so the stylist can access what they need quickly and easily, without leaving the client.

- **Storage:** Effective space utilization can improve the efficiency and inventory control for the salon. Design your storage area so that it is effortless for your staff to find what they need and easy to monitor inventory.

- **Future Expansion:** When designing and space planning, analyze all potential expansions and make allowances for them in your design.

- **Style:** A brand is what attracts your clients and makes them feel they are in the right place. The brand starts with the design of the salon and the experience you want to create and flows through everything else. Make sure each of the following elements communicates the salon's brand:

  - Logo

  - Staff

  - Marketing/advertising

  - Overall look of the salon

  - Shape and style of the reception desk

  - Color on the walls

  - Artwork and other accessories

Here are some tips to help you pull everything together when laying out each area and your departments:

★ Five-Point Salon Design System ★

POINT #1: The Entrance (Doorway/Front Desk/Waiting Area)

- Make sure the desk is properly designed for all components: computer, printers, credit card machine, and a telephone system.
- There should be a counter with space on the desk for clients to write checks, sign credit card slips or search through their purse easily.
- Don't forget counter space at different heights to accommodate for clients in wheel chairs or of shorter stature (as covered in the Universal Design chapter).

POINT #2: The Store Inside Your Salon (Retail Area)

- Install good lighting for exposure of the products, with clear signage and highlight areas for special promotions.
- Displays or shelving should be easy to reach and not too low to the floor or too high. Keep in mind if the customers can't see, reach it, touch and feel it. They will not buy it.

POINT #3: Your Bread & Butter (Service Area)

- Styling station - provide proper storage and utility holders for all tools. Enough outlets to plug in all your utensils.
- Shampoo area - insure storage for products and towels, close to the shampoo bowls.
- Service areas, such as shampoo, manicure, pedicure or facial rooms, should be near the bathroom or near your hot water heater. Designing this properly could save you thousands in plumbing expenses.

POINT #4: Let Your Color Shine (Color & Dispensary Area)

- Plan for plenty of cabinets to house color and mixing bowls.
- Install a stainless steel sink for color wash down. Other man made materials will stain.
- Lighting is important for your stylist to see what colors they are mixing and also to insure less waste of color mixing products.
- Do not make color storage unreachable. Your staff will use lower drawers as step stools to reach products for treatments.

POINT #5: Behind the Scenes (Utility Area)

- Lighting is important in this area. If you are using this as a storage place or if you are accepting packages or inventory in this area, you will want to make sure you can see what is being delivered and what you have in stock. Also, if your staff is using this as a place to keep their personal belongings, you'll want any closet or locker areas to be well-lit.

- Combine utilities into a single area including a commercial hot water heater with a quality washer and dryer for towels.

- Do not put staff or customer's lockers or coat hooks next to electrical panels.

- Water and electric do not mix. Any items that need to be plugged in should be no less than five feet from sinks, wash basins or slop sinks.

Common Design Mistakes

Let's take a close look at these floor plans, all based on rectangular storefronts, and analyze salon elements. At the end of the book, you'll find all the plans for salons of all sizes, including work stations for various number of service providers.

Reception Area

This zoomed in area of a salon design features an impressive reception area. It dominates the vision of the clients as they enter the building and is very welcoming. The reception (or front desk) is set back far enough so that the client can get fully into the store. This exposes clients to the retail that is on both sides of the front desk. If the wall behind the reception is a half-wall, then there could be sightlines into the rest of the salon for an open feeling. However, it does say that it's a logo wall. So, it's likely that this if a full wall. The desk is big enough to serve more than one client for all transactions and its rounded shape is more friendly and stylish than a rectangular shape. Clients could be directed into the service area from the right of the desk and escorted out from the left, to keep a circular flow throughout the salon. Using a directional flow would expose them to the product displays on both sides of the salon.

However, the waiting area seems a little limited. It only seats two people, off in the corner. This salon owner may have figured no more than two people would be waiting at a time, or may have wanted others waiting to be moving around to look at the product displays in the retail area. Is this a mistake, blunder, or great idea?

In this salon design, the limited seating keeps any new customers coming in with nothing more to do than to shop and look around the retail area. If they are standing, walking around, and looking at retail, then there is more of a chance that they will buy. If they are sitting, they are probably not shopping. One could argue that leaving your customers standing too long and waiting is not a good thing and not courteous. On the other hand, if they arrive on time and they are waiting for more than a few minutes for their appointment, then the salon management practices may need to be looked at—not necessarily the design itself.

Wise Use of Space

Here is a very small salon which has used space wisely. Despite their size, they have included four kinds of services: shampoo, style, makeup, and waxing. They have even managed to create a small retail area out of a corner. The retail area is visible from the outside of the window. It's important to keep the window space as open as possible, especially with a smaller salon. The waiting area is small, which encourages clients to cross the room to visit the retail area. However, this space does not allow for a dryer and the work stations are tight on space. Is this a mistake, blunder, or great idea?

They say good things come in small packages. This salon layout accomplished everything the salon owner wanted. They were limited on space. So, the styling stations are a bit tighter than normal. Also, the front desk is smaller and may not be functional at its size. Overall, this is not a bad space when you considering the overall square footage.

Spacious & Open

On the other end of the spectrum, here is a large salon.

Note that the styling areas have been placed on an angle for style and visual privacy. This salon owner values his employees and knows the more comfortable they are the better job they will do. He has given them both a break room and a staff room. The waxing room is very private and might be able to double as a massage area. The color room is very complete with lots of storage.

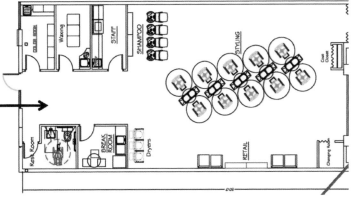

If you look closely at the layout of the salon, you will see that there is no functioning front desk. Is this a design mistake, blunder, or great idea? In this case, this design is for a booth rental salon. Each of the stylists (booth renters) is responsible for greeting their client and bringing them to their styling station. This is not a major design mistake. It is common for booth rental salons to not include a front desk. However, what happens if the stylist is running behind with their previous appointment? Unfortunately with this design, there is no reception area for clients to sit and wait for their stylist. We think that no matter how big or small the salon, you must have a space for your clients to sit and wait. Murphy's Law seems to always strike and no one can run on a perfect schedule. The Five-Point Design System lays out the importance of the reception area for your salon, clients and staff. This salon would fall under the design blunder category because it is missing two very important features in the Five-Point Design System for the reception area.

Top 10 Common Design Mistakes

1. No windows that can open to allow you to let in the fresh air. This is important to include in a utility room or in a color area when possible.

2. Poor Heating, ventilating and air conditioning (HVAC) planning.

3. Insufficient electrical/not enough outlets. It can be a nightmare if stylists do not have enough outlets for styling tools at their stations.

4. Running pipes all over the building instead of grouping water needs together. Plumbing is extremely expensive, especially when the plumber has to cut a concrete floor to install waste and water lines.

5. Storage not convenient for service providers.

6. Doors open into each other, or block a walkway when they are open.

7. Sacrificing function for design, especially at the front desk. The front desk is the heart of the salon. Yes, it's important for it to look beautiful. But, it also needs to be functional.

8. Desk, retail area, hallways, and bathrooms not handicap accessible. Remember your clients come in all shapes and sizes and some may have physical limitations. You must consider all of your clients in the design stages of the salon build out.

9. Not enough area for retail. If you are not carrying retail, then you will not be a profitable salon. Remember to add enough retail space in your salon design.

10. Salon not designed for the clientele in the area. For instance, in a community with many senior citizens, more hair dryers are required than in an area with younger demographics. Or, if the area is big into color services, then give more prominence and space for color services.

Did the three salon designs that we just reviewed make any of the common mistakes? Of the 10 most common mistakes, think about the effect on:

1. Profitability
2. Cost Management

3. Client Satisfaction

4. Employee Satisfaction

5. Owner Frustration

Take a look at the following picture. What is missing? What choices would you consider a mistake or blunder based on what you know and have learned so far by reading this book?

That's right! The retail area is missing. Without the retail area within or viewable from the waiting area, the opportunity for product sales is lost. Secondly, the sleek lines of the couches may look pleasing to the eye; however, clients may be uncomfortable sitting closely to strangers. Individual seats with arms are something to keep in mind as you choose your seating for your waiting area.

Hopefully, it was helpful to take a critical look at different designs and to think about some of the common mistakes or flaws.

Ready, Set, Go! Expert Advice!

Planning your space is not only for comfort and style, but also for profit. Yes, the look is very important to keep old clients and attract new clients. However, your salon's layout has to maximize every square inch. Making money is a top priority. Using the Five-Point Salon Design System will enable you to incorporate every detail into your design plan. You pay for every square inch of your space. Using all of your salon's square footage to your advantage will be the key to your salon's success.

Expert Advice!

Jeff Owen, CFO Keamark Salon Furnishings

Picture this: You are just on the verge of being recognized as a pinnacle salon in your market. You have built a sustainable team of professionals and a full book of business. But your salon's perceived reputation among the targeted A-List clientele and stylists lags in perception just below the pinnacle you aspire to occupy. Could it be your salon lacks that buzz, it factor, cache or social momentum that is conferred by the A-Listers to only a select? This buzz cannot be achieved via self-promotion, even if it is the truth. Obtaining an IT factor is something that is granted.

Today's market demands excellence in all aspects of business – including design, function, and image. When creating your Signature Salon, no detail is too small. While the considerations that go into a salon are countless, the goal is quite singular . . . when you first step inside each day you should feel at home. To that end, your furniture partner should painstakingly craft your salon to create an environment to reflect the emotions you wanted to achieve and give you a sense of confidence and well-being. You deserve to be at the top, now show the world you mean it and look the part.

CHAPTER 10

Incorporating Design Through Furniture & Equipment Choices

"Design is the method of putting form, content and
* furniture together.*
Design, just as art, has multiple definitions; there is no
* single definition.*
Design can be art. Design can be aesthetics.
Design is so simple, that's why it is so complicated."

—Paul Rand

Have you ever redesigned a space in your home? You probably started with some inspiration. Whether it was something you saw in a magazine or whether your design centered on a unique piece of pottery or art, you had something that helped you keep your choices aligned with your inspiration. Designing your salon space and choosing your furniture and equipment is exactly the same type of experience. You'll be amazed—and possibly overwhelmed—by all the choices. So, you need to have a really firm grasp on your brand, the clientele that you want to attract, and the experience that you are trying to create.

How to Choose the Right Furniture & Equipment for Your Salon

When shopping for salon furniture and equipment, there are many things to consider. Selecting the appropriate furniture can add to your salon's business and growth. The kind of furniture and equipment you choose determines the environment of your business. The style and look you choose will determine what type of clients your salon will draw. Quality salon furniture and equipment, placed in an inviting atmosphere, is the perfect complement to a great salon environment.

When choosing furniture and equipment, you should consider working with a designer who specializes in salon layouts. You may also want to have someone with you who shares your vision and can give you feedback. This will be helpful as the salon designer presents different options that meet your budget and design vision. A suitable salon designer should be able to make the design and purchasing experience simple, exciting, and memorable.

You'll have to decide on styles, sizes, colors, laminate designs, and finishes (wood, metal, stained, painted, or natural). There are so many different laminates and veneers to choose from; however, durability is a must. Here are some factors to consider when making your choices:

- Veneers are RARELY used in the salon setting except for in areas that are not affected by hairspray or color. The hairspray and chemicals eventually wear away at the veneers/wood causing the salon owner to have to replace these pieces sooner than if a different material had been used.

- Real wood and veneers do not hold up well as compared to laminate.

- Seating can be cotton, plush, natural fiber, and more. Keep in mind that the fabrics and colors you choose must stand up to water and hair dye.

  - The most common material used in the salon setting for seating is VINYL. It has endured many tests for durability and wear-ability, making it the most popular selection for styling and color areas.

  - Choosing lighter colors, such as white, yellow, and pink for a fabric can make your salon pop and truly look special. However, black is the most common color for styling chairs and reception furniture in salons to hide stains.

NOTE

Design Specialist, Kimber Atkinson of Kimber Design's states, "As a designer people want to go with other colors besides black. When salon owners choose lighter colors, they may have to cover their seats with plastic or choose a two-tone style to bring in lighter colors. If you don't like the idea of setting aside extra time to remove stains from your chairs, then it might not be worth the hassle for you."

Once again, your salon designer should be able to guide you through making the right decision and help you choose the styles, designs, and finishes that you will love.

Let's look at some of the most common design styles and how your choices in furniture/ equipment, finishes, and colors can play into the characteristics of the style. What you choose is based on what you like. Usually, the design and style of your furniture emulates your own personal likes when it comes to the final look you are trying to create in your salon.

Style	Style Characteristics	Furniture / Equipment	Finishes	Colors
Contemporary	Sleek lines, clean look, modern feel	Everything hidden, no wires/cords, light and simplistic	Black, stainless steel, dark woods	Black, white, silver, pop of bold color, wood look
Traditional	Mixture of curvy and straight lines, classic design	Heavier look, bigger pieces	Wood, granite look, marble look	Cherry or lighter wood tones, soft colors, blues, greens, browns

Style	Style Characteristics	Furniture / Equipment	Finishes	Colors
Industrial	Cold feeling, very open and exposed, durable	Bigger pieces, not a lot of detail or design	Metal finishes, concrete look, rough finishes	Blacks, browns, monotone scheme, silver/gray
Glam	High-end feeling, glitzy, luxurious	Petite, stylish, detailed, comfortable	Shiny, glossy, mirror look	White, pewter, pop of bright color
Eclectic	Variety of styles combined in one area, random	Mixture, not all the same style or look, re-purposing items	Wood and metal, texture and smooth, color and bland	No particular color scheme, wide variety

Buying Furniture & Equipment

Buying your furniture and equipment is a big expense. If you go too cheap, you'll suffer the consequences by having to deal with less than ideal wear and tear, expensive repair, and replacement costs. You can buy new or used. In the next couple pages we'll provide you with information for each source and what you can expect.

Manufacturers and/or Distributors

The furniture and equipment manufacturers and/or distributor will be able to furnish you with catalogs, swatches, and color samples of their products. They will also walk you through the different sizes and shapes of the furniture and equipment. They will be able to discuss competitive pricing, customer service, warranty, and repair policies.

- **www.takarabelmont.com**
- **www.collinsmfgco.com**
- **www.minervabeauty.com**
- **www.saloncentric.com**

Shopping Online

You can shop online to find great deals and the different looks that you want to create. However, return shipment fees can get expensive. It's difficult to assess the quality, feel, and texture of an item that you are buying online. If you are not happy with the quality or the selection you made, you will have to ship the product back to the company. The cost to ship it back is always going to be your expense. It is not cheap sending back styling chairs and furniture. The cost to ship these items back may exceed what you paid for them in the first place. There also may be a restocking fee for the items returned.

Used Furniture & Equipment

When buying used furniture, stay local so that you can test and look closely at the merchandise before you buy it. However, it is important to realize that there are limitations to used equipment because there will not be a warranty and you may not be able to get parts. For instance, we don't recommend buying used for the following:

- Plumbing products (unless you have the history on the item)
- Electrical products (such as a multifunction skincare machine)

That being said, we do recommend considering used for extra chairs, skincare tables, or workstations. If you are mixing and matching old and new, plan on putting the used items in private rooms.

If you happen to find someone local who is remodeling their salon and desperate to get rid of their old furniture and equipment, you might be able to get a better price because they might be more willing to bargain with you.

Sources for used salon furniture and equipment:

- **Craigslist (craigslist.com):** Find your local or regional area on the site. A lot of times, people remodeling want to get rid of what they have. The equipment dealer in the area offered them "next to nothing" for it so they decide to sell it on their own. Here is a good opportunity to save some money.
- **Local newspapers:** Go to the classified section and look under furniture.
- **EBay:** Check out the site, you might find some used furniture available.
- **Salon furniture supplier:** You never know when they might have clearance or gently used items for sale.

> ### Salon Owners Talk About . . . the Good, the Bad, and the Ugly
>
> *"I found used massage tables and facial equipment on Craig's List. It was almost brand new at a third of the price. It allowed me to experiment with spa services at a fraction of the cost. I had two empty rooms; now, they produce revenue that I did not expect."*
>
> —Sue Holmann, All About You Hair and Nail Spa

The whole process of picking the right furniture should be a fun process. However, always consider the following when it comes down the final decision.

- **Durability**—The furniture you choose must be durable. Although you may love what you choose and spend a fortune buying it, your clients and staff may not have the same appreciation and may not be used as delicately as needed. The salon atmosphere on any furniture is not "handle with care" it's usually "handle with a hammer." It will not be uncommon for a client or one of your employees to sit on, pull on, tug on, drag objects across, and put their feet up on your prized salon furniture.

- **Color**—Lighter colors can be protected with coverings. Beware, your stylists will get color on your white styling chairs, and your clients will spill coffee on your beautiful yellow couch.

- **Size Matters**—You may find the most beautiful antique piece for a retail display. You might be shocked that what looks "small" in an antique store is much larger than the space you have available. Always take measurements before you buy.

- **Mixed Bag of Tricks**—Mixing and matching furniture takes talent. You may be the best colorist in town. However, you may not be the best "interior" designer. If your attempts to mix and match start to look like a jumbled mess, then it's time for help from a professional. You want your design to work to your advantage and every dime that you spend needs to be put to good use.

Furniture/Equipment Type, Style, & Finish Checklist

What furniture and equipment choices will you make to enhance the characteristics of the style that you have chosen for your salon?

My salon's style is: _____

	Choices to Enhance the Characteristics of My Salon's Style
Furniture/ Equipment	
Finishes	
Colors	

Where will I shop for my furniture/equipment?

_____

_____

_____

PART II

HEAD-TO-TOE – SUCCESS IS IN THE DESIGN DETAILS

CHAPTER 11

A Bright Idea: Salon Lighting

"A rooster crows only when it sees the light. Put him in the dark and he'll never crow. Show as many people the light and they will all crow."

—Muhammad Ali

Light is essential for life, growth, health, beauty, and selling! So much can be done with the direction, color, and intensity of the lighting choices for your salon. Do you know or have you thought about how lighting affects your clients?

- Lighting will change the feel and mood of a room:
    - Harsh overhead lights creates an intimidating feeling and dark shadows.
    - Soft, diffused light from around the room, makes it feel safe, warm, and welcoming.
- If your lighting makes your clients uncomfortable—either too bright and harsh or too dark—they will not stick around and spend money.
- Lighting makes your client's hair shine and gives their skin a smooth and fresh look.
- New lighting systems, like Peter Millard Color Lighting, render accurate colors within the salon environment, enabling your stylists to create the exact color that your clients want.
- Accent lighting can put your clients in a buying mood by showing off new retail items
- Good lighting will make your clients look gorgeous, and they'll come back for more!

Builders usually only concern themselves with adequate overhead lighting and they may not be thinking about how to properly light a salon. In fact, inadequate or improper lighting in a salon environment can have serious consequences and cause the following:

- A dirty or even unsanitary salon.
- Safety hazards.

- Haircutting mistakes by stylists.

- Hair color misjudgments.

- Overlooking products that might otherwise be purchased.

- Wrong product purchases and product exchanges.

- Dissatisfaction with the service results provided by the stylist/colorist/makeup artist.

- Undercharging or overcharging clients.

- Mislabeling products or incorrect placement of products on displays.

- Poor control over inventory.

- An unsafe situation for low-vision clients.

The trick with choosing your lighting is to know enough to make the right decisions for directing your contractors, designers, and/or buyers. You must be involved in these decisions because your salon's lighting will improve employee productivity, retail sales, safety and security, brand identification, revenue, and profit.

Lighting at Each of the Five Points

Understanding how to use light can make your business much more effective and help you avoid the serious consequences of inadequate lighting. Maintaining and growing a retail business means always showing off the best aspects of your products and services. Therefore, effective lighting is important in all five areas of the business. Here's a look at the Five-Point Salon Design System areas and some key points about lighting these areas:

★ POINT #1: The Entrance (Doorway/Front Desk/Waiting Area)

- Invites patrons into your salon.

- Sets a tone.

- Directional lighting helps clients to see when checking out and making appointments.

★ POINT #2: The Store Inside Your Salon (Retail Area)

- Illuminates and spotlights products to get client's attention.

- Helps clients to read product signage, labels, and prices.

- Improves sales.

★ POINT #3: Your Bread & Butter (Service Area)

- Help service providers to see what they are doing and provide the exact color and hair style the client is expecting. (Lighting for color is extremely important).

- Flatters clients' facial features and skin tones.

- Provides the right atmosphere for the given service area. For example, massage rooms and spa areas should have dimming capabilities for a more relaxing experience.

★ **POINT #4: Let Your Color Shine (Color/Dispensary Area)**

- Staff and clients are more engaged and in sync during the color selection and application process because everyone can "see" the color choices more accurately.

- Less mistakes and higher client satisfaction levels—meaning fewer complaints from clients whom are unhappy about bad haircuts or hair color.

★ **POINT #5: Behind the Scenes (Utility Area)**

Your utility room, restrooms, and changing rooms need the right lighting.

- Utility rooms should be bright, in order to:

    - Reenergize your staff.

    - Keep chemicals for cleaning visible to staff and maintenance people.

    - Light up the electrical panel or plumbing fixtures for routine maintenance.

    - Perform inventory management/control of product/retail storage.

- Restrooms can be softly lit for your clients, but you'll want the ability to increase lighting for cleaning and sanitizing.

- Changing rooms should have dimmable lighting so that you can keep a relaxed atmosphere for spa services.

Remember, there are times when you will want to have the capability to brighten up your entire salon even more, such as after hours to ensure thorough cleaning, for painting touch ups, and/or when servicing furniture and equipment.

Lighting for Beauty

Natural light is the best for applying makeup and choosing hair color. However, it's not usually available throughout an entire salon. When choosing lighting, you'll want to replicate natural light as much as possible. Here are some goals for lighting for beauty:

- The light needs to be bright, yet diffuse.

- It must not cast shadows on the face.

- It must not have too much of a tint. Fluorescents are a no-no with their harsh blue-green color.

- Incandescent lights, especially softly colored bulbs, are good.

- Many small bulbs are better than one big one.

- For makeup artists, it's good to have some lights on dimmers, to see how the makeup looks in the different light conditions that the client might encounter once she walks out the door.

- Do not fully illuminate and flood an area with light, use only directional spotlights, lighted mirrors, or scones to cast the right amount of light. Dark paint can be used in combination with lighting patterns for dramatic effects.

Natural Light

Natural lighting is the light that shines through the windows of your store from the sun. This is the broadest possible spectrum. It's provides "warm" lighting tones and it comes free of charge. A large window can bring a nice feeling into a salon. In fact, a retail store designer may suggest using natural light as a means of showing off your retail products. In most cases, there are too many obstacles and issues with natural light. For instance:

- A huge bank of windows can allow in a lot of heat and even create an unpleasant greenhouse effect inside. Consider UV blocking tinting for the glass on the windows or light, diffusing shades that also blocks UV light. This will protect the interior of your salon from the heat and damage that comes with long-term sun exposure.

- Available daylight tends to change in intensity throughout the day, with inclement weather, and during each season.

- Window space must also be used for displaying products to the passer-by.

- Interior salons or ones that are inside a mall may not have any windows to the outside.

- Your salon will be open during times when it is dark outside.

Because it's free, you definitely want to find a way to bring in natural light. Don't block off all your windows. All we are suggesting is that, given the challenges and obstacles of natural light, it is best to have a "backup" lighting scheme.

Setting Up Your Salon's Lighting

One issue that you must determine early in your design and space planning process is adequate power for not only the functional operations of the salon, but also the lighting. In an older building, this may mean updating the breaker box to add more breakers. It probably means adding outlets. But, it could mean that you need some serious services from a licensed electrician to run more wiring for the fixtures that you'd like to install.

There are many lighting resources available to retail store owners. Most people get the bulk of the information from local lighting stores. These stores have sales people that are well versed in setting up stores or at least guiding you to make the right decisions when choosing your stores retail lighting. We recommend hiring a lighting professional if your electrician or architect cannot assist you with the lighting design for your retail store. Many lighting stores have lighting designers that will help you for free if you buy your fixtures from them. Also, most electric supply stores will be able to assist you or recommend someone to help with your project.

Your lighting scheme will be made up of task, ambient, and directional lighting.

- The task lighting will be lights directed at the reception desk or the styling chair for maximum visibility in a defined area.

- The ambient lighting can vary according to style but should provide enough light so that everyone can move about the salon.

- The directional lighting will put spotlights on retail displays and possibly art or signage.

Lighting Fixtures & Bulb Types

Your lighting scheme will include a combination of fixtures and lightbulbs. The fixtures that you'll choose from serve different lighting purposes as do the lightbulbs that you choose for your fixtures.

Lighting Fixtures

The lighting fixtures you choose have both design and functional components. The fixtures will enhance the characteristics of the style that you have chosen for your salon. In addition, they'll serve some type of function. They may light up the entrance, showcase products, allow service providers to see while working on clients, and more. For an introduction to the different types of fixtures, you can go to Lowes or Home Depot. Home Depot has some great Buyer's Guides, including one that covers all Ceiling Lighting. However, we've also provided the following information for how the fixtures would be used in a salon environment.

- **Track**—Give off a starlight effect. Track lighting is also good to show off a specific area. You may be highlighting retail displays that are high-selling items or the name of your salon. One downside of track lighting is the amount of heat that they give off. If used in the styling area, the stylists or clients could end up feeling hot and uncomfortable. They also burn out quickly if kept on for long periods of time.

- **Recessed**—No matter what size your store is you must always consider your electric bill. If your retail store or salon is located in a mall you may be required to be open the same hours as the mall which is seven days a week and as much fourteen hour days. Your electric bill could be outlandish if you don't choose the right lighting. Since you often have to install a large number of lights at a retail location, look into energy efficient fixtures. Recessed fixtures sit within the ceilings of the store while standard fixtures hang and are sometimes adjustable. Energy efficient light fixtures contain lamps that use less energy compared to standard lighting options.

- **Chandeliers**—Great for a grand entrance of a salon. If you have the space and the height, using a Chandelier will make any entrance elegant and certainly make your salon quite different than others in the area. However, they tend to be expensive. Finding one that fits your budget may be a tough task. Consider thrift stores and antique shops to find that one that best fits your salon entrance and your budget.

- **Sconces**—Sconces add such a nice touch and soften any room. These are used in hallways in many spas or treatment rooms. They give off the feeling of elegance, yet softness— making clients feel relaxed and welcomed. They are also used to make a room look formal. Formal is good—as long as you are not dressing up a room to much. Sconces can also be put on dimmers. So, if you are looking for softer lighter or to darken down a room, then these do work well. You will also find that sconces fit into most budgets for lighting.

- **Spotlights**—Plan to feature certain items or have a display case that you want to use in a specific area of the salon for hot new items or sale items. For these areas spot lights can be very effective. A spotlight is an ideal way to draw attention to specific items or an area. The spotlight shines from the ceiling or wall toward its target. You can also install task or accent lighting, which puts a smaller spotlight on certain items on your selling floor, like items on a shelf or inside a cabinet.

- **Floor Lights**—Floor lights are used in hallways and in treatment rooms to set the mood and heighten the ambiance of a room being used for spa services. They are also used as a safety feature if hallways are too dim. Putting lights in the floor is not cheap and are a pain to change once they blow out. It may sound like a good idea in the planning stage; but, most salons and spas that do have them wish they didn't install them in the first place.

- **Task Lights**—Tasks lights are very effective in all areas of a salon, including the front desk, manicure department, pedicure department, styling department, spa treatment rooms, and the utility room. They are simply called task lights because they are used for a specific task, such as mixing color, manicuring and painting nails, cutting hair, setting appointments, doing paperwork, making change, etc. They can be turned on and off when needed and are usually placed exactly where the task is being performed.

- **Lamps**—Lamps are not used in many salons. You may find them in some treatment rooms in salons or spas as a necessary tool for a specific treatment. Lamps tend to get in the way and may be dangerous if knocked over or left on when the salon is closed. With so many different applications of lighting today, lamps are not one we would recommend in the salon environment.

- **Candlelight**—They don't have enough lumens to be very effective in a salon; but, at 2000K, they are the softest, most flattering light and they can make a place feel cozy and natural. If that's the kind of feeling you'd like in your salon, place them in a safe place and light them in a safe area.

Types of Lightbulbs

Lights come in different colors and intensities. Getting a little familiar with the types of lights you might use goes a long way toward that first lighting design session with your designers, contractors, and lighting specialists. You can find great info on the types of lightbulbs through an internet search. The guides for lightbulbs available through

Lowes and the lighting shopping center at Home Depot can help make quick work of your research and education. In addition, here's an introduction to the different types of lightbulbs and some tips about using them in your salon:

- **Fluorescent**—These are tubes filled with mercury that give off a very bright light. Because of their brightness, they are great for cleaning. They do NOT, however, belong in the styling area during business hours because they are harsh and unflattering.

- **Incandescent**—These are the most common bulbs. They come in various colors. The "soft" bulb can be flattering.

- **Halogen**—These bulbs are sometimes used in spotlights. They tend to be expensive and their intensity fades with time. However, most salons use a combination of incandescent and halogen bulbs, which create a lighting tone, that's bright enough, soft enough, and broad enough to be clear, accurate, and flattering.

- **Compact Fluorescent Light (CFLs)**—These are required in some cities. They are considered to be wide spectrum and economical (in the long run). Like fluorescents, they can be a little harsh. So, read the label and make sure they are "corrected" to 2700 to 3000K, to best match the softness of the incandescent lightblulb.

- **Specialty Bulbs**—Can vary in size, shape, and color. Colored spots can be directed at walls and other design features for dramatic effect.

- **Light Emitting Diodes (LEDs)**—Can be another economical way to light specific areas of the salon. They have a long life. They come in a variety of color temperatures. They offer natural looking light, which can bring out the best in virtually all retail products. LED's have been praised by many interior designers for providing the most authentic looking light, and you will find that neutral white LEDs can provide the closest mirror to what an item would look like under bright, natural sunlight. Some municipalities require a certain number of LEDs in new construction.

Lighting Maintenance

The lighting in your retail will slowly get worse overtime. It may not be noticeable but once you clean and or replace your bulbs, you will immediately notice a big difference. Keeping a scheduled maintenance of cleaning or replacing the lights will keep your lighting at peak performance.

Improving your lighting system can be as easy as 1, 2, or 3:

1. **Clean them.** Lamps and luminaries, like any other surface, collect dust and dirt over time. When these lamp surfaces become dirty, they lose the luster and intensity of the light that they give off. They are working harder to give off the light they would

normally give when clean. They become overheated and draw more energy, despite giving off lower levels of light. To properly clean your fixtures follow these guidelines:

- Make sure your lights are off.

- If using a ladder set to the side of the fixtures (do not set directly underneath a florescent bulb or light fixture) Fluorescents can easily come crashing down when slightly loosened. If you are standing to the side you will be out of danger.

DO NOT USE WATER ON ANY BULBS OR FLUORESCENTS. ELECTRIC AND WATER DO NOT MIX. YOU MAY CAUSE THE BULB TO BLOW UP; OR, EVEN WORSE, GET ELECTROCUTED.

2. **Replacing the bulb.** Bulbs lose their lumens with age and stop working as efficiently during the latter stages of their lives. We recommend group replacement, which involves replacing all the bulbs at the same time. This will guaranty the light levels in your retail store are above par at all times.

3. **Replacing the fixture.** You may have inherited the lighting fixtures when you took over the space for your salon. Unfortunately, you may have been stuck with what was already in the space because they were attached to the ceiling or walls and the cost would have been too great to replace. The good news is the lighting industry has come a long way in the past few years. The lamp efficiency and brightness has increased dramatically. By replacing one lamp type with a more efficient version will enhance light and also reduce your overall energy costs. So, it might be worth it to put together a budget for replacing your fixtures.

Spot lights in an area of muted light are very stylish. Note the black ceiling.

**Salon Owners Talk About . . .
the Good, the Bad, and the Ugly**

"The worst thing in your retail store is 'dark spots.' As a retailer, I know that if the customer can see it, they will pick it up. Then it's up to my team to sell it. If clients can't see it, like in your dark spots, they keep walking and you have no chance at the sale."

—Harrison Sasser, Gentlemen's Corner, Wilmington, NC

"I have almost 16' of retail. I use LED lighting that is the most brilliant white light on the market. And I have an expression in my salon: If a client is walking and talking through the retail area, they're not buyers, but the minute they stop, you've got them. Give them good lighting, let them see your products and they'll stop, buy, and come back for more."

—Juliann Gahr, Juliann's Styling Salon, Point Pleasant, NJ

"The most important lighting is over the guest. It makes them the star of the show. But your retail lighting needs to be bright and effective. We change bulbs regularly to maximize product visibility. Lighting can be the Achilles heel of your retail environment."

—Chris Planson, Mistic Hair, Tampa, Fl.

"Lighting is the key to salon success. The better the lighting, the happier your clients. They'll see the correct color of their hair and get a real view of how great they look. The correct lighting dynamics will change your hair color business and take your retail out of the shadows."

—David Osgood, R.G. Skakoun Salons, Nashua, NH

Source: Peter Mallard Salon Lighting
(Used with permission.)

Ceiling Lighting

The most cost-effective type of ceiling lighting is the standard 2x2 or 2x4 acoustical ceiling lights. This is the most popular lighting in the salons around the country today. They may not be the most attractive, but they will save you thousands of dollars in a year. The standard ceiling is usually included when you take the store. If it's not new construction, you may need to replace the covers for the typical fluorescent lights. They may be yellow and look unsightly. You may not have enough lighting in the styling area and have to add more lights, not something many people realize. These can be negotiated with the landlord if you realize the shortage or the yellowing before you sign your lease.

Halogen Lighting

We have seen clients use many types of halogen lights. Halogen lights work very well, but this will really increase your electric budget. They only convert a small portion of the electric to light the rest they waste as heat.

LED Bulbs

LED bulbs are a gigantic improvement over regular bulbs. LEDs last 25 times longer than regular bulbs and even fluorescents. They turn out the best white light, which is great for salons that do a lot of color services. They do not burn out over time they just lose some of their brightness. They also consume far less electricity compared to other options. The good news is that you pay less and pollute less when using LED in your salon.

★ Five-Point Salon Design System ★
(Point-by-Point Assessment)
What is your lighting plan for each area?

POINT #1: The Entrance (Doorway/Front Desk/Waiting Area)

POINT #2: The Store Inside Your Salon (Retail Area)

POINT #3: Your Bread & Butter (Service Area)

POINT #4: Let Your Color Shine (Color & Dispensary Area)

POINT #5: Behind the Scenes (Utility Area)

CHAPTER 12

If the Walls Could Talk

*"The whole difference between construction and creation is
exactly this: that a thing constructed can only be loved after it is
constructed; but, a thing created is loved before it exists."*

—Charles Dickens

When early humans first had walls, in caves, they saw the opportunity to draw and communicate their life story. Whether for decoration or for holding information, early humans couldn't resist drawing on their cave walls. Similarly, the humans of today are still communicating information through our walls.

Our walls, however, are man-made and come in different shapes and can be covered in paint, wallpaper, tile, and more. Within the salon, the treatments of your walls have both functional and aesthetic benefits. In this chapter, you'll learn about all the different options that you have including shapes, surfaces, and colors.

Wall Shapes

Walls are walls, right? They separate rooms, provide structure and support for ceilings, and conceal wires, cables, ductwork, pipes, insulation, etc. Can they really be part of the overall design and change the look of a salon? Sometimes wall treatments are overlooked as an important or decorative feature. Savvy salon designers, however, will show you how to use them to enhance your salon.

For example, a designer may suggest half walls to the separate manicure department from the stylist department while keeping sightlines open. Or, maybe a glass wall will be used to let light flow into the salon or brighten a dark room. Walls, with the artful eye of a designer, can be shaped, textured, designed, cut, decorated, angled, stained, painted, or wallpapered to bring out the best in your design. Designers also know where to place your walls to set up the flow of your salon. And, they know when to use walls as a statement and when they should simply fade into the background

That being said, walls come in many shapes and sizes and any good designer will use them as a painter uses a canvas to separate, enhance, and beautify a room. Here's a review of the different shapes:

- **Rectangular**—Standard, expected, practical. These are the least expensive; and, therefore, the most typical wall shape. These are also the most amenable to housing pre-fabricated shelves, styling stations, and cabinets.

- **Rounded**—Rounded walls are more modern and give a softer, friendlier feeling. They are particularly stunning if they are glass. Rounded walls are a little more expensive to put into a design and usually more functional on one side versus the other. The downside is that it's hard to add shelving, styling stations, and cabinets to a rounded wall.

- **Angles**—Angles are unnatural in a building. So, if you are designing your salon from ground up —and decide to add in a few unusual angles in your walls—you're communicating to your customer that your salon is modern, stylish, and fearless. Angled walls can be a little unsettling; so, use them sparingly. Good design of shelving on angled walls could yield a very dramatic retail area.

- **Half Walls**—These are great for separating areas of a salon, while not impeding sight lines. They can be made of glass or stone or post and beam construction. They can be permanent elements, or can be just a set of book/display shelves placed to form a barrier.

Wall Surfaces

You can go with bold or subtle textures. The textures and finishes that you choose for your salon will change the form and create the "vibe" you are trying to achieve in your salon. Your salon's vibe showcases your style and leaves a vivid, lasting impression. Let's look at different textures that you can incorporate into your salons walls:

- **Paint**—This is the least expensive way to "decorate" your salon; and, it's the most easily changed. Use white or lighter colors to increase light levels. Use darker colors for mood and emphasis.

- **Brick/Rock**—These surfaces communicate that the business is solid and reliable. They are generally low maintenance, but are not easy to change. Bricks could be painted for a new look. More expensive than a plain, painted wall.

- **Glass**—Glass reflects light and can be used very effectively. It shows fingerprints, but is easy to clean. Cost can be a concern.

- **Textured**—These walls can be stylish, but are not easy to clean. Some can be repainted with an airbrush.

- **Wallpaper**—Wallpaper comes and goes in popularity, but it can be used to accent an area. It is often easy to clean. If tastefully done, it can have a large impact. You will have to keep an eye out for peeling wallpaper and fix it or replace it right away.

Wall Colors

Colored walls can make up for boring architecture. It's more popular to choose a color for one or more walls or the ceiling of your salon. If your salon has no design style, it can be made to look more stylish by manipulating color.

- White walls are the standard. White is great. It's reflective. It's clean.

- Vibrant colors, such as orange, red, yellow, can energize the salon.

- Muted, earth colors, such as blue, green, and tan, are calming.

- Darker colors can emphasize lighting design. Darker colors will require special lighting in the salon, and more lumens since the surface does not reflect. If there is a large window bringing in natural light, a darker paint might be preferable to control the light and give the salon a more intimate feel. Darker painted walls will require more paint to turn them back into light walls.

- A single black wall, or painting the walls of the retail area black, is a very good way to highlight the area. Using black makes the area more intimate, while offering a contrast for the actual fixtures used to house the retail products you are selling and making your retail product jump off the shelves.

- Be careful of bright colors and colors that are less natural, they will not reflect well for viewing makeup and hair color. Bright colors or bold, industrial colors are not suited for a salon that caters to an older clientele. Harsh lighting and stark contrast is best for young faces.

- Chose a "signature" color and repeat it throughout the salon as part of your brand.

- Walls must match the floor. Consider both at the same time.

- Ensure that your salon furnishings also flow with your colors.

- Complimentary colors are good, or creating a unicolor salon with varying degrees of saturation is also a stylish choice and can make a salon look larger, plus help emphasize brightly colored retail areas.

- Save some of the paint (or wallpaper) and keep it on hand for touch ups.

Ready, Set, Go! Expert Advice!

Paint Choices

Certain locations in your salon will demand different types of paint. For example, your styling area will tend to get marked up due to the high volume of traffic. If you are concerned about having it hold up longer, then choose sheen or gloss paint. The higher a paints sheen or gloss, the more washable and durable it is, but the shinier it is, the more flaws you'll notice. If you have to touch up an area that is painted with high-gloss paint, you will notice the spot you touched up. So, be prepared to paint the whole wall.

Unexpected Obstacles

Every demolition is sure to have its share of "surprises". It is not uncommon to see covering up of old walls (or floors/ceilings/roofing) in strip malls and old retail/commercial spaces. It's cheaper to cover over walls, floors, ceilings, etc. rather than tearing it out. So, if you are thinking of tearing something up, you might be surprised to find that there are multiple layers that need to be ripped out. So, what seemed like a good idea may turn out to be an expensive and more time-consuming project than expected. All project decisions come down to time and money. Just realize that the "unplanned and unexpected" can happen and that it's a good idea to have some additional funds identified to cover these types of project challenges.

Salon Owners Talk About . . . the Good, the Bad, and the Ugly

"I have a small salon. The space is 1,000 square feet with six stylists. You enter the front of the salon under a trellis that places you right in the retail area. This puts the guest in the mood to understand they are in a professional coiffure. They don't go to the market to buy their hair products because they understand that we sell and are educated in retail. We have retail displayed everywhere in the salon."

—Annamarie Lignori, Bellas Coiffures, Milan, Italy

★ **Five-Point Salon Design System** ★
(Point-by-Point Assessment)
What is your plan for walls in each area?

POINT #1: The Entrance (Doorway/Front Desk/Waiting Area)

POINT #2: The Store Inside Your Salon (Retail Area)

POINT #3: Your Bread & Butter (Service Area)

POINT #4: Let Your Color Shine (Color & Dispensary Area)

POINT #5: Behind the Scenes (Utility Area)

Ready, Set, Go! Expert Advice!

Create Openness with Partial Walls

To open up the room-to-room flow that encourages social engagement, limit the number of walls that you use to define separate spaces. A wall that drops like a curtain from the ceiling to the floor offers a backdrop, separating the styling area and the shampoo area, but permits the flow of light and sightlines to different areas of the salon.

CHAPTER 13

Trim It Out

"Chiefly, the mold of a man's fortune is in his own hands."

—Francis Bacon, Sr.

Trim has been used for centuries to accentuate architectural features, provide focus, and enhance visual interest. In today's world, you can affordably encase otherwise boring rooms with interesting and aesthetically pleasing trim elements to give a majestic, palace like look. Most salons look the same. You walk in the door, see the front desk and stations lined up along the walls—nothing different, nothing special. But, with the right trim touches, your salon can stand out.

Using different forms of trim (crown molding, door and window trim, and baseboards) creates an ambiance and a style that can be unique in each area. When deciding on what trim and molding to use, think about where you live and your demographics. For example:

- Are you in the Washington D.C. area? If so, you can choose molding to give your salon a "authentic colonial" feel

- Are you in Massachusetts? Then, go for a "Bostonian flavor".

- Are you in New York City? Then, take your loft salon and bring in a contemporary flair.

Accent trim was, at one time, quite expensive. However, with pre-fabrication and advanced manufacturing techniques, it has become relatively inexpensive to add different trim accents. The best part about trimming out your salon is that, with a good carpenter, it can happen quickly. Following are some ideas on how you can "look different" by adding trim touches to your salon.

Crown Molding

Crown molding usually creates depth in any home or business. Without it, your business has a much "boxier" look, with no character. The molding gives a softer feel and you can use different sizes of the same type in each department of your salon. Following are several of the most popular styles of crown molding that can be used. They vary in price all depending on the width and design. A price per foot is associated with each crown mold.

Crown Molding Type	What It Looks Like	Style Type
Palmetto Smooth 3"H x 3"P x 41/4"F x 941/2" L ~$1.39 per foot		Contemporary Traditional
Crendon Bead & Barrel 3"H x 3"P x 41/4"F x 941/2" L ~$1.61 per foot		Contemporary Traditional
Attica Acanthus Leaf 51/4"H x 51/4"P x 71/2"F x 941/2"L ~$3.86 per foot		Old World/Greek
Monique 51/4"H x 61/4"P x 81/4"F x 941/2"L ~$4.67 per foot		Old World/Tuscan
Dentil 23/4"H x 23/4"P x 37/8"F x 945/8" L ~$1.37 per foot		Contemporary Traditional
Rosetta 9"H x 9"P x 121/2"F x 941/2"L ~$11.22 per foot		Old World/Roman

Additional Accents

If you want to accent even more, you can use crown molding blocks and corners. The average price starts at $5.00 can go up to $50.00 per corner, depending on the design. Following are a couple of samples.

Image Source: www. architectualdepot.com

(Used with permission.)

It's best to hire a carpenter who has experience in installing crown moldings and specialty trim. Involve your carpenter in your plans; and, of course, get at least three quotes. It can be tricky to get the angles just right. A professional installer will usually charge an hourly fee, ranging from $15 to $30 per hour. Remember, carpenters need to cover not only a fee for their work, but also the cost of the wear and tear of their tools and cutting blades. So, don't be alarmed if it is on the higher side. You can expect them to install about 400 to 600 running feet of molding per day. Always price check your cost of materials by comparing your options from different stores, distributors, and manufacturers.

Door & Window Trim

Door and window trim can also enhance your salon, spa, or barbershop. This can give your door or window an elegant or classic look. Following are examples of door and window trims.

Cost for material on this door is $200.00   *Each window cost for material is $75.00*

For exterior molding or trim, make sure the installer uses an adhesive for all types of weather and secures it properly. For interior molding and trim, consult with a representative at your neighborhood hardware store.

Floor Baseboards

Floor baseboards can also enhance your establishment. In most cases, the normal baseboard for a commercial location is vinyl baseboard. This is an unsightly look and gives no character to the salon. When you lease a location, it is usually comes with tan, gray, or black vinyl molding and in most cases has a "caulked" look to it because of the drywall work that has been done around it.

We recommend that you put a wood baseboard down, which will give your salon a more "expensive look" and cleaner feel. Baseboard is very inexpensive and can be bought in a white finish so you don't even need to paint it. However, you will have to caulk or fill in the holes from where the nail gun was used to tack it to the wall. The cost for basic baseboard from either Lowes or Home Depot starts at $.75 per foot. To keep it simple, you can use composite plastic, which is very easy to keep clean—it just washes easily with soap and water.

Trim at Each of the Five Points

In today's world of pre-manufactured products, you can spend a few thousand dollars and make it look like a million!! Understanding the different trim options that are available and how to use them in your salon can give you the finishing touches to the look you want to create in your salon.

The Five-Point Salon Design System was created for the salon owner to break down each specific area of the salon. Using this system enables you to visualize each area and not forget about how you could use trim to enhance your style and design. The following ideas are not all for one style. Because everyone is different and the styles they will create are different, we wanted to give different ideas for all styles.

You salon should flow from one area to another—we do not recommend switching styles for each area. Like and interior of a home you will find that the same trim is used throughout. That being said, it would be difficult and unusual to see an old world roman style in one area and a contemporary style in another area of the same salon. You should choose a style and keep it coherent and cohesive with your trim choices throughout your salon.

Here's a look at the Five-Point Salon Design System areas and some key points about using trim in each of these areas:

★ POINT #1: The Entrance (Doorway/Front Desk/Waiting Area)

Colonial style molding is used in 75 percent of commercial and residential spaces. Imagine a front entrance encased with large, 6-inch molding opening to a salon that is decked out with the same richness on the inside as on the outside. The entrance is your "doorway to wealth" (as we call it at Ready, Set, Go Publishing). Once inside, this is the area where people can meet, gather, feel a sense of warmth, and not worry about their everyday problems! This style begs for a more intricate crown molding around the ceiling, heavy trim that matches the crown molding around doors and windows, and baseboards that wrap around along the floor and extend higher up on the walls. This look gives a feeling of grandness, authenticity, and richness.

★ POINT #2: The Store Inside Your Salon (Retail Area)

What about a contemporary look? Let's imagine a contemporary retail space. Close your eyes and imagine smooth lines along the floors and ceiling that create an open, youthful, yet chic feeling. It's a modern space that feels clean and together and entices clients to purchase hair care, skin care, and beauty products.

★ POINT #3: Your Bread & Butter (Service Area)

What about a traditional salon? How would you use trim pieces to create a traditional feeling? The trim pieces in the space would be thicker, but not too detailed. They would be stained or painted in dark or warm tones. Statements would be made by framing out each styling station with trim that flows from one station to the next. This look is professional, yet homey. It gives feelings of stability, warmth, safeness, and community.

★ POINT #4: Let Your Color Shine (Color/Dispensary Area)

Let's go back to contemporary again. How would it look in this area? Close your eyes and think about this area being out in the open and how you will treat your clients in this area. They'll feel like they are "part of the process," like they are the "star of the show." You want them to feel relaxed in the space and like all their troubles are being washed away. For this sense of renewal, try bringing in elements of flowing water, the beach, and the crispness of fresh air. With this design in mind, your trim could give a cottage type feel, consider planked walls stained or painted white and accenting some of the trim with blues. It gives a carefree, "beachy" feel; yet, at the same time, it's also a rich and pampered feel.

★ POINT #5: Behind the Scenes (Utility Area)

For this all-purpose area, you'll want to use plastic or vinyl—materials that are easy to clean and can take some abuse before needing to be replaced. This may be the only room that your staff can use an escape to reenergize. You want it to be comfortable enough, but it's really a more functional space than anything else. You don't want to encourage your staff to hang out here, that's for sure. You want them in the salon, being productive, and making money for them and for you. Make sure that you still trim out around the floor, doors, and cabinets.

★ Five-Point Salon Design System ★
(Point-by-Point Assessment)
What is your plan for trim in each area?

POINT #1: The Entrance (Doorway/Front Desk/Waiting Area)

POINT #2: The Store Inside Your Salon (Retail Area)

POINT #3: Your Bread & Butter (Service Area)

POINT #4: Let Your Color Shine (Color & Dispensary Area)

POINT #5: Behind the Scenes (Utility Area)

Ready, Set, Go! Expert Advice!

After you decide on what trim you will be using in the salon, it is important to add an extra 3–5 feet of molding when figuring your final measurements of how much trim is needed. You will need extra molding for waste when cutting to fit corners and angles. Even the best carpenters need some extra trim to work with to account for any mistakes.

CHAPTER 14

Look Up: Salon Ceilings

"The ceiling is the least thought about when it comes to design;
without it, what will hold up the walls of the salon?"

—Jeff Grissler

One of the most famous ceilings of all time is Michelangelo's masterpiece on the ceiling of the Sistine Chapel in Vatican City, Italy. This is one ceiling that cannot go unnoticed. In comparison, most ceilings may go "unseen" even though they have a huge impact on a room. So, although beautiful, ceilings do not have to have grand works of art painted on them to make a statement.

In your mind, the biggest priority when planning your salon is more tied up in how to fit everything in the space—without much concern for what to do with the ceilings. Even though the ceiling in your salon may be thought of as "out of sight, out of mind," there are still times when your clients will be looking up, such as when they are at the shampoo sinks or when getting a massage or facial. So, it's important to spend some time and money on a ceiling that is pleasing to the eye.

In fact, designers are putting a new emphasis on ceiling planning and feel that ceilings are a valuable design element of the room. Without treating the ceiling, designers often feel that a room looks incomplete.

When you think of every square inch as "real estate" for your business, then the ceiling becomes part of the equation. It is the same size of the floor; and, just like the flooring you choose, the treatment of your ceilings can change the overall look of any room. Subtle, simple, and affordable decisions, such as shapes, colors, textures, and geometric design can make the most of your ceilings. And, many manufacturers have developed ceiling solutions that can dramatically change the appearance of your salon and assist with blending the whole atmosphere of the salon design together.

Ceiling: To See or Not To See

One of the first decisions you'll need to make is whether to leave any areas exposed or to close up the ceilings. It may be that you'll decide on a little of both. Read on for more information on both options.

- **Exposed**—It's fashionable to have the duct work exposed in the ceiling, especially for a contemporary, modern, or industrial style salon. One drawback is the salon may be noisier with an exposed ceiling because there is nothing to dampen the sound. Also, there will be additional expense for heating and air-conditioning due to the open space. Here are some questions and tips to consider:

  - Is your ceiling high enough to leave it exposed? No one wants the feeling that they will bump their head on a pipe.

  - How much will it cost to give it a "finished" look? What are the short-term painting costs to paint the entire ceiling and thoroughly cover all the pipes and fittings?

  - Can I afford to spend money on specialty services to clean the dust that will accumulate on the exposed surfaces? Pipes, electric conduits, ventilation ducts and sprinkler systems will all be exposed and need visual maintenance if there is no drop ceiling.

  If you don't know what to expect to pay for these services or if you don't know all that is involved, be sure to find out before you go with an exposed ceiling. We would recommend professional cleaning and maintenance of exposed ceilings at least once a year or when you see that it needs it.

- **Closed**—One big reason to have a dropped ceiling is energy conservation. A ceiling that is 12 to 18 feet may be open, but it is air space that needs to be heated and/or cooled. As you know, heat rises. To heat a building with high ceilings, you will spend a lot of money to warm and/or cool an unused area. Installing ceilings, when there are none, will reduce the area of air to manage.

  - **Dropped**—Dropped ceilings conceal overhead electrical and plumbing; but, still provide access should you need to service them. They present a neat surface. It is also a traditional look for a salon. There are other advantages to a dropped ceiling, such as:

    - **Easy Access for Maintenance, Service, & Expansion**—With electrical and plumbing concealed, but not closed up behind drywall, it makes it much easier to service anything that is broken or to add on new electrical or plumbing if you expand or remodel.

    - **Noise Dampening**—Dropped ceilings are usually made of material that absorbs noise.

  - **Dry Walled**—Drywall is the common name for sheetrock. Most commercial spaces, 10 years or older, may have drywall (sheetrock).

    - **Con:** The problem with sheetrock on the ceiling is getting behind it if you have to fix a leak or need to get at any electrical wiring. To get at anything behind the sheetrock, will require you to cut a hole. After the plumbing repair or electrical job is completed, you will be left with a gaping hole that will need to be patched and repainted. Sometimes, the whole ceiling will need to be repainted when you are finished with patching the hole.

- **Pro:** Sheetrock does look great with a fresh coat of paint on it and does make the room look larger if you use a brilliant white paint.

Ceiling Treatments

The look of a ceiling and how dramatic you may be able to make it really comes down to two things—the height of the ceiling and your budget. The average ceiling height in a commercial space is 10 to 12 feet. If your ceiling is 8 to 9 feet (standard residential ceiling height), then it limits the opportunities and options in designing your salon space. Let's look at the different types of ceiling options.

Consider the height of the ceiling when deciding on a treatment. A low, metal ceiling could make the place feel like a tin can. A high popcorn ceiling could be hard to clean. Here are some ceiling treatment options to consider:

- **Acoustic Ceiling**—A busy salon, depending on the substances used in the walls and floor, can be very noisy. A noisy salon loses the feeling of intimacy that a client often wants with their stylist. An acoustic ceiling can help reduce some of the noise. Tiles are easy to replace and can be painted. A ceiling does not need to remain the standard color that the acoustic tiles come in straight out of the box. Included in this chapter are the steps for making the process of painting ceiling tiles doable for just about anyone.

- **Popcorn Ceiling**—A "popcorn" ceiling has lost favor in the past 30 years, but is still found in some businesses. It is somewhat costly to remove, but it can be painted, and some companies can add sparkles to add to the reflectance of a ceiling. Popcorn ceilings can need dusting.

- **Painted Ceiling**—Painting the ceiling is a great way to bring color into the salon without it detracting from the color of retail products or adding visual chaos. The color of the ceiling can contribute to the mood of the salon.

- **Black Ceiling**—A ceiling painted black or a very dark color is not an unusual choice for a retail or salon. It can be very dramatic and very stylish, while in a practical way controlling the amount of ambient light. The best environment for a black ceiling is when the ceiling is very high and there is lots of natural light. Usually, black is used on an open ceiling application—where everything is exposed and plumbing, air-condition ducts, electrical cables, etc. are all painted black. This gives an industrial, techy feeling.

- **Metal**—The industrial look is in, so a metal ceiling is consistent with a certain style of salon. It is easy to clean, but does show drops of product and dust. It also contributes to the noise level in the salon.

- **Wood**—Depending on how you use wood for a salon, you can give it a traditional, cottage, or rustic look. Wood ceilings, although not very common in salons, look great and are easy to maintain. However, there will be some significant material and labor expenses to include in your budget.

This salon has an exposed ceiling. Everything is painted black so the details do not catch the attention of the viewer. It works because the ceiling is very high.

Updating Ceiling Tiles

If your space already has a dropped ceiling that you are planning to keep, then we recommend a quick update to your ceiling tiles. Although durable, ceiling tiles may develop a worn-out look over time, become cracked, or develop stains. In such scenarios, you need to either replace them or paint them. Changing ceiling tiles can be a quick fix. By painting the tiles, you can give your salon a more completed look almost instantaneously. To remove, paint, and replace your ceiling tiles, use the following information:

Step 1—Removing Ceiling Tiles

Position a ladder under the drop ceiling. Prepare yourself with plastic gloves. Drop ceiling tiles are set within a frame or a tiling grid. When removing ceiling tiles, you need to handle them with care to ensure that they are not damaged. Damaged tiles are unfit for reinstallation in its framework. The edges of the tile might be compacted with dust or grime. Use the tip of a flat screwdriver covered with cloth to scrape off the debris and push along the edges. Slightly push one end of the tile. You need to slide the tile along its frame. After pushing the tile forward, twist it to create an angle within the horizontal grid. Now, slide out the tile from its frame. If you find any loose wires, cover them with twist-on wire connectors or electrical tape.

Step 2—Examining Ceiling Tiles

Place the removed tile on a sheet of newspaper. Use a dry cloth to clean the tile. Examine the edges of the tile. Look for broken edges, cracks on the surface of the tile, staining, and/or water damage. Place it in a "to replace" or an "okay to paint" pile. Continue removing all of the tiles so that you know how many you need to replace.

Step 3—Purchasing Replacement Ceiling Tiles

Replacement drop ceiling tiles are available at hardware supply stores. If you know the specific manufacturer and stock number for the tile, then purchasing becomes easy. If you do not have any information about the tiles, then take one of the damaged tiles to your local hardware store and find the closest match. We recommend using a damaged tile so that you don't damage a good tile when transporting it to the store. If you are converting a space that already has a dropped ceiling, be sure to check to see whether there are extra tiles in the utility area. Don't forget to purchase a couple of extra tiles for future replacements. The existing drop ceiling tile design may be replaced with a new design. Having tiles on reserve is a wise option.

Step 4—Painting Ceiling Tiles

Now that you have all the tiles that you need, you are ready to paint. Use a Shellac stain blocker as your primer or tint it to if you want to use the Shellac primer as your final coat. The Shellac stain blocker will keep your ceiling tiles looking nicer a lot longer by blocking out stains that might occur over time. You can also use a latex paint over the top of the primer. You can use a paint roller or a paintbrush, depending upon the texture of the tile. Paint rollers are better for plain surfaces, while a brush helps to dab into the crevices of tiles with textured exteriors. Match the color to your design or use a bright white. It is best to protect the edges of the tile with masking tape when painting it, as painted edges might hamper the fitting of the tile into its designated slot. Allow the painted tile to dry for a few hours.

Step 5—Reinstalling Replacement/Painted Ceiling Tiles

Carry your replacement/painted tile up the ladder. Hold it in such a way that the finished/painted side is facing downward. Tilt the tile upward, and angle it into the grid. Allow nearly half of the ceiling tile to pass the grid's frame. Now, start to position the tile in a horizontal manner, ensuring that the tile's edges are tightly fitted along the frame.

Ceilings are a major component of the salon. You can let it exist as is or incorporate it as a component of the salon design. Without a doubt, most of your attention and the largest part of your budget will go to the interior walls, the floor, and the furniture/equipment. However, to make your salon complete, don't forget about including the ceiling in the plans for your salon.

Ready, Set, Go! Expert Advice!

Ceiling tiles are not "100%" sound-proof. Some tiles will absorb 80% of the sound and reduce sound transmission. This can be a true blessing in any busy salon. Make sure you shop around and speak to a ceiling expert about which tiles will offer the best sound-proofing results.

★ **Five-Point Salon Design System** ★
(Point-by-Point Assessment)

What is your plan for the ceiling in each area?

*Remember you can have different types of ceiling treatments
in each of the five areas of your salon.*

POINT #1: The Entrance (Doorway/Front Desk/Waiting Area)

What type of ceiling?	◯ Exposed ◯ Open
What material will you use?	◯ Ceiling Tiles ◯ Drywall ◯ Wood ◯ Other
What color will you use?	
What design/feeling are you going for?	

POINT #2: The Store Inside Your Salon (Retail Area)

What type of ceiling?	◯ Exposed ◯ Open
What material will you use?	◯ Ceiling Tiles ◯ Drywall ◯ Wood ◯ Other
What color will you use?	
What design/feeling are you going for?	

POINT #3: Your Bread & Butter (Service Area)

What type of ceiling?	◯ Exposed ◯ Open
What material will you use?	◯ Ceiling Tiles ◯ Drywall ◯ Wood ◯ Other
What color will you use?	
What design/feeling are you going for?	

POINT #4: Let Your Color Shine (Color & Dispensary Area)

What type of ceiling?	◯ Exposed ◯ Open
What material will you use?	◯ Ceiling Tiles ◯ Drywall ◯ Wood ◯ Other

What color will you use?	
What design/feeling are you going for?	
POINT #5: Behind the Scenes (Utility Area)	
What type of ceiling?	◯ Exposed ◯ Open
What material will you use?	◯ Ceiling Tiles ◯ Drywall ◯ Wood ◯ Other
What color will you use?	
What design/feeling are you going for?	

Ready, Set, Go! Expert Advice!

Ceiling space today is not to be ignored. Many new salons around the world are going with the open ceiling look. This gives the salon a loft-like, techno feel. The upside is your salon will look enormous and retro; the downside is you will have more space to heat or cool. Your space will also tend to be loud and noisy. Remember ceiling tile absorbs most of the noise in the salon. It all comes down to the look you are attempting to create.

CHAPTER 15

Watch Your Step: Salon Flooring Options

"If no one ever took risks, Michelangelo would have painted the Sistine floor!"

—Neil Simon

Whether your salon is large or small, it is important to choose the right flooring. Your floor should look nice—it should show that your establishment is clean and professional. Keep in mind that you need to balance short-term and long-term costs, comfort, durability, and safety.

Flooring is a substantial design element, most of the time one of the last things discussed when designing a salon or spa. It is also the one area in the salon that can save a large sum of money when building out a newly designed salon space. More affordable flooring options, placed in the right areas, can meet your needs and save a ton of money. There is no reason to choose one type of flooring for the entire salon. In fact, we'll cover what flooring options are best for each area and why.

Just remember that cheap is not always feasible; and, beautiful is not always sensible. In commercial businesses, the flooring gets more traffic than in a typical home. Sometimes, the more beautiful styles, textures, and materials that are used in residential homes may not be an option because they are too costly—or, they will not withstand the amount of traffic in a salon.

Choosing the right flooring will save you money in the long run because you'll be able to keep it in place longer, avoid early replacement costs, and reduce daily maintenance and cleaning costs.

Many new salon owners prefer to spend more on their salon furniture than they budget for flooring. Yes, the furniture is extremely important for the look and feel of the salon. However, your floor is just as important and needs to be thought about just as much as your furniture. Think about it this way. If your beautiful salon furniture is sitting on flooring that is showing signs of wear, then the overall look of the salon will get dragged down by the inferior flooring choice.

What Flooring Is Right for Your Salon

You may have decided that only wood will do. That laminate is easier to look after. Or that vinyl is more practical. But when you see the extraordinary range of finishes and styles you will realize that the possibilities are endless. There are a myriad of flooring choices today. Many floors today come with surface technology that eliminates scratching, staining that are beautiful to look at, easy to clean, and durable. You'll want to keep these considerations in mind when you decide on your flooring:

- How much traffic will the floor get? Think of each area of the salon.
- How visibility is it to the client?
- Is it aesthetically pleasing?
- What are the unique needs of each area of your salon? Think about the perspective of the client and the staff.
- What is your budget?
- How durable is the material? Will it scratch? Will it stain easily from hair color? Will it break or crack? How easily can it be repaired?
- How comfortable is it for standing? (Remember: concrete flooring is extremely hard on the feet, legs, and back—staff may complain)
- What areas need a more posh, luxurious feel?
- What maintenance is required to keep it looking its best?
- How easy is it to clean and to keep clean?
- Is it slip resistant? (Remember: tile and even wood surfaces can be slippery when wet.)
- Is it water resistant? (Remember: hardwood flooring and water do not mix well.)

The last thing you want in your salon or spa is to spend every minute worrying about stains, cleaning, and wear spots in your salon high traffic areas. By choosing a floor that suits the area, you will cut down on the cleaning and general care you have to provide. Next, take a look at the different types of flooring and the pros and cons of the material.

Types of Flooring

- **Porcelain, Quarry (or Stone) and Ceramic Tiles**—These are lovely, durable, and easy to clean. They are popular in many businesses. Very hard on the feet, legs, and backs of employees who stand for the majority of the day. They can also be expensive. In addition, grout lines may discolor, and they may become slippery when wet. A stone entry area can be impressive and practical. For porcelain or ceramic tiles, be sure to get "through-and-through" tiles that have the same color all the way through, so that chips are less noticeable.

- **Hardwood Floors**—These can be beautiful, good for the backs and legs of your employees that are on their feet all day, and easy to clean. The prices vary with the wood used. This kind of floor could make an impressive entryway, but you'd have to consider your local climate. If incoming traffic brings in too much water from rain and snow, then you'll have to cover up your beautiful wood flooring with mats to soak up the water. It is also not well suited for areas that use water or chemicals, such as in the shampoo department and in the color/dispensary areas or in the restrooms. Used in an area with water and chemicals, this kind of floor may need frequent maintenance and/ or replacement.

- **Laminate Flooring**—This is a man-made material that can be made to look like wood or tile. It's easy to clean and durable. They can be noisy, and small areas cannot be replaced; the whole area must be replaced.

- **Concrete Floors**—Concrete flooring is a new trend where the concrete slab itself is sanded, colored, and covered with an epoxy. These floors are clean and dramatic (especially with bright colors). However, they can be as expensive as a ceramic floor. Be sure of your color choice; they are expensive to change. Need to be maintained occasionally with new sealant.

Wooden flooring: Lovely, but susceptible to water and chemicals.

- **Vinyl Flooring**—These man-made floors are the least expensive and can be very durable and easy to clean. There are nearly infinite color and pattern choices. Buy high-end vinyl, low-end vinyl looks cheap and can tear easily. Have an expert install it; poorly installed vinyl will peel up, especially in a moist environment.

- **Carpeting**—This is not a typical flooring choice for a salon because it is harder to keep clean. It might be preferable only if you had a waiting area that was very discreet from the rest of the salon (such as in a separate spa area), or your style was either homey or pure comfort.

Watching Your Step at Each of the Five Points

Flooring decisions should be based on traffic, visibility, and the unique needs of each area. Most flooring materials today look beautiful to the eye and ensure comfort and durability. However, different areas of your salon and/or spa have their own special requirements that you should consider when making your choice. Here's a point-by-point look at flooring, what we recommend, and why.

The Five Points	Recommended Flooring	Why?
POINT #1: Doorway, Front Desk, & Waiting Area	Stone is the best flooring option for this area. Although stone is an expensive flooring choice, it wouldn't be used in other areas of the salon. Stone would be too uncomfortable for employees to stand on all day. So, use something different behind the front desk or purchase anti-fatigue mats for use by your front desk staff if they'll be standing on stone. The types of stone flooring include: • Travertine • Marble • Granite • Slate • Limestone	This is a high-traffic area, which puts special demands on the floor. You'll have clients, mail service, delivery people, sales people, and staff coming and going all day long. They will bring in dirt, water, and snow that will destroy less durable flooring materials. The bottom line is that stone wins with: • Durability • Slip resistance • Ease of cleaning • Aesthetics
POINT #2: Retail Area	See above.	See above.
POINT #3: Service Area	The service area will see high volume of traffic. Water is the major factor that changes what type of flooring you should choose in this area. **In the Styling Area:** The flooring should be a durable surface, but needs to be fashion focused. Keep in mind this is the largest open area of the salon. So, the flooring is going to be highly visible to your clients. You also have to remember your stylists. They are on their feet all day. Anything hard like ceramic tile, stone or stained concrete will be extremity hard on their feet, legs, and backs. Therefore, hardwood floors and or inlaid tile is very popular in the styling area of the salon. **In the Shampoo Area:** The flooring should be slip-resistant ceramic tile or something that looks like ceramic or wood flooring. Water and shampoo make this a very dangerous area. You must keep safety and the possibility of leaking water in mind when picking your flooring choice.	This flooring takes up the majority of the square footage in your salon. So, it's visible to the client; therefore, it should be attractive and consistent with the style of the salon. These flooring options provide: • Comfort • Ease of cleaning • Durability • Slip resistance

The Five Points	Recommended Flooring	Why?
	In Spa/Treatment Rooms: The top suggestions for these rooms are commercial grade carpet or hardwood flooring. These choices will warm up the room and make the customer feel comfortable if they are barefoot.	
POINT #4: **Color/** **Dispensary Area**	The dispensary will also see high volume of traffic. Recommendations: • Low gloss, anti-slip ceramic tile • Low gloss, anti-slip stone	Water is the major factor that changes what type of flooring you should choose in this area. These flooring options provide: • Ease of cleaning • Durability • Slip resistance
POINT #5: **Utility Area**	**Utility Room** Many salons leave this area without any type of finish. It is not uncommon to see this area in the salon as a rough concrete finish. As long as there aren't any safety concerns, you may decide to leave it as is when you take over the lease. Why spend the money on flooring this area, unless it is combined with your break room.	Utility areas have the lowest traffic and visibility. Operative words: • Affordable • Easy to clean • Durable
	Break Room The break room should keep with the consistency of whatever you are using throughout the salon space.	If you have a separate break room for staff, then you just need something functional that is easy to clean. Bright colors are preferable to keep employees alert.
	Restrooms There is nothing better in a restroom than ceramic tile.	Restrooms are visible to the client. So, they should look clean and neat. This might be an area for its own unique style, but practical is fine, too. The key words are: • Easy to clean • Able to sanitize
	Changing Rooms Changing rooms can have commercial carpet on the floor. Many spas use this type of application.	Changing rooms need to have a warm, at-home type atmosphere. But, they also need to be easy to clean, which is why commercial grade carpeting is the best for this area. You get the comfort with the ability to clean and sanitize if needed.

★ Five-Point Salon Design System ★
(Point-by-Point Assessment)
What is your plan for flooring in each area?

POINT #1: The Entrance (Doorway/Front Desk/Waiting Area)

POINT #2: The Store Inside Your Salon (Retail Area)

POINT #3: Your Bread & Butter (Service Area)

POINT #4: Let Your Color Shine (Color & Dispensary Area)

POINT #5: Behind the Scenes (Utility Area)

Ready, Set, Go! Expert Advice!

Ceramic Tile Flooring

The most popular sizes are 12x12, 13x13, 16x16, and 18x18 inches. These measurements will be important numbers to remember when choosing your tile. Larger tile looks wonderful if the space is wide and deep. Larger tile also covers larger space quickly and easily for the flooring installers. To save money, look for tile that is discontinued. However, always buy an extra 5-10% to replace damaged tiles.

CHAPTER 16

Accessorizing

"Don't spend time beating on a wall, hoping to transform it into a door."

—Coco Chanel

I t's perfectly natural for a new or existing salon owner to worry about the look of their salon. Now more than ever—with all the competition and the fragile economy—it's important that your salon has the look and feel of a high-end fashionable business establishment. Yes, you may have the best stylists, but to have the entire package. You must have the posh feel of a fashion-forward salon. So, how do you pull this off? You may have spent a small fortune on design and salon furniture; but, you feel that your salon is still missing something. What is that little added punch that will put your salon over the top?

Many of us have the capability to pick out the colors, furniture, and the flooring. But, sometimes it's the finer details—the accessories—that become the showcase in a remodel or new salon. Accessories make the room and finish the look—much like the vase you put your fresh cut flowers in. Used like a secret weapon, designers use accessories to close up the look they are trying to create. When everything is pulled together, your salon will look smart, chic, unified, and complete.

How to Get Started

Designers would tell you to follow the look and feel you are trying to create in the salon when choosing the types of accessories that you will use. While this is true, there are many other factors to keep in mind:

- Furniture type and style
- Wall colors
- Flooring
- Lighting
- Size of the salon
- Personal taste

- Clientele
- Seasonal décor

From there, you can follow the ideas found here to jump start your creative side.

Choose Your Colors

Before picking accessories choose your color scheme. Choose one or two accessories that add interest and add coordination with your furniture and wall colors. If your wall coloring is neutral, pick out accessories that are bold to add vibrancy to the room.

For Example:

If you choose chocolate brown walls and your styling stations are white, you may accessorize with a large painting in a white frame with a lime green vase with a single white flower. BAM! Now, that will make any room pop! You can hang two or three paintings like this together.

Go With What You Love

Start with an object that brings you joy. Choose other accessories that are inspired by or complement the object. You will most likely be happy with the result when you begin with a much loved item or an accessory that has special interest or meaning to you.

But, remember, you have to work in the salon every day. So, keep in mind that you will have to look at what you choose every day and you are attempting to satisfy your tastes, while keeping it pleasing for your staff and clients. Be smart about what you pick. Here are some examples of things that you may love, but that just might not work and why.

- **Love of Hunting:** You may have a huge interest in hunting, but a large moose head hanging over your reception desk would probably not be a good idea to use as an accessory.

- **Love of Family:** Everyone loves their children, but your family photos don't belong in your salon. If put into the right context, photos with members of your family might work. For example, you could showcase pictures of:

  - You or one of your stylists cutting your child's hair

  - Your newborn baby in a shampoo sink

  - Your parents, grandparents, or other relatives who were or are also in the hair business

  Regular, family photos are more for you than for your clients and belong in your home, not in your salon.

- **Favorite Hobbies:** Some salons have tried incorporating their favorite hobbies as accessories. However, your interests may not be the interests of the majority of your staff and clients. One person's passion certainly may not be the like of others.

Stick With a Theme or Style

If you are going for a theme or style, pick accessories that coordinate with the theme or style.

For Example:

If you live in a beach town or near the ocean and you want the feel of the "beach" in your salon, then look for accessories that fit the look. Shells, sea glass, and large paintings of the ocean, or children frolicking in the sand may bring together the look you are trying to accomplish.

Or, for a modern design, choose streamlined accessories that mesh with contemporary salon furniture. The key is to keep your theme and style in mind to achieve a cohesive look.

Photos

If you have the wall space and you really want to be different, take pictures of your staff and clients with the best hair styles or color. Blow the best ones up in black and white and have them professionally framed. The nice thing about this is that you can change them from time-to-time and as styles come and go.

Why not have a photo shoot with your staff, put the best work in the frame and change it monthly or quarterly. The pictures must be large. They must make a statement.

How cool would that look hanging on the wall behind your front desk or in the window of the salon for passersby to see? Make no mistake; photos taken and framed by professionals can really put the finishing touch on your salon. Personalized pictures will not only make your staff happy, but will also get you star recognition with your clients.

Framing a large photo will add visual interest to a bare, uninteresting wall. This will also help you if you have gone over budget on your furniture and construction.

Plants & Flowers

There is nothing prettier then fresh cut flowers on your front desk. Fresh flowers and plants are beautiful but if you don't upkeep them they can quickly turn into an eyesore. Unkempt plants drop leaves and pedals on the floor of the salon.

If you don't have a green thumb or the time to keep up with live or fresh-cut plants, then go with artificial. You can use them to introduce color and life into a room. But, keep in mind that artificial plants and flowers need upkeep as well. They tend to be a dust magnet and look drab if they are not dusted off regularly.

Throw Pillows & Small Carpets

You may not have many places to put colorful pillows in you salon. The one area where the colors, patterns, and textures of pillows would be nice is in your reception area. You can really make your salon seating pop with some cool, colorful throw pillows.

If you have the space and an area that is not high traffic, you can introduce a small colorful throw rug to enhance an entrance or a particular area in the salon. If it's going to be put in a high traffic area, it may end up being more of a hazard than a slick accessory. Be careful with small carpets and selective with where you place them.

Mirrors

Of all the architectural décor pieces available on the market today, decorative mirrors are the most functional and are a perfect complement to any salon. They are usually the most affordable accessory item that you can purchase and come in a variety of shapes and sizes. Mirrors can give your salon a dramatic effect by reflecting color and light. They can make the smallest of rooms look considerably larger if hung in the right places. Additionally, when you use mirrors as wall art, they complement any salon area with a decorative touch.

Lighting

Lighting can add instant impact to any room. Pick light fixtures that add design style and match your salon furniture. Remember what we said earlier in the chapter, you need to keep things consistent for symmetry in the salon. Lighting choices—chandeliers, wall sconces, antique lamps, or colorful recessed lighting—will change the look and feel of any room. Light fixtures can add color and illuminate a dark dreary room as soon as you turn on the switch. A wide spectrum of wall lighting fixtures is available in different materials, such as: metals, woods, glass, and ceramic. Using lighting as an accessory can give you the "designer" look that you are trying create in your salons interior.

Metal Wall Art & Sculptures

Installing medal wall art and sculptures on the walls of your salon can instantly make a style statement. Metal wall art and sculptures offer an exclusive look to the walls of your room and leave an everlasting impression to every quest's mind. Cooper metal art offers a brilliant look to a room. Depending on the time of the day your medal wall art can change color naturally. You can find many different medal wall art pieces on line. What's nice about this type of accessory is that you do not have to break the bank if you choose to go with this look.

Accessorize to Finalize

Accessorizing finalizes your salon remodel or opening. It will complete the look of your salon by adding charm, beauty, and character to the overall symmetry of the room. Once finished you will have an overall feeling of accomplishment, your staff will be happy as well as your customers.

Many times, we will start a project, get halfway done with it, and fail to finish it. You may get bored, run out of time, or lack the know-how to complete the task at hand. But, think about this. Your salon is your place of business—it is a reflection of you. Not only that, but you and your staff probably spend just as much time in the salon as you do at your own homes—maybe more. So, this is one of the projects you must get done because you'll feel good knowing that it's a finished project and that you can walk into your salon and have it feel completely finished.

Have fun with accessorizing. If it doesn't work the first time, try again and until you are on the right track. You'll know you are there when you can step back and say, "It's finished and I love it!"

Accessories Checklist

When you pick your accessories, remember that you:

- Don't have to break the bank to choose items that fit in your salon.
- Should use colors that pop when mixed with neutral colors.
- Can use mirrors to make a room look inviting and larger than it really is.
- Should consider wall sconces to add beauty and charm to your walls.
- Need to consider style statements like metal art.
- Can achieve a warm, homey atmosphere with fresh-cut flowers.
- Need to keep it simple. In many cases, less is more.

Salon Owners Talk About . . . the Good, the Bad, and the Ugly

"I wanted my salon to be different and to be truly unique. I didn't want that cookie cutter salon that everyone is used to. So when it came to accessorizing I shopped and searched through antique stores, flea markets, thrift stores, garage sales until I finally found the pieces I needed to complete my salon. My staff and clients love the look and feel of my salon. It's a bit country, city and me! Everything I envisioned my salon would always be. Take your time and have fun with it!"

—Mary Washburne, Salon on Fifth, New York City

★ Five-Point Salon Design System ★
(Point-by-Point Assessment)
What is your plan for accessorizing in each area?

POINT #1: The Entrance (Doorway/Front Desk/Waiting Area)

POINT #2: The Store Inside Your Salon (Retail Area)

POINT #3: Your Bread & Butter (Service Area)

POINT #4: Let Your Color Shine (Color & Dispensary Area)

POINT #5: Behind the Scenes (Utility Area)

Ready, Set, Go! Expert Advice!

If you have the wall space, use it. Bare walls make a salon look scarce and naked. Bare walls also show signs of wear and tear and collect finger-print marks and scuff marks from pocket books and other items that regularly hit the walls. Think about all the techniques to enhance a bare wall:

- Painting with accent colors
- Texturizing
- Padding it
- Upholstering
- Wall-papering
- Bricking it or adding natural stone

Hand-painted murals are another option which can become the salon's focal point without taking away from the rest of the salon's design. Murals should be above the waistline to avoid scuffs and marks.

PART III

SHAPING YOUR DREAMS INTO REALITY

CHAPTER 17

Dream It . . . Design It

"Let the beauty that we love be what we do."

—Rumi

Being able to clearly define your personal vision is only one half of achieving your ultimate goal—business success. Let's take a look at your salon from head to toe and define all of the parts that build a lasting business, including the services, products, aesthetics, employees, reputation, and more.

Did you know that the right designs can make ordinary tasks pleasurable and everyday surroundings inspirational? Making the right designs not only makes the functionality of your business work, but also creates an experience that allows you to "leave the world you live in" and step into a whole new experience every day you come to work.

Almost unknowingly, you live in, on, and around design. Your life changes and evolves and so do your possessions. Good design isn't dependent on having lots of space or money; it comes from necessity and desire—increasing short- and long-term satisfaction.

As you work through this chapter, be sure to write down all the details of your dream when answering the questions that are posed in this book or when filling in the blanks. Like you would do with a personal vision or goal, it's recommended that you revisit these questions every six months or every year at the least. This helps you keep your business on track and allows you to revise your mission, goals, and standards to reflect the culture, products, and services of your salon.

This Is My Dream; My Vision; My Salon

When I close my eyes and imagine my salon, I . . .

Example:

I see everything I always wanted in a salon . . . plenty of space, my personal vibe, a creative center for my stylists, a safe-haven for all my clients, homey, loving, and inspirational. I see spring colors. I hear nature, tranquil music. I smell flowers. I feel a touch of my mom.

See . . .	open, calming colors, smiling faces, elegance
Hear . . .	
Smell . . .	~~beautiful~~ clean, fresh, relaxing
Feel . . .	calm, welcomed, relaxed, beautiful

What services will you offer?

The most elegant stations, plenty of room to create, nail stations that allow my manicurist to have the freedom to do what they do best. Beauty, massage, and facials are a must with the most relaxing rooms that make everyone want to stay after their service to unwind.

Hair	~~cutting color~~ Men's & Women's services. Cutting, color, highlights, extensions, smoothing treatments.
Nail	manicure, pedicure, massage, gel-shellac
Beauty	Waxing, make up, eyebrows, eye treatments, tight skincare
Body	spray tanning

134

What products will you sell?

I will offer only the best for my clients. If my staff and I don't use them, why would I sell them? Look on the first pages of Allure magazine. Those are the best brands; those are the ones I want to sell!

Hair Care	
Nail Care	
Beauty Tools	
Cosmetic/Skin Care	

Describe Your Ideal Client

Let's shoot for the stars, like Madonna, Jennifer Lopez, and Beyoncé. But, let's not forget the soccer moms, school teachers, policemen, firemen, sisters, brothers, moms, kids, grandmas, aunts, and uncles.

Appearance	
Favorite Places to Shop	
Owns	
Wears	
Drives	
Income	
Desired Salon Products	

Describe the Client Experience at Your Salon

I want every one of my clients to walk away and say, "Wow! That was just amazing!" From the moment they walk into my place of business to the minute they leave, each guest will feel as if they are a King or Queen in a castle. All the planning of the design will create an experience of comfort and renewal. Everything will be easy and relaxing . . . from the time they arrive until the time they leave. Each step of the way, they'll enjoy the full amenities of the salon and the ability to purchase high-quality salon products. They'll be pampered with comfortable chairs and a warm cup of coffee.

What will they feel like when the services are completed?	
What will they think about your salon?	
What will they say to others about their experience?	
Why will they recommend your salon to their friends?	
What will they purchase before they leave?	
What will they expect of the products that they purchase?	
Why will they return?	
What new services will they take advantage of the next time they return?	
Why will they become loyal clients?	

Describe Each Area of Your Salon

Now that you have described the services and products and ideal clients for your salon, go through the five-point salon design system. As you go through the point-by-point assessment, think about what you need to work into your design in order to fulfill the senses, feelings, and special offerings that will allow you to attract and retain your ideal clients.

★ Five-Point Salon Design System ★			
(Point-by-Point Assessment)			
The Five Points	**Senses** (Appearance/Sounds/ Smells)	**Feeling** (For Clients / Employees)	**Special Offerings** (Services / Products)
POINT #1: **Doorway / Front Desk / Waiting Area**			
POINT #2: **Retail Area**			
POINT #3: **Service Area: Stylists**			
Service Area: Specialized Treatment Areas			
Service Area: Manicure/ Pedicure			
POINT #4: **Color / Dispensary Area**			
POINT #5: **Utility Area**			
Break Room			
Restrooms			
Changing Rooms			

CHAPTER 18

Ready-to-Use Floor Plans & Pricing Models

"A goal without a plan is just a wish."

—Antoine de Saint-Exupery

Floor plans are diagrams that provide a top view of the layout of a structure. Your designer, contractor, architect, and furniture/equipment person will all need a detailed layout of your salon. For a typical floor plan, the detailed plans will include the location of:

- Interior and exterior walls
- Windows
- Door frames
- Utilities (heating/air conditioning units, hot water heaters, washers/dryers, sinks, etc.)
- Closets
- Restrooms
- Entrances/exits
- Cabinetry
- Salon furniture/equipment

Depending on the intended use of the floor plans, the detail may include all electric, air conditioning lines and ducts, and plumbing. This is reffered to as a mechanical drawing.

- Styling stations outlets
- Window light outlet
- Exterior sign lights
- Restroom lights

- Front desk outlets
- Heating and air conditioning power
- Light switches
- Hot water heater power
- Display lighting for retail
- Overhead ceiling plans

Floor plans are an important part of building plans. Depending on the overall size of the salon and the depth of the construction of the project it is all most impossible for anyone to give you an idea of what your salon may look like without them. These plans usually include details on all aspects of the structure from both a horizantal and a vertical perspective. Within the setting, floor plans often serve as blueprints to keep the building project on course when it comes to laying out the interior space of the salon. The plans included in this book are to scale, making these plans ready for you to easily use and or give to your builder to translate into a constructed salon.

If you are altering an existing space to fit the needs of your salon or if you are just renovating your current salon, you will need a good floor plan. These plans serve as a means to arranging the spacific areas of the salon to best suit your needs. Using the Ready, Set, Go! Five-Point Salon Design System will enable you to work with your architect and/or designer to create your dream salon. You'll have great layouts and examples that are designed for comfort and accessibility in each of the five areas:

★ **POINT #1:** The Entrance (Doorway/Front Desk/Waiting Area)

★ **POINT #2:** The Store Inside Your Salon (Retail Area)

★ **POINT #3:** Your Bread & Butter (Service Area)

★ **POINT #4:** Let Your Color Shine (Color/Dispensary Area)

★ **POINT #5:** Behind the Scenes (Utility Area)

So, the plans in this chapter were drawn especially for you—with the intent that you may actually use the plans as-is or make a few changes to them to better fit your salon space. Therefore, we included 13 floor plans which range from smaller to larger square footage. The various versions will work in strip mall designs and for older buidlings. The designs were drawn by an expert designer in the beauty field who has designed award-winning salons around the country.

The designs also feature salon furniture/equipment costs and building material/labor costs to give you a true understanding of what it will take, financially, to design, build-out, and furnish your salon. No other book in the world has these features. So, take these designs and visuallize your new salons space as you see it.

These samples are ready to use. However, if you'd like a downloadable PDF of these floor plans to email and/or print and take to your designer, architect, and/or contractor, then go to http://readysetgobooks.com. Each floor plan is available to purchase at a nominal fee.

	Floor Plan Name	Operators	Square Feet	Find It
1	Itty Bitty Baby Salon	1-2	121	Page 142
2	Heads & Tails Salon	2	450	Page 146
3	A Cut Above Salon	4	750	Page 150
4	Salon 101	5	1176	Page 155
5	Hair Color Studio	6	1200	Page 160
6	The Hair House	8	1200	Page 165
7	Studio 495	10	2400	Page 170
8	Cutting Edge Salon	18	3500	Page 175
9	Heads Up Hair Salon (Booth Rental)	18	3021	Page 180
10	Strip Mall – Plan A (Skinny Salon)	10	1244	Page 185
11	Strip Mall – Plan B (Strip Mall Styles)	8	1280	Page 190
12	Strip Mall – Plan C (Signature Strip Mall Salon)	5	1380	Page 195
13	Blow Out Salon & Retail Store	2	2000	Page 200

1. Itty Bitty Baby Salon | 1-2 Operator Salon | 121 Square Feet

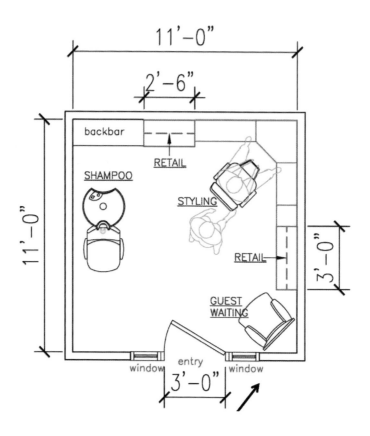

Itty Bitty Baby Salon - Furniture & Equipment Budget

	Quantity	Budget	Total	Mid	Total	High End	Total
Styling Chair	1	$175	$175	$400	$400	$1,200	$1,200
Custom Styling Station	1	$500	$500	$1,500	$1,500	$3,000	$3,000
Shampoo Cabinet	1	$300	$300	$600	$600	$1,000	$1,000
Dryer	1	$200	$200	$200	$200	$200	$200
Reception Chairs	1	$80	$80	$200	$200	$400	$400
Retail Unit Wall	2	$250	$500	$900	$1,800	$2,000	$4,000
Floor Mats	1	$80	$80	$120	$120	$190	$190
Grand Total			**$1,835**		**$4,820**		**$9,990**

Itty Bitty Baby Salon ★ Five-Point Salon Design System ★	
POINT #1: **Doorway / Front Desk / Waiting Area**	This suite set up is simply a room rented by the stylist. There is a common area in the front of the building that acts as the reception/waiting area. It is here that customers can be "buzzed" back to the stylists' studios for their appointment. As you can see, there is also one guest waiting chair inside the room itself. This plan can also be used as an in-home salon setup.
POINT #2: **Retail Area**	Retail displays have been placed along the wall, providing a visual upon entering the space. They have been strategically placed to be easily accessible to both the stylist and the guest. In addition, the display cases were designed with a drawer below for extra product storage, making optimal use of the space.
POINT #3: **Service Area**	The styling area is nestled into the corner of this salon suite. The mirror extends fully around the entire L-shaped space to provide the necessary visuals for the customer, but also to make the room appear larger.
POINT #4: **Color / Dispensary Area**	Since this is a ONE room salon, all the typical features are multifunctional. For example, the shampoo back bar area doubles as the color/dispensary area. The stylist uses the counter top for mixing and there is also additional storage on both sides of the styling chair for overflow.
POINT #5: **Utility Area**	Similar to the common reception and waiting area in the front of the building, the utility area is all in one space for the building. Single room salons who are essentially "booth renting" will share the same utility area. The utility area houses hot water heaters, washers/dryers, and a break room. The building is also outfitted with restrooms for your clients.

Itty Bitty Baby Salon - Materials & Labor Cost Break Down					
	Qty. / Sq. Ft. / Days	Low Estimate	Total	High Estimate	Total
Flooring					
Ceramic Tile *(Prices Higher on Imported Italian Tile)*	121 sq. ft.	$3/sq. ft.	$363	$6/sq. ft.	$726
Hardwood, Oak, Cherry	121 sq. ft.	$5/sq. ft.	$605	$7/sq. ft.	$847
Vinyl *(Prices can vary on manufacturer, style, thickness)*	121 sq. ft.	$2/sq. ft.	$242	$5/sq. ft.	$605
Installation *(Labor Costs)*	121 sq. ft.	$2/sq. ft.	$242	$8/sq. ft.	$968
Ceiling					
Decorative drop ceiling with metal brackets *(standard)*	121 sq. ft.	$3/sq. ft. *(installed)*	$363 *(installed)*	$8/sq. ft. *(installed)*	$968 *(installed)*
Paint					
Commercial Grade Paint *(Note: 1 gallon =1 coat for every 400 sq. ft.)*	121 sq. ft. *(<1 gallon)*	$20/gal.	$20	$40/gal.	$40
Ceiling Paint *(Price it, if applicable)*					
Trim & Door Paint *(Price it, if applicable)*					
Painter *(Labor Costs)*	2 days	$150/day	$300	$150/day	$300
Trim					
Baseboards	41 linear ft.	$1.50/ft. *(simple)*	$61.50	$4.50/ft. *(big/fancy)*	$184.50
Door/Window Trim *(1 window & 1 door)*	40 linear ft.	$1.50/ft. *(simple)*	$60	$4.50/ft. *(big/fancy)*	$180
Installation *(Labor Costs)*	1 day	$200/day	$200	$250/day	$250
Signage					
Non-Illuminated *(installed)*	1	$2,000/ sign	$4,000	$4,000/ sign	$4,000
Illuminated Block Letter *(installed)*	1	$3,000/ sign	$7,000	$7,000/ sign	$7,000
Lighting *(Note: Price your lighting and enter your estimates here.)*					
Overhead					
Task					
Accent					
Other					
Illuminated *(Labor Costs)*					

Itty Bitty Baby Salon - Materials & Labor Cost Break Down		
Accessories *(Note: Price your accessories and enter your estimates here.)*		
	Low Estimate	**High Estimate**
POINT #1: The Entrance (Doorway/Front Desk/ Waiting Area)		
POINT #2: The Store Inside Your Salon (Retail Area)		
POINT #3: Your Bread & Butter (Service Area)		
POINT #4: Let Your Color Shine (Color/Dispensary Area)		
POINT #5: Behind the Scenes (Utility Area)		

NOTE: These prices and installation costs are based on a general pricing structure that is subject to change depending on demographics and overall budget of the salon owner. The material pricing is based on a high traffic material cost that will withhold the normal wear and tear of heavy salon traffic. It is recommended to add approximately 10% to each of the above totals to cover costs of spoilage of materials or human error.

2. Heads & Tails Salon | 2 Operator Salon | 450 Square Feet

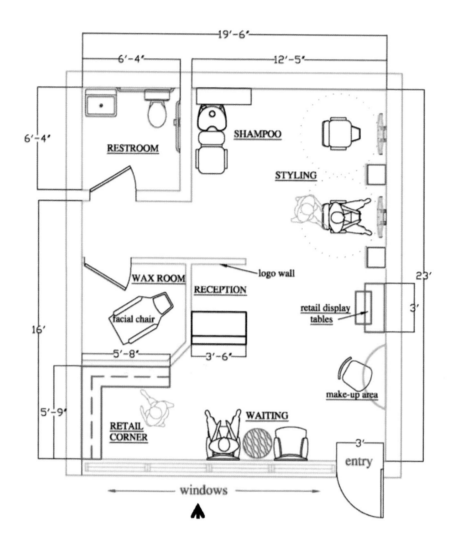

Heads & Tails Salon	
★ Five-Point Salon Design System ★	
POINT #1: **Doorway / Front Desk / Waiting Area**	The front desk is minimized, because the stylists also act as the receptionists. The reception desk has just enough room for a computer and some storage. The waiting area has (2) oversized chairs for added comfort.
POINT #2: **Retail Area**	Due to the small square footage, displays have been kept low so that there is an open feeling. The styling area is open to the reception/ retail area, creating a visual interest. The retail area has been purposely divided and not placed directly in the view of the waiting area to encourage clients to move around the retail area, which should lead to more product sales.
POINT #3: **Service Area**	The styling area consists of two complete operator set ups. It's easily seen from the front area due to the open concept of the space.
POINT #4: **Color / Dispensary Area**	Because this space has more of a studio concept, there is no designated color area. Color storage is kept right at the styling station making it easily accessible.
POINT #5: **Utility Area**	The utility area is a shared area with the surrounding businesses. The idea of this salon is similar to renting out a salon suite.

Heads & Tails Salon - Furniture & Equipment Budget							
	Quantity	Budget	Total	Mid	Total	High End	Total
Styling Chair	2	$175	$350	$400	$800	$1,200	$2,400
Styling Station	2	$150	$300	$500	$1,000	$2,000	$4,000
Custom Cabinets (Retail)	1	$1,200	$1,200	$2,400	$2,400	$4,800	$4,800
Shampoo Cabinet	1	$300	$300	$600	$600	$1,000	$1,000
Stools	2	$75	$150	$150	$300	$300	$600
Shampoo Shuttles	1	$600	$600	$1,200	$1,200	$2,500	$2,500
Reception Desk	1	$400	$400	$1,000	$1,000	$3,000	$3,000
Reception Chairs	2	$80	$160	$200	$400	$400	$800
Retail Unit Freestanding	1	$250	$250	$500	$500	$2,000	$2,000
Floor Mats	2	$80	$160	$120	$240	$190	$380
Roller Carts	2	$70	$140	$150	$300	$300	$600
Mirrors	2	$75	$150	$150	$300	$300	$600
Massage / Facial Table	1	$400	$400	$800	$800	$2,500	$2,500
Make Up Cabinet	1	$400	$400	$1,000	$1,000	$2,500	$2,500
Make Up Chair	1	$130	$130	$330	$330	$550	$550
Grand Total			**$5,090**		**$11,170**		**$28,230**

Heads & Tails Salon - Materials & Labor Cost Break Down

	Qty. / Sq. Ft. / Days	Low Estimate	Total	High Estimate	Total
Flooring					
Ceramic Tile *(Prices Higher on Imported Italian Tile)*	450 sq. ft.	$3/sq. ft.	$1,350	$6/sq. ft.	$2,700
Hardwood, Oak, Cherry	450 sq. ft.	$5/sq. ft.	$2,250	$7/sq. ft.	$3,150
Vinyl *(Prices can vary on manufacturer, style, thickness)*	450 sq. ft.	$2/sq. ft.	$900	$5/sq. ft.	$2,250
Installation *(Labor Costs)*	450 sq. ft.	$2/sq. ft.	$900	$8/sq. ft.	$3,600
Ceiling					
Decorative drop ceiling with metal brackets *(standard)*	450 sq. ft.	$2/sq. ft. *(installed)*	$900 *(installed)*	$5/sq. ft. *(installed)*	$2,250 *(installed)*
Paint					
Commercial Grade Paint *(Note: 1 gallon =1 coat for every 400 sq. ft.)*	450 sq. ft. (2 gal.)	$20/gal.	$40	$40/gal.	$80
Ceiling Paint *(Price it, if applicable)*					
Trim & Door Paint *(Price it, if applicable)*					
Painter *(Labor Costs)*	3 days	$150/day	$450	$350/day	$1,050
Trim					
Baseboards	89 linear ft.	$1.50/ft. *(simple)*	$133.50	$4.50/ft. *(big/fancy)*	$400.50
Specialty Trim *(Price it, if applicable)*					
Installation *(Labor Costs)*	2 days	$150/day	$300	$350/day	$700
Signage					
Non-Illuminated *(installed)*	1	$2,000/ sign	$2,000	$4,000/ sign	$4,000
Illuminated Block Letter *(installed)*	1	$3,000/ sign	$3,000	$7,000/ sign	$7,000
Lighting *(Note: Price your lighting and enter your estimates here.)*					
Overhead					
Task					
Accent					
Other					
Illuminated *(Labor Costs)*					
Accessories *(Note: Price your accessories and enter your estimates here.)*					
		Low Estimate		**High Estimate**	
POINT #1: The Entrance (Doorway/Front Desk/ Waiting Area)					
POINT #2: The Store Inside Your Salon (Retail Area)					
POINT #3: Your Bread & Butter (Service Area)					

Heads & Tails Salon - Materials & Labor Cost Break Down		
POINT #4: Let Your Color Shine (Color/Dispensary Area)		
POINT #5: Behind the Scenes (Utility Area)		

NOTE: These prices and installation costs are based on a general pricing structure that is subject to change depending on demographics and overall budget of the salon owner. The material pricing is based on a high traffic material cost that will withhold the normal wear and tear of heavy salon traffic. It is recommended to add approximately 10% to each of the above totals to cover costs of spoilage of materials or human error.

3. A Cut Above Salon | 4 Operator Salon | 750 Square Feet

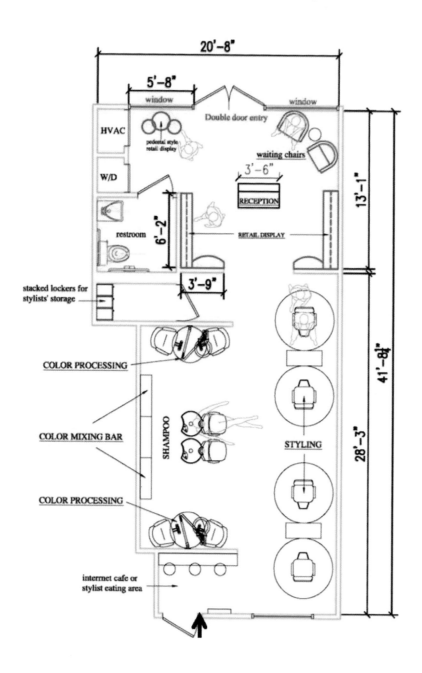

A Cut Above Salon ★ Five-Point Salon Design System ★	
POINT #1: **Doorway / Front Desk / Waiting Area**	The reception area is very grand. The idea here is to make it look like a retail store front instead of a salon. The reception desk has been placed front and center to create a welcoming atmosphere. Minimal waiting chairs have been provided to encourage customers to be up and about the retail displays.
POINT #2: **Retail Area**	The overall salon space has been distinctly divided between a specifically designed retail area and the service/styling floor itself. The two large windows up front allow for a great view into the retail section of the salon. This retail layout has been designed in an inviting way to encourage walk-in traffic.
POINT #3: **Service Area**	The service area has been created with back-to-back styling stations. All storage is behind the mirrors which acts as a space saver. The styling area is directly across from the shampoo/color area making the the space functional and efficient.
POINT #4: **Color / Dispensary Area**	The color display and mix bars are located on both sides of the shampoo back bar. These are exposed units that display the color boxes in a fashionable manner. Also, two processing tables have been placed on both sides to provide extra application/processing points.
POINT #5: **Utility Area**	The washer and dryer have been placed in a closet next to the restroom. Directly on the other side is another closet housing the HVAC system. The stylists have a small space for storage/lockers and an eating counter in the back of the salon.

A Cut Above Salon - Furniture & Equipment Budget							
	Quantity	Budget	Total	Mid	Total	High End	Total
Styling Chair	8	$175	$1,400	$400	$3,200	$1,200	$9,600
Freestanding 2-Sided Styling Station	2	$795	$1,590	$1,595	$3,190	$3,000	$6,000
Custom Cabinets *(Internet Cabinet)*	1	$1,000	$1,000	$2,000	$2,000	$3,000	$3,000
Color Mixing Bar *(Custom)*	1	$1,800	$1,800	$3,600	$3,600	$7,200	$7,200
Stools	4	$75	$300	$150	$600	$300	$1,200
Dryer	2	$200	$400	$200	$400	$200	$400
Color Processing Tables	2	$150	$300	$250	$500	$600	$1,200
Shampoo Shuttles	2	$600	$1,200	$1,200	$2,400	$2,500	$5,000
Reception Desk	1	$400	$400	$1,000	$1,000	$3,000	$3,000
Reception Chairs	2	$80	$160	$200	$400	$400	$800
Retail Unit Freestanding	3	$250	$750	$500	$1,500	$2,000	$6,000
Retail Unit Wall	2	$600	$1,200	$1,500	$3,000	$3,000	$6,000
Lockers	3	$200	$600	$200	$600	$200	$600
Magazine Rack	1	$130	$130	$130	$130	$300	$300
Washer/Dryer	1	$800	$800	$1,200	$1,200	$3,000	$3,000
Floor Mats	4	$80	$160	$120	$480	$190	$760
Grand Total			**$12,350**		**$24,200**		**$54,060**

A Cut Above Salon - Materials & Labor Cost Break Down					
	Qty. / Sq. Ft. / Days	Low Estimate	Total	High Estimate	Total
Flooring					
Ceramic Tile *(Prices Higher on Imported Italian Tile)*	750 sq. ft.	$3/sq. ft.	$2,250	$6/sq. ft.	$4,500
Hardwood, Oak, Cherry	750 sq. ft.	$5/sq. ft.	$3,750	$7/sq. ft.	$5,250
Vinyl *(Prices can vary on manufacturer, style, thickness)*	750 sq. ft.	$2/sq. ft.	$1,500	$5/sq. ft.	$3,750
Installation (Labor Costs)	750 sq. ft.	$2/sq. ft.	$1,500	$8/sq. ft.	$6,000
Ceiling					
Decorative drop ceiling with metal brackets *(standard)*	750 sq. ft.	$2/sq. ft. *(installed)*	$1,500	$5/sq. ft. *(installed)*	$3,750
Paint					
Commercial Grade Paint *(Note: 1 gallon =1 coat for every 400 sq. ft.)*	750 sq. ft. (2 gal.)	$20/gal.	$40	$40/gal.	$80
Ceiling Paint *(Price it, if applicable)*					
Trim & Door Paint *(Price it, if applicable)*					
Painter *(Labor Costs)*	3 days	$150/day	$450	$350/day	$1,050
Trim					
Baseboards	144.5 linear ft.	$1.50/ft. *(simple)*	$216.75	$4.50/ft. *(big/fancy)*	$650.25
Specialty Trim *(Price it, if applicable)*					
Installation *(Labor Costs)*	3 days	$150/day	$450	$350/day	$1,050
Signage					
Non-Illuminated *(installed)*	1	$2,000/ sign	$2,000	$4,000/ sign	$4,000
Illuminated Block Letter *(installed)*	1	$3,000/ sign	$3,000	$7,000/ sign	$7,000
Lighting *(Note: Price your lighting and enter your estimates here.)*					
Overhead					
Task					
Accent					
Other					
Illuminated *(Labor Costs)*					
Accessories *(Note: Price your accessories and enter your estimates here.)*					
		Low Estimate		**High Estimate**	
POINT #1: The Entrance (Doorway/Front Desk/ Waiting Area)					
POINT #2: The Store Inside Your Salon (Retail Area)					
POINT #3: Your Bread & Butter (Service Area)					

A Cut Above Salon - Materials & Labor Cost Break Down		
POINT #4: Let Your Color Shine (Color/Dispensary Area)		
POINT #5: Behind the Scenes (Utility Area)		

NOTE: These prices and installation costs are based on a general pricing structure that is subject to change depending on demographics and overall budget of the salon owner. The material pricing is based on a high traffic material cost that will withhold the normal wear and tear of heavy salon traffic. It is recommended to add approximately 10% to each of the above totals to cover costs of spoilage of materials or human error.

4. Salon 101 | 5 Operator Salon | 1176 Square Feet

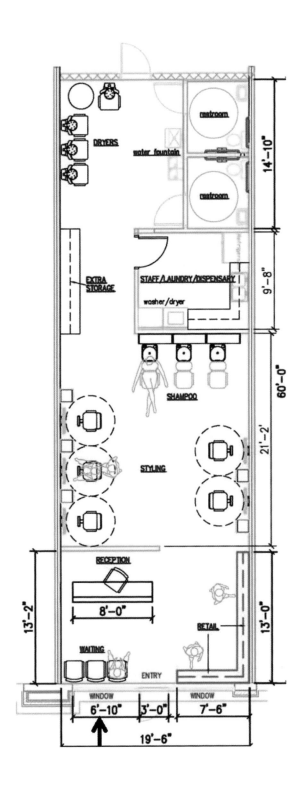

Salon 101 ★ Five-Point Salon Design System ★	
POINT #1: **Doorway / Front Desk / Waiting Area**	The front area is very basic. The design includes a decent-sized front desk and minimal waiting chairs, with more space devoted to retail. A wall has been created behind the reception desk to act as a divider, but it also displays the salon's logo.
POINT #2: **Retail Area**	Even though this is a narrow space, it still feels quite open with the retail nook opening into the styling floor and service area. The long wall of retail displays create a dramatic effect as well as a focal point when looking into the salon through the window.
POINT #3: **Service Area**	This five operator salon floor plan saves money on build-out costs. All plumbing is toward the back with the shampoo bowls tapping into the plumbing from the staff area.
POINT #4: **Color / Dispensary Area**	Most of the color storage is kept behind closed doors in the staff/utility area. However, an extra storage unit has been created just outside this room for easier access to commonly used products/color.
POINT #5: **Utility Area**	The utility area doubles as the staff area and break room. This room houses a full-size washer and dryer, cabinetry storage, a sink, and a refrigerator.

Salon 101 - Furniture & Equipment Budget							
	Quantity	Budget	Total	Mid	Total	High End	Total
Styling Chair	5	$175	$875	$400	$2,000	$1,200	$6,000
Wall Styling Station	5	$250	$1,250	$500	$2,500	$1,200	$6,000
Wall Mirrors	5	$75	$375	$110	$550	$250	$1,250
Color Mixing Dispensary	1	$1,800	$1,800	$3,600	$3,600	$7,200	$7,200
Stools	4	$75	$300	$150	$600	$300	$1,200
Dryer	4	$200	$800	$200	$800	$200	$400
Dryer Chairs	4	$150	$600	$300	$1,200	$600	$1,200
Shampoo Wall Sinks	3	$175	$525	$325	$975	$600	$1,800
Shampoo Cabinets	3	$250	$750	$500	$1,500	$2,000	$6,000
Reception Desk	1	$400	$400	$1,000	$1,000	$3,000	$3,000
Reception Chairs	3	$80	$240	$200	$600	$400	$1,200
Retail Unit Wall	1	$2,000	$2,000	$4,000	$4,000	$7,000	$7,000
Lockers	3	$200	$600	$200	$600	$200	$600
Storage Cabinet	1	$600	$600	$1,000	$1,000	$2,000	$2,000
Washer/Dryer	1	$800	$800	$1,200	$1,200	$3,000	$3,000
Grand Total			$11,915		$22,125		$49,450

Salon 101 - Materials & Labor Cost Break Down					
	Qty. / Sq. Ft. / Days	Low Estimate	Total	High Estimate	Total
Flooring					
Ceramic Tile *(Prices Higher on Imported Italian Tile)*	1176 sq. ft.	$3/sq. ft.	$3,528	$6/sq. ft.	$7,056
Hardwood, Oak, Cherry	1176 sq. ft.	$5/sq. ft.	$5,880	$7/sq. ft.	$8,232
Vinyl *(Prices can vary on manufacturer, style, thickness)*	1176 sq. ft.	$2/sq. ft.	$2,352	$5/sq. ft.	$5,880
Installation (Labor Costs)	1176 sq. ft.	$2/sq. ft.	$2,352	$8/sq. ft.	$9,408
Ceiling					
Decorative drop ceiling with metal brackets *(standard)*	1176 sq. ft.	$2/sq. ft. *(installed)*	$2,352	$5/sq. ft. *(installed)*	$5,880
Paint					
Commercial Grade Paint *(Note: 1 gallon =1 coat for every 400 sq. ft.)*	1176 sq. ft. (6 gal.)	$20/gal.	$120	$40/gal.	$240
Ceiling Paint *(Price it, if applicable)*					
Trim & Door Paint *(Price it, if applicable)*					
Painter *(Labor Costs)*	3 days	$150/day	$450	$350/day	$1,050
Trim					
Baseboards	270 linear ft.	$1.50/ft. *(simple)*	$405	$4.50/ft. *(big/fancy)*	$1,215
Crown Molding	270 linear ft.	$2.00/ft. *(simple)*	$540	$6.00/ft. *(big/fancy)*	$1,620
Carpenter/Installer	5 days	$150/day	$750	$350/day	$1,750
Signage					
Non-Illuminated *(installed)*	1	$2,000/ sign	$2,000	$4,000/ sign	$4,000
Illuminated Block Letter *(installed)*	1	$3,000/ sign	$3,000	$7,000/ sign	$7,000
Lighting *(Note: Price your lighting and enter your estimates here.)*					
Overhead					
Task					
Accent					
Other					
Illuminated *(Labor Costs)*					
Accessories *(Note: Price your accessories and enter your estimates here.)*					
		Low Estimate		**High Estimate**	
POINT #1: The Entrance (Doorway/Front Desk/ Waiting Area)					
POINT #2: The Store Inside Your Salon (Retail Area)					

Salon 101 - Materials & Labor Cost Break Down		
POINT #3: Your Bread & Butter (Service Area)		
POINT #4: Let Your Color Shine (Color/Dispensary Area)		
POINT #5: Behind the Scenes (Utility Area)		

NOTE: These prices and installation costs are based on a general pricing structure that is subject to change depending on demographics and overall budget of the salon owner. The material pricing is based on a high traffic material cost that will withhold the normal wear and tear of heavy salon traffic. It is recommended to add approximately 10% to each of the above totals to cover costs of spoilage of materials or human error.

5. Hair Color Studio | 6 Operator Salon | 1200 Square Feet

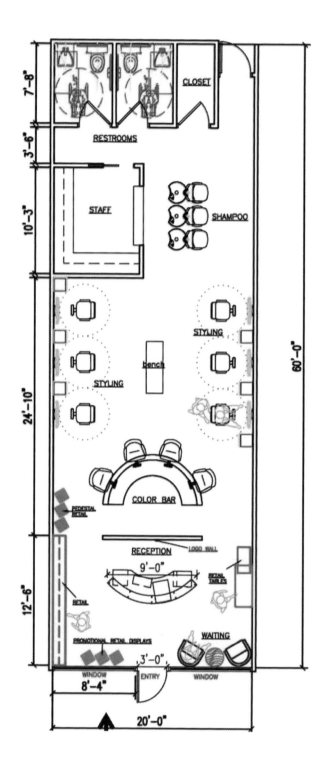

Hair Color Studio ★ Five-Point Salon Design System ★	
POINT #1: **Doorway / Front Desk / Waiting Area**	Minimal waiting chairs were placed in the waiting area to encourage guests to interact with the various retail displays
POINT #2: **Retail Area**	The retail area extends into the salon area to fill unused wall space. Plus, this slight extension allows clients, who are receiving salon services, to maintain a visual of retail products at all times.
POINT #3: **Service Area**	In this salon design, the shampoo area and the staff area directly correspond to each other for a practical reason. The shampoo back bar has been inserted into the staff room wall. It is accessible from both the shampoo side AND the staff room. For operator ease, to minimize traffic, and to keep the area visually tidy, the staff can empty dirty towel baskets and restock supplies all from the staff area.
POINT #4: **Color / Dispensary Area**	A full color bar and processing area has been created directly behind the reception wall. The shape of the color bar mimics the shape of the reception desk. The color bar has processing chairs on one side while the back side houses the color storage and mix area.
POINT #5: **Utility Area**	The staff area has a large amount of storage, hook ups for a washer/dryer, and enough room to house the hot water heater. A closet has been created just outside the restrooms that could double as utility overflow if necessary.

Hair Color Studio - Furniture & Equipment Budget

	Quantity	Budget	Total	Mid	Total	High End	Total
Styling Chair	10	$175	$1,750	$400	$4,000	$1,200	$12,000
Styling Station	6	$150	$900	$500	$3,000	$2,000	$12,000
Portable Dryer on Wheels	2	$200	$400	$200	$400	$200	$400
Staff Stools	3	$100	$300	$200	$600	$300	$900
Staff Lounge (Custom Counter)	1	$600	$600	$1,200	$1,200	$3,000	$3,000
Shampoo Shuttles	3	$600	$1,800	$1,200	$3,600	$2,500	$7,500
Custom Reception Desk	1	$3,000	$3,000	$5,000	$5,000	$8,000	$8,000
Reception Chairs	2	$80	$160	$200	$400	$400	$800
Reception Benches (in Styling Area)	1	$300	$300	$500	$500	$1,000	$1,000
Retail Unit Freestanding	7	$250	$1,750	$500	$3,500	$2,000	$14,000
Custom Retail Units	2	$1,800	$3,600	$3,600	$7,200	$6,000	$12,000
Color Bar	1	$2,500	$2,500	$5,000	$5,000	$9,000	$9,000
Floor Mats	6	$80	$480	$120	$720	$190	$1,140
Roller Carts	6	$70	$420	$150	$900	$300	$1,800
Mirrors	6	$75	$450	$150	$900	$300	$1,800
Magazine Rack	1	$130	$130	$130	$130	$300	$300
Closet-sized, Stacking Washer/Dryer (Optional)	1	$800	$800	$1,200	$1,200	$3,000	$3,000
Shampoo Back Bar	1	$1,200	$1,200	$2,400	$2,400	$5,000	$5,000
Grand Total			**$20,540**		**$40,650**		**$93,640**

Hair Color Studio - Materials & Labor Cost Break Down					
	Qty. / Sq. Ft. / Days	Low Estimate	Total	High Estimate	Total
Flooring					
Ceramic Tile *(Prices Higher on Imported Italian Tile)*	1200 sq. ft.	$3/sq. ft.	$3,600	$6/sq. ft.	$7,200
Hardwood, Oak, Cherry	1200 sq. ft.	$5/sq. ft.	$6,000	$7/sq. ft.	$8,400
Vinyl *(Prices can vary on manufacturer, style, thickness)*	1200 sq. ft.	$2/sq. ft.	$2,400	$5/sq. ft.	$6,000
Installation (Labor Costs)	1200 sq. ft.	$2/sq. ft.	$2,400	$8/sq. ft.	$9,600
Ceiling					
Decorative drop ceiling with metal brackets *(standard)*	1200 sq. ft.	$2/sq. ft. *(installed)*	$2,400	$5/sq. ft. *(installed)*	$6,000
Paint					
Commercial Grade Paint *(Note: 1 gallon =1 coat for every 400 sq. ft.)*	1200 sq. ft. (6 gal.)	$20/gal.	$120	$40/gal.	$240
Ceiling Paint *(Price it, if applicable)*					
Trim & Door Paint *(Price it, if applicable)*					
Painter *(Labor Costs)*	3 days	$150/day	$450	$350/day	$1,050
Trim					
Baseboards	287 linear ft.	$1.50/ft. *(simple)*	$430.50	$4.50/ft. *(big/fancy)*	$1,291.50
Crown Molding	287 linear ft.	$2.00/ft. *(simple)*	$574.00	$6.00/ft. *(big/fancy)*	$1,722
Carpenter/Installer	5 days	$150/day	$750	$350/day	$1,750
Signage					
Non-Illuminated *(installed)*	1	$2,000/ sign	$2,000	$4,000/ sign	$4,000
Illuminated Block Letter *(installed)*	1	$3,000/ sign	$3,000	$7,000/ sign	$7,000
Lighting *(Note: Price your lighting and enter your estimates here.)*					
Overhead					
Task					
Accent					
Other					
Illuminated *(Labor Costs)*					
Accessories *(Note: Price your accessories and enter your estimates here.)*					
		Low Estimate		**High Estimate**	
POINT #1: The Entrance (Doorway/Front Desk/ Waiting Area)					
POINT #2: The Store Inside Your Salon (Retail Area)					

Hair Color Studio - Materials & Labor Cost Break Down		
POINT #3: Your Bread & Butter (Service Area)		
POINT #4: Let Your Color Shine (Color/Dispensary Area)		
POINT #5: Behind the Scenes (Utility Area)		

NOTE: These prices and installation costs are based on a general pricing structure that is subject to change depending on demographics and overall budget of the salon owner. The material pricing is based on a high traffic material cost that will withhold the normal wear and tear of heavy salon traffic. It is recommended to add approximately 10% to each of the above totals to cover costs of spoilage of materials or human error.

6. The Hair House | 8 Operator Salon | 1200 Square Feet

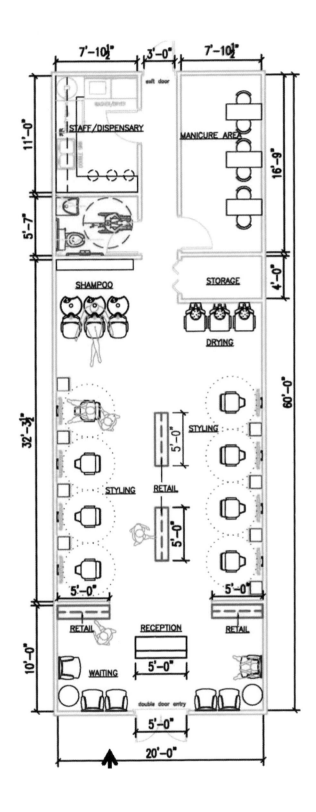

The Hair House ★ Five-Point Salon Design System ★	
POINT #1: **Doorway / Front Desk / Waiting Area**	There is a distinct separation between the reception/waiting area and the styling/service area, but nothing impedes the slightlines from the reception area to the extra retail display area.
POINT #2: **Retail Area**	The walls behind the retail units in the front were existing when this space was acquired. There was on 10 feet of depth for the reception area. So, additional retail displays were placed directly on the cutting room floor. Having the retail units right in the styling area also allows the stylists to promote the products being used on their clients during a visit.
POINT #3: **Service Area**	The service area/styling floor is very open with a great traffic flow. The retail units that are placed in the salon area act as a natural division between the stylists on both sides and create wide walkways. The shampoo bowls are nestled in the back corner to share the plumbing with the restroom, keeping build-out cost down.
POINT #4: **Color / Dispensary Area**	All color storage and mixing is done in the back dispensary. The salon owner preferred retail displays in the center of the salon instead of doing a color bar. Thus, the color/dispensary room became extremly important when designing to meet the needs of staff and clients.
POINT #5: **Utility Area**	The dispensary/staff area also doubles as the utility area which includes a full-size washer and dryer, hot water heater, and a sink. An extra storage space has been inserted for the stylists to store personal belongings.

The Hair House - Furniture & Equipment Budget

	Quantity	Budget	Total	Mid	Total	High End	Total
Styling Chair	8	$175	$1,400	$400	$3,200	$1,200	$9,600
Styling Station	8	$150	$1,200	$500	$4,000	$2,000	$16,000
Floor Mats	8	$80	$640	$120	$960	$190	$1,520
Reception Tables	2	$150	$300	$300	$600	$500	$1,000
Shampoo Cabinet	1	$900	$900	$1,800	$1,800	$3,600	$3,600
Stools	6	$75	$300	$150	$900	$300	$2,700
Dryer Chair	3	$150	$450	$400	$1,200	$800	$2,400
Dryer	3	$200	$600	$200	$600	$200	$600
Shampoo Shuttles	3	$600	$1,800	$1,200	$3,600	$2,500	$7,500
Reception Desk	1	$500	$500	$1,200	$1,200	$3,000	$3,000
Reception Chairs	6	$80	$480	$200	$1,200	$400	$2,400
Retail Unit Freestanding	2	$250	$500	$500	$1,000	$2,000	$4,000
Retail Unit Wall	2	$250	$500	$900	$1,800	$2,000	$4,000
Dispensary Furniture	1	$2,000	$2,000	$3,000	$3,000	$7,000	$7,000
Nail Tables	3	$140	$420	$400	$1,200	$800	$2,400
Roller Carts	8	$70	$560	$150	$1,200	$300	$2,400
Mirrors	8	$75	$600	$150	$1,200	$300	$2,400
Washer/Dryer	1	$800	$800	$1,200	$1,200	$3,000	$3,000
Grand Total			**$13,950**		**$29,860**		**$75,520**

The Hair House - Materials & Labor Cost Break Down

	Qty. / Sq. Ft. / Days	Low Estimate	Total	High Estimate	Total
Flooring					
Ceramic Tile *(Prices Higher on Imported Italian Tile)*	1200 sq. ft.	$3/sq. ft.	$3,600	$6/sq. ft.	$7,200
Hardwood, Oak, Cherry	1200 sq. ft.	$5/sq. ft.	$6,000	$7/sq. ft.	$8,400
Vinyl *(Prices can vary on manufacturer, style, thickness)*	1200 sq. ft.	$2/sq. ft.	$2,400	$5/sq. ft.	$6,000
Installation (Labor Costs)	1200 sq. ft.	$2/sq. ft.	$2,400	$8/sq. ft.	$9,600
Ceiling					
Decorative drop ceiling with metal brackets *(standard)*	1200 sq. ft.	$2/sq. ft. *(installed)*	$2,400	$5/sq. ft. *(installed)*	$6,000
Paint					
Commercial Grade Paint *(Note: 1 gallon =1 coat for every 400 sq. ft.)*	1200 sq. ft. (6 gal.)	$20/gal.	$120	$40/gal.	$240
Ceiling Paint *(Price it, if applicable)*					
Trim & Door Paint *(Price it, if applicable)*					
Painter *(Labor Costs)*	3 days	$150/day	$450	$350/day	$1,050
Trim					
Baseboards	287 linear ft.	$1.50/ft. *(simple)*	$430.50	$4.50/ft. *(big/fancy)*	$1,291.50
Crown Molding	287 linear ft.	$2.00/ft. *(simple)*	$574	$6.00/ft. *(big/fancy)*	$1,722
Carpenter/Installer	5 days	$150/day	$750	$350/day	$1,750
Signage					
Non-Illuminated *(installed)*	1	$2,000/ sign	$2,000	$4,000/ sign	$4,000
Illuminated Block Letter *(installed)*	1	$3,000/ sign	$3,000	$7,000/ sign	$7,000
Lighting *(Note: Price your lighting and enter your estimates here.)*					
Overhead					
Task					
Accent					
Other					
Illuminated *(Labor Costs)*					

Accessories *(Note: Price your accessories and enter your estimates here.)*		
	Low Estimate	**High Estimate**
POINT #1: The Entrance (Doorway/Front Desk/ Waiting Area)		
POINT #2: The Store Inside Your Salon (Retail Area)		

The Hair House - Materials & Labor Cost Break Down		
POINT #3: Your Bread & Butter (Service Area)		
POINT #4: Let Your Color Shine (Color/Dispensary Area)		
POINT #5: Behind the Scenes (Utility Area)		

NOTE: These prices and installation costs are based on a general pricing structure that is subject to change depending on demographics and overall budget of the salon owner. The material pricing is based on a high traffic material cost that will withhold the normal wear and tear of heavy salon traffic. It is recommended to add approximately 10% to each of the above totals to cover costs of spoilage of materials or human error.

7. Studio 495 | 10 Operator Salon | 2400 Square Feet

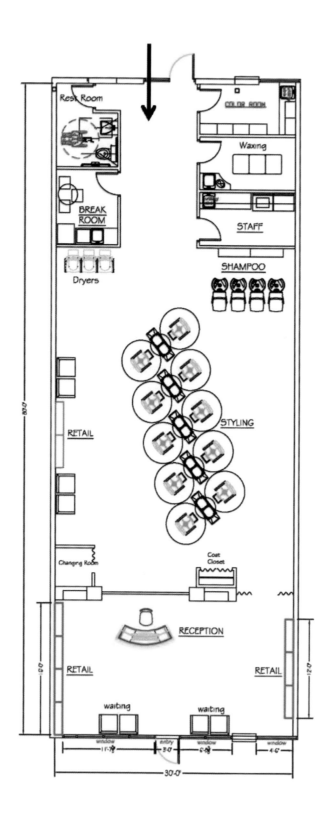

Studio 495 ★ Five-Point Salon Design System ★	
POINT #1: **Doorway / Front Desk / Waiting Area**	The front desk has been placed in the center to act as a focal point. Directly behind the desk is a glass wall with an etched logo to provide some visual interest.
POINT #2: **Retail Area**	The product displays have been placed on both sides of the reception area to distinguish between two separate product lines. These displays have also been placed on wheels to allow for easy mobility and quick rearranging for a fresh look.
POINT #3: **Service Area**	In the service area, back-to-back styling stations have been placed in a long run at an angle to have a dramatic effect. Included in this area are additional retail and a few waiting chairs to achieve a more welcoming and homey atomosphere.
POINT #4: **Color / Dispensary Area**	A color mix room/dispensary has been created separate from the staff and break areas. This keeps overall noise level down as staff is not all crowded into one area.
POINT #5: **Utility Area**	The utility area has been placed directly behind the shampoo bowls to share plumbing lines and drains.

Studio 495 - Furniture & Equipment Budget							
	Quantity	Budget	Total	Mid	Total	High End	Total
Styling Chair	10	$175	$1,750	$400	$4,000	$1,200	$12,000
Freestanding 2 Sided Styling Station	5	$795	$3,950	$1,595	$8,000	$3,000	$15,000
Shampoo Cabinet	2	$300	$600	$600	$1,200	$1,000	$2,000
Wax Table	1	$250	$250	$600	$600	$1,600	$1,600
Wax Room Cabinet	1	$400	$400	$800	$800	$1,500	$1,500
Dryer Chair	3	$150	$450	$400	$1,200	$800	$2,400
Dryer	3	$200	$600	$200	$600	$200	$600
Shampoo Shuttles	4	$600	$2,400	$1,200	$4,800	$2,500	$10,000
Reception Desk	1	$600	$600	$1,200	$1,200	$4,000	$4,000
Reception Chairs	8	$80	$640	$200	$1,600	$400	$3,200
Retail Unit Wall	9	$250	$1,750	$900	$8,100	$2,000	$18,000
Coffee Station	1	$125	$125	$300	$300	$750	$750
Color Caninets in Color Room	1	$2,500	$2,500	$5,000	$5,000	$7,000	$7,000
Break Room	1	$500	$500	$1,500	$1,500	$3,000	$3,000
Floor Mats	10	$80	$800	$120	$1,200	$190	$1,900
Roller Carts	10	$70	$700	$150	$1,500	$300	$3,000
Washer/Dryer	1	$800	$800	$1,200	$1,200	$3,000	$3,000
Grand Total			$18,815		$42,800		$88,950

handwritten: 24,000

handwritten: 1600

Studio 495 - Materials & Labor Cost Break Down

	Qty. / Sq. Ft. / Days	Low Estimate	Total	High Estimate	Total
Flooring					
Ceramic Tile *(Prices Higher on Imported Italian Tile)*	2400 sq. ft.	$3/sq. ft.	$7,200	$6/sq. ft.	$14,400
Hardwood, Oak, Cherry	2400 sq. ft.	$5/sq. ft.	$12,000	$7/sq. ft.	$16,800
Vinyl *(Prices can vary on manufacturer, style, thickness)*	2400 sq. ft.	$2/sq. ft.	$4,800	$5/sq. ft.	$12,000
Installation *(Labor Costs)*	2400 sq. ft.	$2/sq. ft.	$4,800	$8/sq. ft.	$19,200
Ceiling					
Decorative drop ceiling with metal brackets *(standard)*	2400 sq. ft.	$2/sq. ft. *(installed)*	$4,800	$5/sq. ft. *(installed)*	$12,000
Paint					
Commercial Grade Paint *(Note: 1 gallon =1 coat for every 400 sq. ft.)*	2400 sq. ft. (12 gal.)	$20/gal.	$240	$40/gal.	$480
Ceiling Paint *(Price it, if applicable)*					
Trim & Door Paint *(Price it, if applicable)*					
Painter *(Labor Costs)*	5 days	$150/day	$750	$350/day	$1,750
Trim					
Baseboards	372 linear ft.	$1.50/ft. *(simple)*	$558	$4.50/ft. *(big/fancy)*	$1,674
Crown Molding	372 linear ft.	$2.00/ft. *(simple)*	$744	$6.00/ft. *(big/fancy)*	$2,232
Carpenter/Installer	7 days	$150/day	$1,050	$350/day	$2,450
Signage					
Non-Illuminated *(installed)*	1	$2,000/sign	$2,000	$4,000/sign	$4,000
Illuminated Block Letter *(installed)*	1	$3,000/sign	$3,000	$7,000/sign	$7,000
Lighting *(Note: Price your lighting and enter your estimates here.)*					
Overhead					
Task					
Accent					
Other					
Illuminated *(Labor Costs)*					
Accessories *(Note: Price your accessories and enter your estimates here.)*					
		Low Estimate		**High Estimate**	
POINT #1: The Entrance (Doorway/Front Desk/ Waiting Area)					
POINT #2: The Store Inside Your Salon (Retail Area)					

Studio 495 - Materials & Labor Cost Break Down		
POINT #3: Your Bread & Butter (Service Area)		
POINT #4: Let Your Color Shine (Color/Dispensary Area)		
POINT #5: Behind the Scenes (Utility Area)		

NOTE: These prices and installation costs are based on a general pricing structure that is subject to change depending on demographics and overall budget of the salon owner. The material pricing is based on a high traffic material cost that will withhold the normal wear and tear of heavy salon traffic. It is recommended to add approximately 10% to each of the above totals to cover costs of spoilage of materials or human error.

8. Cutting Edge Salon | 18 Operator Salon | 3500 Square Feet

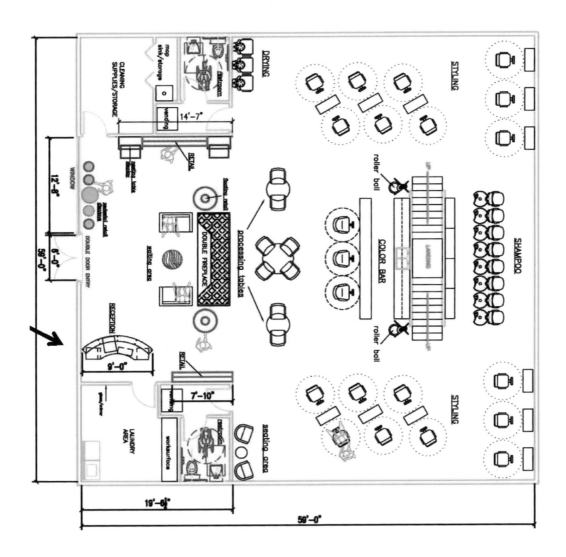

Cutting Edge Salon ★ Five-Point Salon Design System ★	
POINT #1: **Doorway / Front Desk / Waiting Area**	The salon owner wanted to create a cozy, comfortable feeling in the reception area. The design begain with a double-sided fireplace as a focal point.
POINT #2: **Retail Area**	The "homey" feel to the retail area, which is created by the fireplace, attracts walk-in traffic and additional business. There are several groupings of retail units to keep the clients up on their feet and browsing while waiting for their appointment.
POINT #3: **Service Area**	The service area flanks both sides of the color area. Minimal walls have been built to keep the space open and exposed. The shampoo area is hidden from sight by simply placing it behind the existing staircase.
POINT #4: **Color / Dispensary Area**	The exposed color bar and processing area is another great feature of this salon (and another way to sell more retail). The color storage and display is built off of the existing staircase in the space creating a dramatic effect. Not only is the color bar where the color is actually stored, but it also serves as a promotional retail area. As the stylist is applying color to the client's hair, she can also recommend all the products available to maintain color-treated hair. These products will also be visible from the processing tables to initiate conversations about specialty retail products and promotions.
POINT #5: **Utility Area**	Due to the large square footage of this space, the utility area has been separated into two rooms on both sides of the entrance for easier access from all points of the salon.

Cutting Edge Salon - Furniture & Equipment Budget							
	Quantity	Budget	Total	Mid	Total	High End	Total
Styling Chair	18	$175	$3,150	$400	$7,200	$1,200	$21,600
Freestanding 2-Sided Styling Station	6	$795	$4,770	$1,595	$9,570	$3,000	$18,000
Wall Styling Station	6	$150	$900	$500	$3,000	$2,000	$12,000
Wall Mirrors	6	$75	$450	$120	$720	$200	$1,200
Shampoo Cabinet	4	$300	$1,200	$600	$2,400	$1,000	$4,000
Color Styling Chairs	11	$175	$1,925	$400	$4,400	$1,200	$13,200
4-Seat Color Table	1	$250	$250	$500	$500	$900	$900
2-Seat Color Table	2	$200	$400	$400	$800	$600	$1,200
Color Counter Styling Freestanding	1	$1,200	$1,200	$1,800	$1,800	$2,500	$2,500
Rollerball Color Processor	2	$2,400	$4,800	$2,400	$4,800	$2,400	$4,800
Desk Stools	2	$75	$150	$150	$300	$300	$600
Dryer Chair	3	$150	$450	$400	$1,200	$800	$2,400
Dryer	3	$200	$600	$200	$600	$200	$600
Shampoo Shuttles	8	$600	$4,800	$1,200	$9,600	$2,500	$20,000
Reception Desk Curved	1	$1,200	$1,200	$2,200	$2,200	$5,500	$5,500
Reception Chairs	6	$80	$480	$200	$1,200	$400	$2,400
Retail Unit Wall	2	$800	$1,600	$2,000	$4,000	$4,000	$8,000
Retail Units Freestanding	6	$300	$1,800	$500	$3,000	$750	$4,500
Color Bar Work Station	1	$4,000	$4,000	$7,000	$7,000	$12,000	$12,000
Laundry Room	1	$500	$500	$1,500	$1,500	$3,000	$3,000
Floor Mats	18	$80	$1,440	$120	$2,160	$190	$3,420
Roller Carts	18	$70	$1,260	$150	$2,700	$300	$5,400
Washer/Dryer	1	$800	$800	$1,200	$1,200	$3,000	$3,000
Grand Total			**$38,125**		**$71,850**		**$150,220**

15000

4800

2400

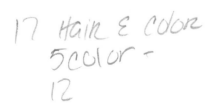

17 Hair & Color
5 color -
12

Cutting Edge Salon - Materials & Labor Cost Break Down					
	Qty. / Sq. Ft. / Days	Low Estimate	Total	High Estimate	Total
Flooring					
Ceramic Tile *(Prices Higher on Imported Italian Tile)*	3500 sq. ft.	$3/sq. ft.	$10,500	$6/sq. ft.	$21,000
Hardwood, Oak, Cherry	3500 sq. ft.	$5/sq. ft.	$17,500	$7/sq. ft.	$24,500
Vinyl *(Prices can vary on manufacturer, style, thickness)*	3500 sq. ft.	$2/sq. ft.	$7,000	$5/sq. ft.	$17,500
Installation *(Labor Costs)*	3500 sq. ft.	$2/sq. ft.	$7,000	$8/sq. ft.	$28,000
Ceiling					
Decorative drop ceiling with metal brackets *(standard)*	3500 sq. ft.	$2/sq. ft. *(installed)*	$7,000	$5/sq. ft. *(installed)*	$17,500
Paint					
Commercial Grade Paint *(Note: 1 gallon =1 coat for every 400 sq. ft.)*	3500 sq. ft. (12 gal.)	$20/gal.	$360	$40/gal.	$720
Ceiling Paint *(Price it, if applicable)*					
Trim & Door Paint *(Price it, if applicable)*					
Painter *(Labor Costs)*	5 days *(2 people)*	$150/day	$1,500	$350/day	$3,500
Trim					
Baseboards	386 linear ft.	$1.50/ft. *(simple)*	$579	$4.50/ft. *(big/fancy)*	$1,737
Crown Molding	386 linear ft.	$2.00/ft. *(simple)*	$772	$6.00/ft. *(big/fancy)*	$2,316
Carpenter/Installer	7 days *(2 people)*	$150/day /person	$2,100	$350/day /person	$4,900
Signage					
Non-Illuminated *(installed)*	1	$2,000/ sign	$2,000	$4,000/ sign	$4,000
Illuminated Block Letter *(installed)*	1	$3,000/ sign	$3,000	$7,000/ sign	$7,000
Lighting *(Note: Price your lighting and enter your estimates here.)*					
Overhead					
Task					
Accent					
Other					
Illuminated *(Labor Costs)*					
Accessories *(Note: Price your accessories and enter your estimates here.)*					
		Low Estimate		**High Estimate**	
POINT #1: The Entrance (Doorway/Front Desk/ Waiting Area)					

Cutting Edge Salon - Materials & Labor Cost Break Down		
POINT #2: The Store Inside Your Salon (Retail Area)		
POINT #3: Your Bread & Butter (Service Area)		
POINT #4: Let Your Color Shine (Color/Dispensary Area)		
POINT #5: Behind the Scenes (Utility Area)		

NOTE: These prices and installation costs are based on a general pricing structure that is subject to change depending on demographics and overall budget of the salon owner. The material pricing is based on a high traffic material cost that will withhold the normal wear and tear of heavy salon traffic. It is recommended to add approximately 10% to each of the above totals to cover costs of spoilage of materials or human error.

9. Heads Up Hair Salon | 18 Booth Rental Set Ups | 3021 Square Feet

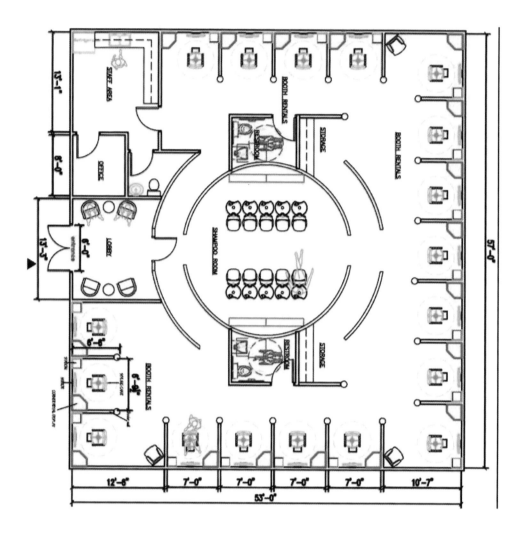

Heads Up Hair Salon	
★ Five-Point Salon Design System ★	
POINT #1: **Doorway / Front Desk** **/ Waiting Area**	The front and waiting area is a shared lobby. Here, customers can buzz back to the stylists' booths or wait for their stylists to come greet them when it's time for their appointment.
POINT #2: **Retail Area**	Because this salon is a booth rental set up, each stylist has their own product/retail display within their booth.
POINT #3: **Service Area**	This design incorporates individual booth rental set ups. Each booth space is separated by divider walls for more privacy. In this salon, all stylists are responsible for supplying their own retail products to sell. Each booth gets a standard corner retail unit to display whatever hair products they desire.
POINT #4: **Color / Dispensary** **Area**	All color is stored and mixed directly in the stylists' booths.
POINT #5: **Utility Area**	The utility area is shared by all booth renters.

Heads Up Hair Salon - Furniture & Equipment Budget						
	Quantity	Budget	Total	Mid	Total	High End	Total
Styling Chair	18	$175	$3,150	$400	$7,200	$1,200	$21,600
Styling Station	18	$300	$5,400	$750	$13,500	$1,500	$27,000
Shampoo Cabinet	4	$600	$2,400	$1,200	$2,400	$2,000	$8,000
Hair Stylist Stools	18	$75	$1,350	$150	$2,700	$300	$5,400
Dryer Wheel Kits	18	$40	$720	$40	$720	$40	$720
Dryers	18	$250	$4,500	$250	$4,500	$250	$4,500
Shampoo Shuttles	10	$800	$8,000	$1,500	$15,000	$3,000	$30,000
Reception Desk (Optional)	1	$600	$600	$1,200	$1,200	$4,000	$4,000
Reception Chairs	4	$80	$320	$200	$800	$400	$1,600
Corner Retail Display	18	$250	$4,500	$600	$10,800	$1,200	$21,600
Coffee Station	1	$125	$125	$300	$300	$750	$750
Color Cabinets In Color Room	1	$2,500	$2,500	$5,000	$5,000	$7,000	$7,000
Floor Mats	18	$80	$1,440	$120	$2,160	$190	$3,420
Roller Carts	18	$70	$1,260	$150	$2,700	$300	$5,400
Washer/Dryer	1	$800	$800	$1,200	$1,200	$3,000	$3,000
Grand Total			$37,065		$70,180		$143,990

Heads Up Hair Salon - Materials & Labor Cost Break Down

	Qty. / Sq. Ft. / Days	Low Estimate	Total	High Estimate	Total
Flooring					
Ceramic Tile *(Prices Higher on Imported Italian Tile)*	3021 sq. ft.	$3/sq. ft.	$9,063	$6/sq. ft.	$18,126
Hardwood, Oak, Cherry	3021 sq. ft.	$5/sq. ft.	$15,105	$7/sq. ft.	$21,147
Vinyl *(Prices can vary on manufacturer, style, thickness)*	3021 sq. ft.	$2/sq. ft.	$6,042	$5/sq. ft.	$15,105
Installation *(Labor Costs)*	3021 sq. ft.	$2/sq. ft.	$6,042	$8/sq. ft.	$24,168
Ceiling					
Decorative drop ceiling with metal brackets *(standard)*	3021 sq. ft.	$2/sq. ft. *(installed)*	$6,042	$5/sq. ft. *(installed)*	$15,105
Paint					
Commercial Grade Paint *(Note: 1 gallon =1 coat for every 400 sq. ft.)*	3021 sq. ft. (16 gal.)	$20/gal.	$320	$40/gal.	$640
Ceiling Paint *(Price it, if applicable)*					
Trim & Door Paint *(Price it, if applicable)*					
Painter *(Labor Costs)*	7 days (2 people)	$150/day /person	$2,100	$350/day	$4,900
Trim					
Baseboards	800 linear ft.	$1.50/ft. *(simple)*	$1,200	$4.50/ft. *(big/fancy)*	$3,600
Crown Molding	800 linear ft.	$2.00/ft. *(simple)*	$1,600	$6.00/ft. *(big/fancy)*	$4,800
Carpenter/Installer	7 days (2 people)	$150/day/person	$2,100	$350/day/person	$4,900
Signage					
Non-Illuminated *(installed)*	1	$2,000/sign	$2,000	$4,000/sign	$4,000
Illuminated Block Letter *(installed)*	1	$3,000/sign	$3,000	$7,000/sign	$7,000
Lighting *(Note: Price your lighting and enter your estimates here.)*					
Overhead					
Task					
Accent					
Other					
Illuminated *(Labor Costs)*					
Accessories *(Note: Price your accessories and enter your estimates here.)*					
		Low Estimate		**High Estimate**	
POINT #1: The Entrance (Doorway/Front Desk/ Waiting Area)					

Heads Up Hair Salon - Materials & Labor Cost Break Down		
POINT #2: The Store Inside Your Salon (Retail Area)		
POINT #3: Your Bread & Butter (Service Area)		
POINT #4: Let Your Color Shine (Color/Dispensary Area)		
POINT #5: Behind the Scenes (Utility Area)		

NOTE: These prices and installation costs are based on a general pricing structure that is subject to change depending on demographics and overall budget of the salon owner. The material pricing is based on a high traffic material cost that will withhold the normal wear and tear of heavy salon traffic. It is recommended to add approximately 10% to each of the above totals to cover costs of spoilage of materials or human error.

10. Strip Mall – Plan A (Skinny Salon) | 10 Operator Salon | 1244 Square Feet

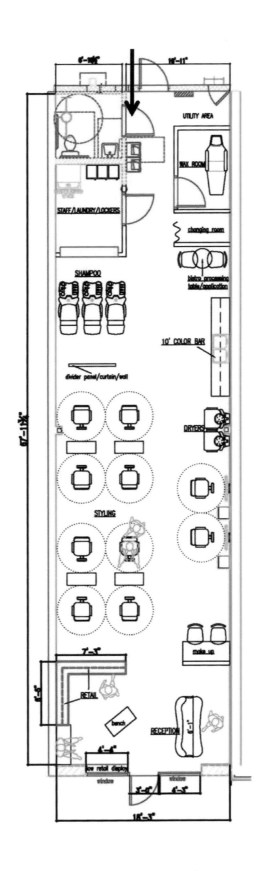

Strip Mall – Plan A (Skinny Salon) ★ Five-Point Salon Design System ★	
POINT #1: **Doorway / Front Desk / Waiting Area**	Due to the small amount of square footage alloted for the reception/retail area in this layout, minimal seating has been provided.
POINT #2: **Retail Area**	The windows up from provide some great natural daylight. So, the retail displays were designed to have glass shelving with no back. You can see straight through the retail area into the service area. Keeping the retail open to the service area avoids making this space feel too "strip mall-y" and allows the overall plan to feel more spacious.
POINT #3: **Service Area**	A combination of back-to-back and wall-mounted styling stations have been used in the space. This breaks up the styling area some, giving the stylists more room to work.
POINT #4: **Color / Dispensary Area**	A color mix and storage bar has been placed directly on the styling floor making it easily accessible for all stylists. Plus, this piece was specifically designed to attract attention of clients and spark conversation.
POINT #5: **Utility Area**	The utility area was existing when this space was turned into a salon. The entire back area was designed around the utility area so that extra money was not spent moving things unnecessarily.

Strip Mall – Plan A (Skinny Salon) - Furniture & Equipment Budget

	Quantity	Budget	Total	Mid	Total	High End	Total
Styling Chair	10	$175	$1,750	$400	$4,000	$1,200	$12,000
Freestanding 2 Sided Styling Station	4	$795	$3,180	$1,595	$6,380	$3,000	$12,000
Wall Styling Station	2	$300	$600	$750	$1,500	$1,500	$3,000
Shampoo Cabinet	1	$600	$600	$1,200	$1,200	$2,000	$2,000
Stool Desk	1	$75	$75	$150	$150	$300	$300
Manicure Table	1	$150	$150	$400	$400	$800	$800
Stool Nail Tech	1	$75	$75	$150	$150	$300	$300
Client Nail Chair	1	$100	$100	$200	$200	$400	$400
Dryer Chair	2	$150	$300	$400	$800	$800	$1,600
Dryer	2	$200	$400	$200	$400	$200	$400
Shampoo Shuttles	3	$600	$1,800	$1,200	$3,600	$2,500	$7,500
Reception Desk	1	$600	$600	$1,200	$1,200	$4,000	$4,000
Reception Benches	2	$150	$300	$300	$600	$600	$1,200
Retail Unit Wall	1	$900	$900	$2,500	$2,500	$4,500	$4,500
Make Up Station	1	$300	$300	$750	$750	$2,000	$2,000
Make Up Chair	1	$150	$150	$300	$300	$500	$500
Color Bar	1	$2,500	$2,500	$5,000	$5,000	$7,000	$7,000
Laundry/Break Room	1	$500	$500	$1,500	$1,500	$3,000	$3,000
Floor Mats	10	$80	$800	$120	$1,200	$190	$1,900
Lockers	3	$200	$600	$200	$600	$500	$1,500
Wax Table	1	$300	$300	$750	$750	$2,000	$2,000
Roller Carts	10	$70	$700	$150	$1,500	$300	$3,000
Washer/Dryer	1	$800	$800	$1,200	$1,200	$3,000	$3,000
Grand Total			**$17,480**		**$35,880**		**$73,900**

Strip Mall – Plan A (Skinny Salon) - Materials & Labor Cost Break Down

	Qty. / Sq. Ft. / Days	Low Estimate	Total	High Estimate	Total
Flooring					
Ceramic Tile *(Prices Higher on Imported Italian Tile)*	1244 sq. ft.	$3/sq. ft.	$3,732	$6/sq. ft.	$7,464
Hardwood, Oak, Cherry	1244 sq. ft.	$5/sq. ft.	$6,220	$7/sq. ft.	$8,708
Vinyl *(Prices can vary on manufacturer, style, thickness)*	1244 sq. ft.	$2/sq. ft.	$2,488	$5/sq. ft.	$6,220
Installation *(Labor Costs)*	1244 sq. ft.	$2/sq. ft.	$2,488	$8/sq. ft.	$9,952
Ceiling					
Decorative drop ceiling with metal brackets *(standard)*	1244 sq. ft.	$2/sq. ft. *(installed)*	$2,488	$5/sq. ft. *(installed)*	$6,220
Paint					
Commercial Grade Paint *(Note: 1 gallon =1 coat for every 400 sq. ft.)*	1244 sq. ft. (7 gal.)	$20/gal.	$140	$40/gal.	$280
Ceiling Paint *(Price it, if applicable)*					
Trim & Door Paint *(Price it, if applicable)*					
Painter *(Labor Costs)*	3 days	$150/day	$450	$350/day	$1,050
Trim					
Baseboards	260 linear ft.	$1.50/ft. *(simple)*	$390	$4.50/ft. *(big/fancy)*	$1,170
Crown Molding	260 linear ft.	$2.00/ft. *(simple)*	$520	$6.00/ft. *(big/fancy)*	$1,560
Carpenter/Installer	5 days	$150/day	$750	$350/day/ person	$1,750
Signage					
Non-Illuminated *(installed)*	1	$2,000/ sign	$2,000	$4,000/ sign	$4,000
Illuminated Block Letter *(installed)*	1	$3,000/ sign	$3,000	$7,000/ sign	$7,000
Lighting *(Note: Price your lighting and enter your estimates here.)*					
Overhead					
Task					
Accent					
Other					
Illuminated *(Labor Costs)*					

Accessories *(Note: Price your accessories and enter your estimates here.)*		
	Low Estimate	**High Estimate**
POINT #1: The Entrance (Doorway/Front Desk/ Waiting Area)		
POINT #2: The Store Inside Your Salon (Retail Area)		

Strip Mall – Plan A (Skinny Salon) - Materials & Labor Cost Break Down		
POINT #3: Your Bread & Butter (Service Area)		
POINT #4: Let Your Color Shine (Color/Dispensary Area)		
POINT #5: Behind the Scenes (Utility Area)		

NOTE: These prices and installation costs are based on a general pricing structure that is subject to change depending on demographics and overall budget of the salon owner. The material pricing is based on a high traffic material cost that will withhold the normal wear and tear of heavy salon traffic. It is recommended to add approximately 10% to each of the above totals to cover costs of spoilage of materials or human error.

11. Strip Mall – Plan B (Strip Mall Styles) | 8 Operator | 1280 Square Feet

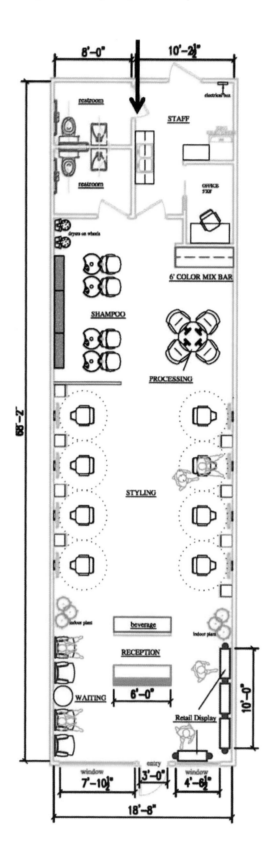

Strip Mall – Plan B (Strip Mall Styles) ★ Five-Point Salon Design System ★	
POINT #1: **Doorway / Front Desk / Waiting Area**	The desk is front-and-center as the focal point of the reception area. Ample seating has been provided on one side while the retail displays are on the opposite side.
POINT #2: **Retail Area**	Due to the high amount of walk-by and foot traffic in a strip mall setting, it's important to display your retail in an inviting way. This encourages people to come inside and make a purchase even if they are not getting a service that day.
POINT #3: **Service Area**	There are two points of entry into the service area. The styling stations are wall mounted, creating one large walkway down the center of the salon floor.
POINT #4: **Color / Dispensary Area**	The back part of this strip mall salon was designed to house a combination shampoo/color area. The shampoo area has a decent amount of storage with an extra back bar for overflow product. The six foot color mix bar has been designed with upper and lower cabinetry for color storage and display. The surface counter can also be used for mixing. A small processing table has been added for clients to relax while their color is being processed.
POINT #5: **Utility Area**	The utility area is in the back of the space next to the existing restrooms.

Strip Mall – Plan B (Strip Mall Styles) - Furniture & Equipment Budget							
	Quantity	Budget	Total	Mid	Total	High End	Total
Styling Chair	12	$175	$2,100	$400	$4,800	$1,200	$14,400
Styling Station	8	$150	$1,200	$500	$4,000	$2,000	$16,000
Shampoo Cabinet	3	$300	$900	$600	$1,800	$1,000	$3,000
Stools	1	$75	$75	$150	$150	$300	$300
Dryer	2	$200	$400	$200	$400	$200	$400
Shampoo Shuttles	4	$600	$2,400	$1,200	$4,800	$2,500	$10,000
Reception Desk	1	$400	$400	$1,000	$1,000	$3,000	$3,000
Reception Chairs	4	$80	$320	$200	$800	$400	$1,600
Retail Unit Freestanding	1	$250	$250	$1,500	$1,500	$3,000	$3,000
Retail Unit Wall	4	$250	$1,000	$900	$3,600	$2,000	$8,000
Coffee Station	1	$125	$125	$300	$300	$750	$750
Color Lab 6'	1	$2,500	$2,500	$5,000	$5,000	$9,000	$9,000
Dispensary Furniture	1	$500	$500	$1,500	$1,500	$3,000	$3,000
Color Table	1	$300	$300	$600	$600	$1,000	$1,000
Floor Mats	8	$80	$640	$120	$960	$190	$1,520
Roller Carts	8	$70	$560	$160	$1,280	$300	$2,400
Mirrors	8	$75	$600	$150	$1,200	$300	$2,400
Washer/Dryer	1	$800	$800	$1,200	$1,200	$3,000	$3,000
Grand Total			**$15,070**		**$34,890**		**$82,770**

Strip Mall – Plan B (Strip Mall Styles) - Materials & Labor Cost Break Down					
	Qty. / Sq. Ft. / Days	Low Estimate	Total	High Estimate	Total
Flooring					
Ceramic Tile *(Prices Higher on Imported Italian Tile)*	1280 sq. ft.	$3/sq. ft.	$3,840	$6/sq. ft.	$7,680
Hardwood, Oak, Cherry	1280 sq. ft.	$5/sq. ft.	$6,400	$7/sq. ft.	$8,960
Vinyl *(Prices can vary on manufacturer, style, thickness)*	1280 sq. ft.	$2/sq. ft.	$2,560	$5/sq. ft.	$6,400
Installation *(Labor Costs)*	1280 sq. ft.	$2/sq. ft.	$2,560	$8/sq. ft.	$10,240
Ceiling					
Decorative drop ceiling with metal brackets *(standard)*	1280 sq. ft.	$2/sq. ft. *(installed)*	$2,560	$5/sq. ft. *(installed)*	$6,400
Paint					
Commercial Grade Paint *(Note: 1 gallon =1 coat for every 400 sq. ft.)*	1280 sq. ft. (7 gal.)	$20/gal.	$140	$40/gal.	$280
Ceiling Paint *(Price it, if applicable)*					
Trim & Door Paint *(Price it, if applicable)*					
Painter *(Labor Costs)*	3 days	$150/day	$450	$350/day	$1,050
Trim					
Baseboards	258 linear ft.	$1.50/ft. *(simple)*	$387	$4.50/ft. *(big/fancy)*	$1,161
Specialty Trim *(Price it, if applicable)*					
Installation *(Labor Costs)*	3 days	$150/day	$450	$350/day/ person	$1,050
Signage					
Non-Illuminated *(installed)*	1	$2,000/ sign	$2,000	$4,000/ sign	$4,000
Illuminated Block Letter *(installed)*	1	$3,000/ sign	$3,000	$7,000/ sign	$7,000
Lighting *(Note: Price your lighting and enter your estimates here.)*					
Overhead					
Task					
Accent					
Other					
Illuminated *(Labor Costs)*					
Accessories *(Note: Price your accessories and enter your estimates here.)*					
		Low Estimate		**High Estimate**	
POINT #1: The Entrance (Doorway/Front Desk/ Waiting Area)					
POINT #2: The Store Inside Your Salon (Retail Area)					

Strip Mall – Plan B (Strip Mall Styles) - Materials & Labor Cost Break Down		
POINT #3: Your Bread & Butter (Service Area)		
POINT #4: Let Your Color Shine (Color/Dispensary Area)		
POINT #5: Behind the Scenes (Utility Area)		

NOTE: These prices and installation costs are based on a general pricing structure that is subject to change depending on demographics and overall budget of the salon owner. The material pricing is based on a high traffic material cost that will withhold the normal wear and tear of heavy salon traffic. It is recommended to add approximately 10% to each of the above totals to cover costs of spoilage of materials or human error.

12. Strip Mall – Plan C (Signature Strip Mall Salon)
5 Operator   I   1380 Square Feet

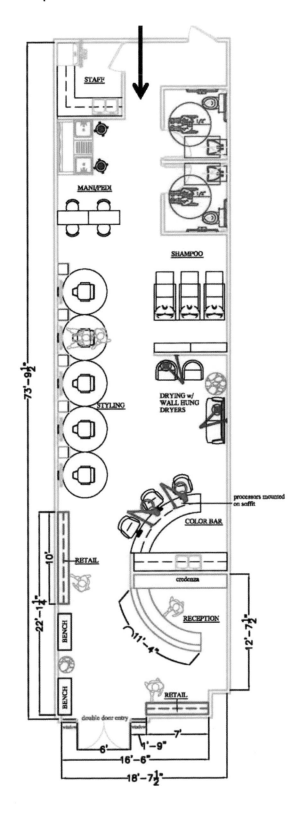

Strip Mall – Plan C (Signature Strip Mall Salon) ★ Five-Point Salon Design System ★	
POINT #1: **Doorway / Front Desk / Waiting Area**	Just because you are opening your salon in a strip mall location does not mean your reception/waiting area has to be minimal or boring. Try angling your front desk to create a nice focal point upon entering the salon.
POINT #2: **Retail Area**	Break up retail displays into different areas to encourage interaction and browsing. Also, display promotional products prominently and viewable from the desk area to encourage impulse sales during check-out.
POINT #3: **Service Area**	The service area is conveniently located next to the color, drying, and shampoo areas. The styling floor is visible from the front reception and retail area making the overall space appear larger.
POINT #4: **Color / Dispensary Area**	The color bar mirrors the reception desk creating an awesome design feature. All color storage is located directly behind the reception wall. Clients process and relax on the other side of the curved portion.
POINT #5: **Utility Area**	The utlity area is all the way in the back along with the rest of the plumbed areas to keep build-out costs down.

Strip Mall – Plan C (Signature Strip Mall Salon) - Furniture & Equipment Budget

	Quantity	Budget	Total	Mid	Total	High End	Total
Styling Chair	8	$175	$1,400	$400	$3,200	$1,200	$9,600
Styling Station	5	$150	$750	$500	$2,500	$2,000	$10,000
Custom Color Bar	1	$1,500	$1,500	$2,500	$2,500	$3,500	$3,500
Custom Desk	1	$1,200	$1,200	$2,000	$2,000	$4,000	$4,000
Shampoo Cabinet	2	$300	$600	$600	$1,200	$1,000	$2,000
Stools	3	$75	$225	$150	$450	$300	$900
Dryer Chair	2	$150	$300	$400	$800	$800	$1,600
Dryer	2	$200	$400	$200	$400	$200	$400
Wall Hung Dryer	4	$600	$2,400	$750	$3,000	$1,500	$6,000
Shampoo Shuttles	3	$600	$1,800	$1,200	$3,600	$2,500	$7,500
Reception Benches	2	$300	$600	$500	$1,000	$1,000	$2,000
Credenza	1	$500	$500	$1,000	$1,000	$2,000	$2,000
Retail Unit Wall	4	$400	$1,600	$900	$3,600	$2,000	$8,000
Coffee Station	1	$125	$125	$300	$300	$750	$750
Color Lab Cabinet Behind Custom Bar	1	$2,000	$2,000	$4,000	$4,000	$8,000	$8,000
Dispensary Furniture	1	$500	$500	$1,500	$1,500	$3,000	$3,000
Nail Tables	2	$140	$280	$400	$800	$800	$1,600
Client Chairs	4	$80	$320	$120	$480	$190	$760
Pedicure Units	2	$600	$1,200	$2,500	$5,000	$10,000	$20,000
Pedicure Stools	2	$130	$260	$130	$260	$330	$660
Roller Carts	5	$70	$360	$150	$750	$300	$500
Floor Mats	5	$80	$400	$120	$600	$190	$950
Mirrors	5	$75	$375	$150	$750	$300	$1,500
Washer/Dryer	1	$800	$800	$1,200	$1,200	$3,000	$3,000
Grand Total			**$19,895**		**$40,890**		**$98,220**

Strip Mall – Plan C (Signature Strip Mall Salon) - Materials & Labor Cost Break Down

	Qty. / Sq. Ft. / Days	Low Estimate	Total	High Estimate	Total
Flooring					
Ceramic Tile *(Prices Higher on Imported Italian Tile)*	1380 sq. ft.	$3/sq. ft.	$4,140	$6/sq. ft.	$8,280
Hardwood, Oak, Cherry	1380 sq. ft.	$5/sq. ft.	$6,900	$7/sq. ft.	$9,660
Vinyl *(Prices can vary on manufacturer, style, thickness)*	1380 sq. ft.	$2/sq. ft.	$2,760	$5/sq. ft.	$6,900
Installation *(Labor Costs)*	1380 sq. ft.	$2/sq. ft.	$2,760	$8/sq. ft.	$11,040
Ceiling					
Decorative drop ceiling with metal brackets *(standard)*	1380 sq. ft.	$2/sq. ft. *(installed)*	$2,760	$5/sq. ft. *(installed)*	$6,900
Paint					
Commercial Grade Paint *(Note: 1 gallon =1 coat for every 400 sq. ft.)*	1380 sq. ft. (7 gal.)	$20/gal.	$140	$40/gal.	$280
Ceiling Paint *(Price it, if applicable)*					
Trim & Door Paint *(Price it, if applicable)*					
Painter *(Labor Costs)*	6 days	$150	$900	$350	$2,100
Trim					
Baseboards	316 linear ft.	$1.50/ft. *(simple)*	$474	$4.50/ft. *(big/fancy)*	$1,422
Specialty Trim *(Price it, if applicable)*					
Installation *(Labor Costs)*	3 days	$150/day	$450	$350/day	$1,050
Signage					
Non-Illuminated *(installed)*	1	$2,000/ sign	$2,000	$4,000/ sign	$4,000
Illuminated Block Letter *(installed)*	1	$3,000/ sign	$3,000	$7,000/ sign	$7,000
Lighting *(Note: Price your lighting and enter your estimates here.)*					
Overhead					
Task					
Accent					
Other					
Illuminated *(Labor Costs)*					

Accessories *(Note: Price your accessories and enter your estimates here.)*		
	Low Estimate	**High Estimate**
POINT #1: The Entrance (Doorway/Front Desk/ Waiting Area)		
POINT #2: The Store Inside Your Salon (Retail Area)		
POINT #3: Your Bread & Butter (Service Area)		

Strip Mall – Plan C (Signature Strip Mall Salon) - Materials & Labor Cost Break Down		
POINT #4: Let Your Color Shine (Color/Dispensary Area)		
POINT #5: Behind the Scenes (Utility Area)		

NOTE: These prices and installation costs are based on a general pricing structure that is subject to change depending on demographics and overall budget of the salon owner. The material pricing is based on a high traffic material cost that will withhold the normal wear and tear of heavy salon traffic. It is recommended to add approximately 10% to each of the above totals to cover costs of spoilage of materials or human error.

13. Blow Out Salon & Retail Store | 2 Operator | 2000 Square Feet

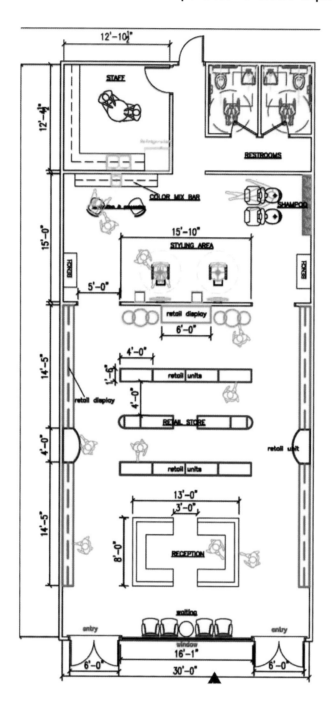

Blow Out Salon & Retail Store ★ Five-Point Salon Design System ★	
POINT #1: **Doorway / Front Desk / Waiting Area**	A very large reception desk sits directly in the middle of the front area. Both sides can be utilized to check clients out which meets the needs of this busy retail setting.
POINT #2: **Retail Area**	The business model for this salon was to make the most of the revenue from product sales. Therefore, the majority of the space is taken up by the retail area, which offers many more product lines than the typical salon. Clients who buy product in the retail area of the store can also make an appointment with the salon.
POINT #3: **Service Area**	In the back of the store, a small salon has been incorporated to offer more services to clients. By adding a small service area to the "store," this salon can create loyalty through expert use and testimonials of the products carried.
POINT #4: **Color / Dispensary Area**	A basic color area has been created in the back salon area. All color is housed and displayed in upper/lower cabinetry pieces. Two processing chairs sit immediately in front of this case, which is a good piece for color application and processing.
POINT #5: **Utility Area**	The utility area is incorporated into the staff area located near the restrooms in the back. All plumbing is located in the back of the salon to keep the costs of running plumbing lines at a minimal cost.

Blow Out Salon & Retail Store - Furniture & Equipment Budget							
	Quantity	Budget	Total	Mid	Total	High End	Total
Styling Chair	4	$175	$700	$400	$1,600	$1,200	$4,800
Styling Station	2	$150	$300	$500	$1,000	$2,000	$4,000
Custom Cabinets (Retail)	1	$5,000	$5,000	$12,000	$12,000	$30,000	$30,000
Shampoo Cabinet	1	$300	$300	$600	$600	$1,000	$1,000
Color Station with mirrors	2	$400	$800	$900	$1,800	$1,800	$3,600
Shampoo Shuttles	2	$600	$1,200	$1,200	$2,400	$2,500	$5,000
Reception Desk	1	$2,500	$2,500	$6,000	$6,000	$11,000	$11,000
Reception Chairs	4	$80	$320	$200	$800	$400	$1,600
Retail Unit Freestanding	1	$250	$250	$500	$500	$2,000	$2,000
Floor Mats	2	$80	$160	$120	$240	$190	$380
Roller Carts	2	$70	$140	$150	$300	$300	$600
Mirrors	2	$75	$150	$150	$300	$300	$600
Dispensary	1	$2,000	$2,000	$3,500	$3,500	$7,000	$7,000
Lunch Table and Chairs	1	$400	$400	$600	$600	$1,000	$1,000
Grand Total			$14,220		$31,640		$72,580

Blow Out Salon & Retail Store - Materials & Labor Cost Break Down					
	Qty. / Sq. Ft. / Days	Low Estimate	Total	High Estimate	Total
Flooring					
Ceramic Tile *(Prices Higher on Imported Italian Tile)*	2000 sq. ft.	$3/sq. ft.	$6,000	$6/sq. ft.	$12,000
Hardwood, Oak, Cherry	2000 sq. ft.	$5/sq. ft.	$10,000	$7/sq. ft.	$14,000
Vinyl *(Prices can vary on manufacturer, style, thickness)*	2000 sq. ft.	$2/sq. ft.	$4,000	$5/sq. ft.	$10,000
Installation *(Labor Costs)*	2000 sq. ft.	$2/sq. ft.	$4,000	$8/sq. ft.	$32,000
Ceiling					
Decorative drop ceiling with metal brackets *(standard)*	2000 sq. ft.	$2/sq. ft. *(installed)*	$4,000	$5/sq. ft. *(installed)*	$10,000
Paint					
Commercial Grade Paint *(Note: 1 gallon =1 coat for every 400 sq. ft.)*	2000 sq. ft. (10 gal.)	$20/gal.	$200	$40/gal.	$400
Ceiling Paint *(Price it, if applicable)*					
Trim & Door Paint *(Price it, if applicable)*					
Painter *(Labor Costs)*	6 days	$150	$900	$350	$2,100
Trim					
Baseboards	327 linear ft.	$1.50/ft. *(simple)*	$490.50	$4.50/ft. *(big/fancy)*	$1,471.50
Specialty Trim *(Price it, if applicable)*					
Installation *(Labor Costs)*	4 days	$150/day	$600	$350/day	$1,400
Signage					
Non-Illuminated *(installed)*	1	$2,000/ sign	$2,000	$4,000/ sign	$4,000
Illuminated Block Letter *(installed)*	1	$3,000/ sign	$3,000	$7,000/ sign	$7,000
Lighting *(Note: Price your lighting and enter your estimates here.)*					
Overhead					
Task					
Accent					
Other					
Illuminated *(Labor Costs)*					
Accessories *(Note: Price your accessories and enter your estimates here.)*					
		Low Estimate		**High Estimate**	
POINT #1: The Entrance (Doorway/Front Desk/ Waiting Area)					
POINT #2: The Store Inside Your Salon (Retail Area)					
POINT #3: Your Bread & Butter (Service Area)					

Blow Out Salon & Retail Store - Materials & Labor Cost Break Down		
POINT #4: Let Your Color Shine (Color/Dispensary Area)		
POINT #5: Behind the Scenes (Utility Area)		

NOTE: These prices and installation costs are based on a general pricing structure that is subject to change depending on demographics and overall budget of the salon owner. The material pricing is based on a high traffic material cost that will withhold the normal wear and tear of heavy salon traffic. It is recommended to add approximately 10% to each of the above totals to cover costs of spoilage of materials or human error.

Ready, Set, Go! Expert Advice!

Group wet areas together and locate the hot water system (HWS) close to the shampoo area. This saves on plumbing and reduces the amount of water going cold in the pipes. It may not seem that important when you first look at your salon's design. But, if your shampoo area is far from the HWS, your clients may get a cold shampoo instead of a hot comfortable one. In today's world, when everyone is paying for water and sewer, the last thing you want your staff to do is to leave the water running just to get hot water to the faucet for their clients. Big energy waste!

PART IV

FROM DESIGN TO BUILD OUT

CHAPTER 19

Matching Your Design Concept to Available Properties

*"Location is the key to most businesses, and the entrepreneurs
typically build their reputation at a particular spot."*

—Phyllis Schlafly

Any realtor will tell you, there are three things important about a property: location, location, location. It's true, the best stylists, the best advertising, and the best designed salon will not make up for a salon that is placed in a poor location. A property may be inexpensive, beautiful, and close to home, but are those the qualities that matter the most? What makes a great location? The following checklist will help give you some things to consider and the POINT-BY-POINT PROPERTY ASSESSMENT guide found later in this chapter will guide you through evaluating your top three properties to find a winner!

Location Checklist

Parking

○ Does the location have ample parking?

○ Is it easy to pull in and out of the parking lot?

○ Is there a traffic light or stop sign that may make it easier for clients to get in and out during high-traffic days?

Traffic/Visibility

○ How much traffic drives by the location? (The Department of Transportation or city traffic department can often provide this information.)

○ How much traffic walks by the location? (Though you want a loyal, returning client base, don't underestimate the buying power of walk-in clients, especially for your retail sales.)

○ How visible would your salon be from the street? From the parking lot?

○ Is your location easy to find?

Signage

○ What are the shopping center's regulations on signage and exterior lighting?

○ Does the city have ordinances over signage?

Neighborhood/Condition & Safety of the Area

○ What other businesses are nearby? (If you are looking for an upscale client, you should surround yourself with upscale stores. If you are looking for a family client base, you should find a location near other family-friendly dining and shopping destinations.)

○ Is the area you're considering under good repair? Are sidewalks clean and unbroken, streetlights maintained, street and parking lot surface maintained and pothole free?

○ Is the area safe at night?

○ Do the price points, product lines and services of neighboring stories fall in line with what you offer?

○ Do any of them compete directly with your retail or service offerings?

○ Are the owners and employees friendly?

○ What do they have to say about their location?

Location Checklist

Convenience

◯ How long will it take you to get to and from work? Are you comfortable with that commute?

◯ How close is your bank?

◯ Is there a place for you and employees to eat lunch affordably?

◯ If you need to take your kids to school, where are their school and afterschool programs located in relation to your salon?

Products/Retail

◯ Have you identified the products you want to carry? Seems like a crazy question when trying to choose a location right? Wrong! If you haven't done the correct demographics, how do you know what your clientele can afford? High-end, expensive retail warrants your clientele to be middle to upper class. This is just another step in picking the right location.

◯ What products are available in your territory? A distributor may not sell you the specific brand of product that you want to carry if they are already established with another salon that is bigger and has a larger clientele. Distributors and manufacturers may not sell to you if the area is already saturated with their products.

◯ Have you made contact with the sales representatives in your area?

◯ Is there enough room for an effective retail area?

◯ Do you have enough storage space for stock and supplies?

Services

◯ Have you decided on your salon's services, beauty treatments, and spa treatments?

◯ Does your ideal location have enough space for the services, treatments, storage, retail and reception areas you desire?

◯ Is there room for a break room/employee lounge?

Expansion Potential

◯ Can it be expanded (into the next storefront or by building onto the existing building) to fit your dream salon? Most entrepreneurs don't think about what happens if the business grows in leaps and bounds. The fact is if you have to move because you didn't plan on expansion possibilities, it will be very expensive and interrupt your current business.

	Property A	Property B	Property B
Contact Information for Leasing Agent and/or Real Estate Agent			
Name of the Property			
Address/ Location			
Total Square Footage			
Age of the Building			
Age & Size of Furnace			
Age & Size of Air Conditioner			
Concrete Slab Floor?			
Electrical Up-to-Date?			
Age of the Roof?			

Overall, you are going to put your three properties into one of the following three buckets. Keep shopping until you get at least one in the #1 spot and at least one in the #2 spot. Run away from any properties that sound like #3. We do not recommend that you start your business with so many negatives and expenses to overcome.

- **#1** – Best location close to home, clients, and family. Meets your budget. Not too big. Doesn't need much tenant improvement. Building not to old. Safe. Plenty of parking. Plenty of signage. Easy to get in and out of from the highway or main road. Great mall for walk in business. Plenty of food and other businesses for clients and staff.

- **#2** – It's located in an older strip mall. A little bit out of the way. Parking is okay, but not great. Center divider in front of the entrance. Need to U- turn to get into the parking area. Signage is minimal. Space can work, but construction will be close to or possibly a little over budget. Bigger or smaller than you wanted. Further from home.

- **#3** – The parking lot is small. It's tough to see the building from the main road. It is way out of the way. Far from existing client base. Borderline neighborhood. Old building; electric and cooling system need updating. Way too big for what you want. Landlord trying to push you to take the spot. Parking lot is a mess with potholes. The entire space needs to be gutted. 35 minutes from your house. No food establishments for your staff. No draw for walk in business.

To help you figure out how you would rank each property, you are going to use the five points to assess each property according to the assessment statements on the following pages. The rating scale is described below:

- **4** = Best Match and Budget Friendly
- **3** = Close Match with Minimal Impact on Budget
- **2** = Not Desirable, But Workable with Medium to High Impact on Budget Costs
- **1** = Worst Match, Deal and Budget Breaker

You'll want to record not only the overall square footage, but any square footage that may currently exist in some way for any of the five areas. Take notes on the amenities and the drawbacks of the property for each area.

POINT #1: The Entrance (Doorway/Front Desk/Waiting Area)

4 = Best Match and Budget Friendly
3 = Close Match with Minimal Impact on Budget
2 = Not Desirable, But Workable with Medium to High Impact on Budget Costs
1 = Worst Match, Deal and Budget Breaker

Things to look for in an entrance . . . (NOTE: If you add more criteria, frame the statement as a positive.)	Properties (Rating Scale: 4, 3, 2, 1)		
	A	B	C
Waiting Area Square Footage			
1. The entry area is roomy.			
2. The entrance is visible from the street			
3. There is plenty of light inside the entry area.			
4. The entrance is dramatic.			
5. There is plenty of glass for open sightlines into the salon.			
6. The entrance has high ceilings and gives a feeling of grandness.			
7. The entrance is already set up for handicap accessibility.			
8. Other:			
9. Other:			
10. Other:			
Total			

Notes:

Property A	Property B	Property C

POINT #2: The Store Inside Your Salon (Retail Area)

4 = Best Match and Budget Friendly
3 = Close Match with Minimal Impact on Budget
2 = Not Desirable, But Workable with Medium to High Impact on Budget Costs
1 = Worst Match, Deal and Budget Breaker

	Things to look for in your retail area . . . (NOTE: If you add more criteria, frame the statement as a positive.)	Properties (Rating Scale: 4, 3, 2, 1)		
		A	B	C
	Retail Area Square Footage			
1.	The space is large enough to house shelving or cabinets for retailing.			
2.	There is plenty of light inside the retail area.			
3.	The retail area can be seen from the outside of the building.			
4.	The electric is adequate.			
5.	The ceiling is high enough for shelving capacity.			
6.	Other:			
7.	Other:			
8.	Other:			
9.	Other:			
10.	Other:			
	Total			

Notes:

Property A	Property B	Property C

POINT #3: Your Bread & Butter (Service Area)

4 = Best Match and Budget Friendly
3 = Close Match with Minimal Impact on Budget
2 = Not Desirable, But Workable with Medium to High Impact on Budget Costs
1 = Worst Match, Deal and Budget Breaker

Things to look for in your service area . . . (NOTE: If you add more criteria, frame the statement as a positive.)	Properties (Rating Scale: 4, 3, 2, 1)		
	A	B	C
Service Area Square Footage			
1. You can fit all your stylists and accommodate growth.			
2. There is plenty of light inside the service area.			
3. Electric for stations or easy access electrical to add more.			
4. Flooring is good or can easily be replaced			
5. Ample space for clients.			
6. Has capability for handicap accessibility.			
7. Other:			
8. Other:			
9. Other:			
10. Other:			
Total			

Notes:

Property A	Property B	Property C

POINT #4: Let Your Color Shine (Color/Dispensary Area)

4 = Best Match and Budget Friendly
3 = Close Match with Minimal Impact on Budget
2 = Not Desirable, But Workable with Medium to High Impact on Budget Costs
1 = Worst Match, Deal and Budget Breaker

Things to look for in your color area . . . (NOTE: If you add more criteria, frame the statement as a positive.)	Properties (Rating Scale: 4, 3, 2, 1)		
	A	B	C
Color Area Square Footage			
1. Easy access to plumbing.			
2. Ceramic tile or another waterproof and slip-resistant material is already in place.			
3. Plenty of lighting or ability to add more lights easily.			
4. Adequate room for staff and clients.			
5. Other:			
6. Other:			
7. Other:			
8. Other:			
9. Other:			
10. Other:			
Total			

Notes:

Property A	Property B	Property C

215

POINT #5: Behind the Scenes (Utility Area)

4 = Best Match and Budget Friendly
3 = Close Match with Minimal Impact on Budget
2 = Not Desirable, But Workable with Medium to High Impact on Budget Costs
1 = Worst Match, Deal and Budget Breaker

Things to look for in your utility area . . . (NOTE: If you add more criteria, frame the statement as a positive.)	Properties (Rating Scale: 4, 3, 2, 1)		
	A	B	C
Utility Area Square Footage			
1. Plenty of light already available.			
2. Access to all utilities.			
3. Room for washer and dryer.			
4. Room for table or separate break room for staff.			
5. Flooring that is easy to clean and durable.			
6. Ventilation to the outside of the building.			
7. Close to exit door.			
8. Decent size slop sink available.			
9. Other:			
10. Other:			
Total			

Notes:

Property A	Property B	Property C

Overall Property Ratings

Bring the totals over for each area and enter them in the table below. Then, add up the scores for each property so that you can see the overall score for each property.

	Square Footage	Scores Point #1 (Waiting Area)	Scores Point #2 (Retail Area)	Scores Point #3 (Service Area)	Scores Point #4 (Color Area)	Scores Point #5 (Utility Area)	Total Score
Property A							
Property B							
Property C							

Okay! So, now you have a good idea for what space best suits you and your new business needs. It's time to go to work.

Ready, Set, Go! Expert Advice!

There is virtually no remedy in picking the wrong location! When choosing a location, do as much leg work as possible to ensure that you are making the right choice. Finally, there are two final steps before you commit to a location:

1. Visit with other tenants in the neighboring stores. Ask them about:

   a. The space you are thinking of leasing. They may have some insider knowledge about the space and any problems that the previous tenants may have had, such as leaks, foundation issues, etc.

   b. Their experience with opening their business and what worked from a marketing/promotion standpoint in the area.

   c. Check their openness to referral/affiliate marketing and cross-promotion of each other's businesses. Remember, you are opening a new salon that will also bring traffic to their businesses.

   d. Their experience with the landlord and how responsive the landlord is when there are issues. If there have been challenges, then they will probably share them with you. Ask for specifics so that you can understand how dealing with the landlord might affect you and the operation of your salon. But, remember, there are always two sides to a story.

2. Visit with the local police department. Ask about the area. Research the area to find out if there have been any crimes in the location or around the store area that you are thinking about choosing for your salon.

CHAPTER 20

Working with Contractors

""If you cannot be on the project each day to check on things,
then you should not try and be your own contractor."

—Robert Metcalfe

At this point, you have a salon design and floor plan and a good idea for the type of furniture and equipment that you want to purchase for your salon. The next step in the new salon process or remodel is to find the right people who will help you build it. If you have leased your space, keep in mind that your landlord or other tenants may be able to direct you to an architect or contractors that they have used when they built their place of business.

Architect

This individual can help you design and space-plan your location. However, businesses that sell salon furniture also have salon designers available who can help you to space-plan your salon more affordably. By taking advantage of our ready-to-use floor plans in this book and the services of a salon designer, you will save time and money. The whole intent of the book was for you to use, dissect, and add on to the designs provided in this book. This enables you to go into a salon designer or an architect with a formal plan. Having a good idea and a solid design plan to start with will save you a ton of time and money. Architects charge by the hour and it will not be cheap, especially if you start out with no concept of what you want to build. The architect, who is not likely to have experience in designing salons, won't have to spend time researching how to space-plan a salon. From the floor plan you provide, they should be able to quickly draw up your blueprint. Add your wish list before your first meeting with your architect. This will also eliminate any guess work and certainly a ton of time by the designer and or architect.

Here are a couple of sources for architects:

- **www.architectfinder.aia.org**
- **www.servicemagic.com**

It is critical for you to spend a lot of time with the architect to make sure he or she puts everything in the right place. The architect is responsible for:

- Transferring your floor plan into a blueprint; work with him/her to ensure that everything is in the right place.

- Creating and providing you with hard copy blueprints for your new space, including:

  - Two "certified plans" for submitting to the city for building permits

  - 15 contractor copies that you can use for getting bids on your project. This may sound like a lot of copies, but your contractor will need to give each one of his subcontractors a set of plans for the work that they will be required to do (plumber, electrician, er, ceiling installer, flooring, drywall installer, HVAC, etc.).

  - You may also be shopping contractors. Each contractor will need a set of plans to give you a quote for the project.

Before you take the finished plan from the architect, it's important to review it and make sure every detail is included.

> **NOTE**
> Do not misplace or mix up the "certified plans" with any other copies.

Builders/Construction Contractors

Once you have the architect's plans, you should move quickly to get some prices on the cost for construction. Why?

- At this stage, you will probably have already signed the lease and the clock is ticking on any "free" rent periods that may have been negotiated for the build-out. Negotiate with the landlord to not pay rent until you get your final "Certificate of Occupancy" (CO) from the city.

- The process might take a couple of weeks to get final bids from your three prospective contractors.

- Your contractor will be the one to submit the plans to the city. In our past experience, this can take anywhere from two to six weeks to submit them and get them approved. The city can also reject the plans, which will have to go back to the architect, redrawn and resubmitted.

> **NOTE**
> Your architect may be able to refer you to some good contractors that they've come to know by working on projects.

Friends, family, and associates can usually recommend a good contractor. You can even ask the owner of a well-built salon what contractor they used. If you cannot find someone you feel comfortable with, you can try these websites:

- **www.1800contractor.com**
- **www.needacontractor.com**
- **www.agc.org**
- **www.angieslist.com**

Quick steps to get started:

1. Identify at least three contractors. Collect as much information as you can about each contractor before you ask for a bid:

    a. Type of Contractor—Find out what their specialties are.

    b. Quality of Work—Visit job sites and/or recently completed projects.

    c. Client Satisfaction—Get list of referrals and call on them.

    d. Licensed/Insured—Get the physical proof of their builder's license and insurance policy. Never hire a contractor who is not licensed and insured.

    e. Stability—Ask how long he/she has been in business. Look for those who have been in business for more than five years.

    f. Project Management—Find out if your contractor will be your main contact and on-site to oversee the work being performed.

    g. Payment Terms—Ensure that you will be accepting with how the contractor will bill and receive payment for services. Never, never, never pay in advance or pay in full.

2. Get bids from the three contractors that you identified.

3. Give each contractor four to five sets of plans. General contractors will most likely give a copy to a plumber, electrician, and an air conditioning company.

4. Assess the bids and choose your contractors. Here are some thoughts around coming to a decision:

    a. Price—Price is a BIG factor, but you must look at each contractor's bid and compare what they are providing and the quality of their work. If you only choose based on price, you could get stuck doing things twice—once the wrong way and again the right way. This can be an expensive lesson learned.

    b. Thoroughness—You must make sure that each bid includes everything on the plan. A contractor is only as good as the plans he works from. If the plan is not complete or is missing something, a contractor will do the additional work, but also charge you for the change in the scope of the project.

    c. Timeline—Look at the overall timeline and when the contractor is saying that work will be completed.

    d. Quality—Do your homework and visit former jobs that the builder/contractor has completed. Check that the customer was satisfied with the process of working with the contractor and with the end product. Inspect the work yourself to ensure that it meets your standards and expectations.

Building the salon of your dreams should be something you always remember with fond memories. You don't want the start of your business plagued by a poor choice in contractors or project overages in time and money. Take your time when choosing the contractor. Do your due diligence by getting references.

Once you have your team in place, you should visit the job site daily. If changes need to be made, catching them sooner rather than later makes a big difference. If you're not watching and keeping an eye on things, rest assured that corners will be cut and problems will arise. Get involved, get your hands dirty, and read up on some of the things that the contractor is doing so that you know what to look for when you are assessing their work. You can get involved with demolition, cleaning the job site, removing trash, ing, and assembling some of your furniture—anything to stay involved and help drive to opening day. For more details about getting involved in the build-out, check out Roll Up Your Sleeves; You're Under Construction.

Salon Owners Talk About . . . the Good, the Bad, and the Ugly

"Choosing a family member as your contractor may save you a few dollars. But what happens when the work is not getting done on time or the quality of the work is not what you expected? I had to fire my wife's brother. It's been two years and he still doesn't talk to me."

—James Giodano, Fancy and Prancy Hair

Ready, Set, Go! Expert Advice!

Deciding on the lowest price is not always the smartest choice when choosing a contractor. Just remember the old adage, "You get what you pay for!" Contractors who lowball a price just to get the job will most likely use subcontractors to get the work done. Sometimes, the subcontractors will not be licensed. And, they may have lowballed their price to the contractor to get the work. In this case, you can expect delays, shoddy work, and a messy job site. A few quick questions to ask when deciding on your contractor:

- Who will be doing the work?
- Is everyone working on the job site licensed and insured?
- Who guarantees the work?
- For how long do you guarantee your work?

CHAPTER 21

Environmental Compliance

"What's the use of a fine house if you haven't got a tolerable planet to put it on?"

—Henry David Thoreau

As you know, a salon business uses chemicals and concentrated soaps, which creates solid waste (such as hair). All of these "byproducts" of a salon need to be dealt with and handled properly for minimal environmental effects. Therefore, federal, state, and local government s have specific compliance requirements that salons must adhere to in order to manage chemicals and detergents that are released from a salon day-to-day.

As a business owner, you will have a "green" responsibility, especially in today's increasingly polluted world, and will incur some expenses to meet environmental compliance requirements. However, it's better to address them on the front end rather than trying to retrofit the salon for compliance. All of the items listed here (in addition to others) may be required by your municipality. So, be prepared and educate yourself on the requirements! Ignorance can be costly and is not excusable for noncompliance. Also, remember the most important thing, you have a responsibility to the planet and to others!

Plumbing Updates for Various Requirements by Some Municipalities

Following are three items that most municipalities require for salons. Meeting these requirements can be costly. Do your research to find suitable products that are cost effective.

Hair Traps

Special units, attached to the waste line of the sink, which catch and collect all of the hair rather than sending it into the sewer system. You will need one hair trap per sink. You can check with your local municipality to see if hair traps are required. However, it's recommended that you put them in whether you are required to or not. Otherwise, hair will clog your drains and cost you more money long-term in plumbing bills.

There are two types that are standard versions sold for the beauty industry:

- Plastic: Cost is around $50 each. Accepted by most municipalities around the country. Carried by: Collins Manufacturing or Marble Products, a division of Takara Belmont.

- Cast Iron: Cost is around $200.

Make sure that you have access to the units so that you can easily get to them for cleaning. Hair traps need to be cleaned out every 30 days. If you don't clean them out regularly, they will clog up and slow the draining of the sink. The trap is shaped as a revised P trap or a cylinder and unscrews from the top for cleaning (see below).

Belvedere HT1 Hair Trap

Marble Products

Vacuum Breakers

To stop water from backing up into the sink, vacuum breakers are installed on the top of the sink, usually next to the spray hose. Presently, there are two types on the market. One is rated (Compliance Safety Accountability or CSA) and the other is unrated. Some municipalities require the rated part. Marble Products carries two CSA rated vacuum breakers:

- Vacuum Breaker Separate from Sprayer: Cost is around $80 each for a vacuum breaker that is separate from the sprayer. So, remember to add on the cost of the sprayer if you go this route.

- Sprayer with Built-In Vacuum Breaker: Cost is around $225 for a self-contained fixture with a sprayer, vacuum breaker, and spray hose.

Marble Products #1729

Takara Belmont #800
fixture with vacuum breaker

Backflow Preventers (BFPs)

This piece of equipment stops contaminated water from backing into the businesses water system. Municipalities have asked business owners to put "BFPs" on each pedicure unit, one for each water line (hot and cold) at an average cost of $220 each. There is an option to put one "BFP" on the back of the building, which will shut all the water off before it enters the building. If the municipality requires this piece of equipment, have your architect clarify what is required. General contractors and plumbers always follow an architect's plan on what they specify. Those plans are approved by the city before anyone does any work. One BFP on the back of the building may run $400-600 depending on the size, which is more cost effective than individual ones, especially for salons with more than one pedicure unit. Below is a typical individual BFP by Watts.

(Image Source:
http://www.watts.com/backflowprevention)

Below is the spec information on the BFP.

Series 009 Reduced Pressure Zone Assemblies prevent the reverse flow of polluted water from entering into the potable water supply due to back siphonage and or backpressure. It consists of bronze body construction (1/4 to 2 in.) or FDA approved epoxy coated cast iron (2 1/2 to 3 in.), two, in-line independent check valves, replaceable check seats with an intermediate relief valve, and ball valve test cocks.

Series 009 is ideal for protection of health hazard cross-connections or for containment at the service line entrance. Check with local water authorities for installation requirements. Maximum Working Pressure: 175psi (12.06 bar).

Watts Backflow Preventer Series 009QT 1/2" (0062094) Features:

• 1/4 to 3 in. (8 to 80mm)

• Single access cover and modular check construction for ease of maintenance

• Top entry - all internals immediately accessible

• Captured springs for safe maintenance

• Internal relief valve for reduced installation clearances

• Replaceable seats for economical repair

• Bronze body construction for durability 1.4" . 2" (8.50mm)

- Fused epoxy coated cast iron body 21.2" and 3" (65 and 80mm)
- Ball valve test cocks, screwdriver slotted 1.4" . 2" (8.50mm)
- Large body passages provides low pressure drop
- Compact, space saving design
- No special tools required for servicing

The Green Salon

It is in vogue and makes business sense to "go green." People are more concerned about the chemicals in and the origin of the products being used on their hair, nails, and skin. Your clients want to patronize a business that is environmentally conscious. As a benefit to you, many "green" business practices will save you money. Here are some simple ways to go green:

- Carry a green product line and make sure your stylists know to recommend it.
- Use the sun to light your salon. It looks lovely and reduces costs.
- Make sure the walls and ceiling are well insulated, which saves on heating/cooling bills.
- Ensure that materials used in construction are local and organic (to prevent off-gassing).
- Check your faucets regularly and tighten them down so that they are not dripping.
- Use ecofriendly coffee cups for customers: either ceramic, to be washed, or biodegradable paper.
- Offer a reusable cloth bag for products purchased (with the salon name on them, of course).
- Don't use more product than necessary when shampooing, coloring, etc.
- Install low-flow toilets.
- Place ferns around the salon. They clean the air and produce oxygen, while making the salon feel fresh.

Many people these days are chemically sensitive. Promote the use of organic materials in the construction of your salon, natural products, and green initiatives. Use these as a point of advertising that might bring in clients who would otherwise shy away from any salon.

All of these products can be costly, but can make a difference in your salon in many ways. It's recommended that you review what the architect draws up for your plans and ask whether there are alternatives that are more cost effective. This chapter should have given you information and options that, in the big picture, will save you money. Remember, doing these preventive measures will not only make your salon run more effective, but will also help the planet stay "green."

Ready, Set, Go! Expert Advice!

So, you're done with the build out of the salon. Your furniture and equipment is installed. You are waiting for the inspectors to come to sign off on your permits so you can open. However, if you did not use the correct backflow preventers that you town or city requires, you will not pass inspection. Make sure your plumber and/or your equipment supplier gives you the correct equipment to meet your town's requirements.

If your architect misses these specified items, you will have a problem when it comes to final inspection and being able to open your salon. It is not up to your equipment supplier to know what your town and city's building code requirements are; this is your architect's responsibility.

CHAPTER 22

Roll Up Your Sleeves; You're Under Construction

"Doing things the way you see it, going by your own heart and soul, that is pure artistic integrity. Whatever the hair is six or sixty inches long, the eyes have make-up or not, the riffs are in 'E' or 'F' sharp, the amps are Marshall or not, all those things don't matter if you are doing it for the right reason, which to me means doing it for yourself!"

—Lars Ulrich

How much of your own time that you spend on your salon startup or remodel construction project is dictated by you (and by your budget). Yes, there is only so much you can do to help move the project along and based on your availability and skills. But, by you doing some of the work yourself, you can save some money. You may not know how to install flooring or trim a window, but you can still roll up your sleeves and get your hands dirty.

Are you not convinced that you need to do some of the work? Construction costs typically are about $60–70 per square foot. If your salon space is 1000 square feet, then the construction of your salon could run between $60,000 and $70,000. Keep in mind that this is an industry standard—your location and the current market will determine what you'll pay in construction costs. Maybe you negotiated a great deal with your landlord who will build out the space you are moving into to meet your needs. Or, maybe it was once a salon and doesn't require much work at all. However, if you have had any kind of construction done or know someone who has, you know that overruns and lack of knowledge on your part can be expensive—making it the riskiest and most costly part of opening your salon.

If unforeseen issues come up and if you don't manage the construction process (and your contractors), then you can easily end up 20–30 percent higher than you budgeted—that amounts to $12,000-21,000 over and above the $60,000–70,000 range that was mentioned earlier. Going over budget is the biggest pitfall when building and starting any business. It can suck away funds that were meant for other things and/or stack up undesirable debt before you even open.

Starting and growing your business is not always an easy task. Once you took your first steps into becoming an entrepreneur, the burden of everything started to weigh on your shoulders. The same is true of the construction of your salon—it's your baby, your responsibility. The fact is that sometimes you just have to jump in—even if it means getting dirty. In fact, for the women readers, you may want to hold off on manicures while you are under construction or at least realize that you won't have a freshly manicured look for long.

Some of the things that you might decide to take on may be new and uncomfortable for you. You might have to rearrange your schedule with your clients, ask for help from family and friends, and secure your new hires early to get them involved. The fact is, by doing some basic things yourself, you can save some money. And, you'll have new skills and a feeling of accomplishment!

CAUTION: Make sure that you have insurance that covers you and anyone who comes in to help you during the construction of your salon. If anyone were to get injured or if property damage were to occur while you or others were in the building working, you'll want to make sure that you have the right insurance coverage.

Now, you might be thinking, "Okay, I get it. I do need to do some of this work myself. But, I see myself more as a creative person! I don't know the first thing about construction!" Being hands on in construction may be a stretch for you; and, that's okay. How you assist with moving your project along may vary based on your skill, availability, and willingness to step out of your comfort zone. In this chapter, you will find some surefire ways that you can:

- Get involved in your construction project.

- Keep your project on track.

- Check in on contractors (while staying out of their way so that you are helping, not hindering their work and progress).

- Save yourself time and money (without losing your existing clients along the way).

Construction Don'ts and Dos

You have decided to "take the bull by the horns" and jump into your salon project. Good for you! If you have never done this before and have no idea where to start, don't worry we've got you covered. Following are some major "DON'TS" so that you don't end up in a heap of trouble:

Don'ts

1. **Don't work without a design and detailed floor plan.** Some projects require an architect and an interior designer to help you build a salon that based on a good, solid floor plan and aesthetically pleasing. A lot of elements interact in a space — put them all on paper and you'll catch problems before they are built. You may be able to build a functional space without a plan, but if you want a functional and beautiful space, hire a designer.

2. **Don't work with contractors without a contract and an agreed upon schedule.** It's important that there is an agreed upon contract and schedule for any project, no matter what this person is doing for you in the salon. The schedule keeps your contractor accountable for getting the finished product completed by the finish date. Remember each day you're not open your paying rent, electric, gas, insurance on a space that you're not making any money in. You also have to worry about any new hires abandoning ship before they start, due to delays on your opening date. Stylists get finicky quickly if you're not open when you say you will you most likely will start the hiring process all over again.

3. **Don't pay contractors in full before they even start the project.** Only pay for materials to start the job. Pay for the labor after the job is completed to your contract terms and satisfaction or after portions of the job are completed.

4. **Don't delay decisions.** If you want your new salon project to go well, the best thing to do is make every single decision before work starts. A good builder can talk you through the list of situations that might come up on your job, but decisions about situations aren't usually what cause delays. Most of the issues are related to decisions about things like paint, trim and salon furniture selections. These may seem small, but when your backwash units are two weeks late because you couldn't decide on which one you wanted, plumbers have to be rescheduled and then a wall has to be moved because you choose a different style that's just a few inches bigger than the original, you'll see how something small can balloon into a week's delay on a five-week project.

Dos

1. **Get involved in demolition and preparing the job site.** One way to save some money is to do the demolition and job site preparation yourself. As long as you prepare the site for construction to begin, most contractors do not get offended if you decide to do any demolition that needs to be done before the construction starts. Just make sure that they did not include demolition and job site preparation in their quote. You don't want to pay for something that you end up doing yourself. What is involved with demolition and job site preparation?

   - Taking down walls

   - Ripping up old flooring

   - Removing cabinets

Keep in mind if you have never done anything like this before it will probably take you three times longer than your contractor. You also have to be careful when you're taking down walls that electric, gas and the roof doesn't come down with it.

So, buy some good gloves and a hardhat if you're taking down walls and a pry bar so you don't hurt your back. This type of work is not easy. If you come across plumbing or electric lines in the wall you are tearing down, don't touch them. Work around them and leave the hard stuff for the professionals.

2. **Visit the job site daily.** Drop in by surprise to see if your contractor is there and who else is working on your salon build out. See for yourself if the plumber, electrician, drywall installer, and/or general contractor are on site and actually working. If you did your due diligence, then odds are you won't have any trouble. However, some contractors will take advantage of you and not show up as promised, especially if they know you are keeping another job while you are building out your salon. Stop in on your way into work, on your way home from work, or when taking a break. If you can't stop in, then call. Vary the times that you check in on the status; it will keep your contractors on their toes.

   So, what do you do if no one is onsite and they are scheduled to be there? Call your contractor(s) immediately and ask them why they are not at the job site and when you can expect to see them. Get specific answers as to what will get accomplished that day, especially if they are behind schedule.

   When you stop in, make a mental checklist on what was and wasn't done. Call your contractor when you get home and discuss the next day's plan. Withhold payment for labor if progress is not being made according to the schedule.

3. **Clean up the job site.** Your contractors should be keeping the site clean for safety reasons and building inspections. But, you might want to do a little extra, especially after the electricians, drywall installers, and plumbers come through—as the jobs tend to get messier as the project progresses. It's hard for workers to do a good job when they are stepping on everyone's garbage and leftover materials. This doesn't cost you anything and keeps the job from becoming a mess. If it's really unreasonably messy, talk with your contractor about stepping it up and helping to keep the job site picked up.

   It might be worth it just to show the contractors how much you care about the project and to keep things moving. When you aren't afraid to jump in and be a part of it, they'll also tend to extend themselves more which will come in handy when you need to ask for small favors.

4. **Dispose of the trash.** Taking away the trash can save you thousands of dollars and save your contractor some valuable time. You can take garbage home and use your home disposal service or put it out into the garbage bin. For bigger jobs with loads of building materials, you'll need to find out where you can take it. Call your local municipality to find out where you can unload building materials. Once you know where you are taking it, rent a pickup truck or trailer from Home Depot or Lowes. The average rental for the day is minimal compared to what your contractor may charge you.

5. **Paint your own walls and trim.** Painting is relatively easy when painting a small room at home, but when it comes to a space that is soon to be your salon can be a huge undertaking. If you have the time before your opening, then it may be worth it in the long run. It may look like an easy job, but can take you way longer than you expected. Things to keep in mind when deciding whether you can take this on:

- Prepping the walls is time-consuming. Repairing any damaged walls, spackling, sanding, and priming the walls are all important steps to a perfect paint job.

- Most ceilings in salons are 10 to 12 feet standard in commercial applications. You will need ladders or maybe scaffolding to speed up the process.

- Standard rollers and brushes will have to be upgraded and you will need to spend a bit more because of the extended use.

- You will need spotlights because most likely you will be painting at night after you leave the current salon you're working in or weekends late into the night. Painting in the dark is a no, no. When you come back the next day you will see all the mistakes and spots you missed. Then back to the drawing board or should I say roller to do it all over again!

- Be realistic about your abilities. If you're not comfortable with these chores, consider hiring a professional. A painting contractor will take care of choosing the right paint, prepping the surfaces, getting the job done in warp speed compared to you.

6. **Checking the list and checking it twice.** Many salon owners or should I say people in general take the contractors word as cast in stone. If you are buying flooring, lighting, bathroom fixtures check online to see if the pricing your contractor is charging you is in the ballpark of where it needs to be. The price structure we have with the plans in the RSG Book is pretty much what the going rate is around the country. Although we don't have the costs for lighting and different materials you may need, you can pretty much check on line to keep your contractors material list in check.

Ready, Set, Go! Expert Advice!

It is not unusual for a contractor to pad cost of materials. He may get a contractor discount on materials. However, he may still charge you the full price of materials and not pass the discount onto you. In essence, he's making 20–25% off of the materials. However, you can negotiate the price on materials and make the deal based on getting them at his discounted price. Keep the money in your pocket, not his!

7. **Follow up on furniture/equipment order for timely delivery.** Most manufacturers work with the person who is ordering and paying for the furniture/equipment. Most likely, that person is you. Delivery dates are essential when running an on-time project. Your contractors have other projects. The whole build-out process can have a domino effect when the date changes for the delivery of your salon equipment. It is up to you to schedule all furniture/equipment delivery and installation so your contractor

knows when he needs the electrician, plumber, and carpenter on the job to install your new, beautiful salon equipment. The minute you find out the date, you need to get on the phone with your contractor. He'll organize his team to meet the truck and accept the delivery when your furniture/equipment arrives.

- Within six to eight weeks from the day you place your order, you can expect your shipment to arrive.

- If you are ordering any custom equipment or special furniture from overseas, it could be as long as 12 to 14 weeks (sometimes longer).

It's important to have someone at the job site to accept the delivery because nine times out of ten, you will have a curb side delivery. This means the truck driver will drop your expensive furniture/equipment at the curb; they do not bring it inside for you. You have to have a crew or team of people ready to accept the delivery and bring it in out of the elements. The problem is you just don't know when it's coming. You know the day, not the time. If you have ever waited for furniture for your home, you've probably experienced the pain of a promised time that passes from morning to afternoon to evening. Most likely, you will have to pay your help for the entire day just to keep them there—unless your equipment happens to arrive first thing in the morning.

> **NOTE**
>
> Most salon equipment manufacturers require a 50 percent deposit when you place your order. You will have to pay the remaining balance in full before it leaves the manufacturer's warehouse! No ifs, ands, or buts about it; that is the policy in the beauty industry when purchasing salon furniture.

8. **Bring in your furniture/equipment.** Most people don't realize how heavy salon equipment is until they have to move it themselves. This usually happens when no one is there to help when the furniture/equipment gets delivered. Styling chairs get delivered in boxes the size of wash machines and can way up to 75 pounds or more. Styling stations are made out of plywood or compressed board. I can't even begin to guess what they weigh. Point here is that you will need help. Don't count on your contractors; in our experience most electricians and plumbers will not assist in moving furniture/equipment. The day before your equipment gets delivered go to Home Depot, Lowes or your local hardware store to pick up a few items.

- **Dolly or Hand Truck**—A hand truck can be wedged under heavy boxes and make it a lot easier to get from the curb to inside the salon. Furniture dollies are also helpful for moving heavy boxes. Hand trucks and dollies range in price between $20 and $150. This will be the best money you ever spent.

- **Utility Knifes**—You will need a few utility knives to open the boxes your furniture is delivered and shipped in.

- **Crowbar**—Some of your equipment might come shipped in wooden crates. You'll need to pry open the boxes which will be held together with nails.

- **Band-Aids**—This is one job where your fingers might get nicked as you are opening boxes and pulling out furniture and pieces and parts. So, it's a good idea to have a box of Band-Aids on hand.

- **Roll of Brown Paper & Duct Tape**—Once your furniture and equipment is out of the boxes, you will need to cover it to keep off dust and to keep it from getting damaged by the contractors who may still be working. It's not uncommon for a tool to drop or a contractor's utility knife to accidentally slice a new styling chair while everyone is rushing to get the build-out complete. Better to cover and protect than to deal with waiting on furniture/equipment reorders due to cuts and scratches or items getting broken.

- **Rented Truck/Trailer**—If you are taking everything out of the boxes on this day, you'll want to rent a truck or trailer to haul away all the trash and broken down boxes.

> **NOTE**
>
> DO NOT drag your new salon styling chairs or heavy styling stations from the curb into your new salon. Not only could you damage your furniture, but you could also damage your new flooring. Making this mistake will cost you a fortune in replacements and/or refinishing and delays in opening your salon.

Although much of what was just covered may seem difficult, just get started and make the most of it. By putting your mind to it, you'll get it done, save money, and open on time! Remember, you're on a mission. By the time you are done with construction, you will have done some or all of the following:

- Learned to relate your vision to architects and designers.
- Donned a hardhat.
- Demoed the space.
- Taken away the trash.
- Led a team of contractors.
- Observed and learned the lingo of electricians and plumbers.

Your doors haven't even opened and you've put your blood, sweat, and tears into the business. You'll sit back and think, "Wow! I really pushed myself and my construction crew to stay on schedule and to build the salon of my dreams. I really did it!" You'll start your new venture in business ownership with a newfound confidence and winning attitude.

CHAPTER 23

Reassessing After Year 1, 3, 5 & Beyond

"We keep moving forward, opening new doors, and doing new things, because we're curious and curiosity keeps leading us down new paths."

—Walt Disney

Your business is running along. But, how well is it running? Have some of your design dreams fallen short of expectations? Can your staff operate efficiently? Does your space need to be freshened up to bring back the excitement and brightness that you had on opening day? Are there are any changes in the market that are making it necessary for you to incorporate some changes so that your business doesn't lose traction with your client demographic?

So, are you ready to check in and find some ideas to help your business to keep up with the latest trends? Check out the section that applies to your salon business:

- Year One
- Year Three
- Year Five or Beyond

Year One: Quick Checkup

First off, congratulations! You've made it past that tricky first year and you have the foresight and courage to review and refresh your business. So many businesses fail in the first year, the fact that you are here means that you've done something right. However, now is the perfect time to review your design and business plan to see your strengths and weaknesses, and turn those weaknesses into strengths. This can be the difference between a business that just makes ends meet year-after-year and one that keeps growing and making money. Quick checkups for year one:

- Do the walls or trim need to be repainted?
- How is the floor holding up?
- Does the salon flow and are your clients comfortable?
- Did you allow enough room for retailing?
- Is your shampoo area designed properly?

239

- Is your front desk in the right spot?

- Do you have enough seating for clients waiting for service?

Year Three: Complacency

You've made it through the crazy, chaotic first year. During your second year, you were building confidence and the work came more naturally. You've learned a few things. You feel like you know your demographic, their spending habits, and what makes them comfortable and loyal. You're on top of your bills. No longer is it a struggle to take home a paycheck. The salon is running pretty smoothly and the retail side is a smashing success. However, the spark that used to get you up and excited every morning is starting to fade. If you're feeling like this, then your staff and your clients might be getting the same vibe. Here are some quick fixes, to reenergize you:

- Look at repainting

- Update your flooring

- Brighten things up with new lighting

- Refocus your retail area to drive interest, engagement, and sales

So, now is really the time that the vigilance of the first year starts to slack and vision starts to dim so you might need to dig deeper into the vision that you originally had for your salon. Go back and review the chapter, "Dream It . . . Design It" and review the worksheet that you created in this book three or four years ago. If you didn't have this book, then revisit any notes that you have from when you designed your salon and improvement notes that you may have been taking over the last few years. Take a critical look at the design and functionality of your salon and see if they can be addressed simply or if they require a redesign. It's also a good idea to gather input/feedback from multiple sources. Here are some ideas:

- Ask your friends and family what your vision was and whether you are living up to it.

- Ask your employees for input:

  - What areas of the salon are looking drab and out-of-style?

  - Are there new services or service areas that need to be added?

  - Are there areas that are awkward to work within? What can be done to fix them?

  - What can you provide to help them with organization of their stations?

  - Find out if employees are working around issues because something is lacking in the salon, such as:

    - Employees are using the rinsing sink for the mop because the utility sink isn't big enough.

    - Clients are waiting in empty styling stations because there's not enough room in the waiting room.

- Ask yourself:

  - To what extent does your current salon match your conception of what kind of salon you wanted?

- Are you ready to expand?
    - Did you allow room for expansion in your plans?
    - Is there an adjacent space that is coming up for lease that you could bump into?
    - Are there services you've been waiting to include until you reached the point of stability?

Year Five & Beyond: Keeping Up

Change is inevitable. Ideally, we would create a business that would last forever and ever just as it was on day one. But, the fact is that a business that lasts forever is the one that changes when and how it needs to by meeting customer demand, the current economy, the latest trends, etc. After five years, you'll need to assess the following:

- **Décor:** The décor may be starting to show its age. It was a sad day when shag carpets and avocado refrigerators went out of style, but it was mandatory to move on. Is there something in your décor that speaks of an earlier time? If so, replace it.

- **Signage:** Are the same banners and posters still hanging from your first year? If so, it's way past time for a change. Products change almost yearly. Be sure that your advertisements reflect the newest versions of your retail products.

- **Wear and Tear:** Review each of the five areas for signs of wear and tear.

- **Habits:** Have you and your employees gotten into any bad habits with messy, disorganized stations? Are you keeping up on daily, weekly, monthly cleaning schedules?

Point-by-Point Design Reassessment

Having been in business for a year, three years, or five years, your perspective should have matured. You'll have a better idea of your clients and their needs, and the things they'll pay for. You may have really wanted a waxing room, only to find that waxing is no longer in vogue, but exfoliating is. It's important to be able to let go of the kind of business you may have wanted to run and move toward the business you can be successful at. Overall, there are some questions that you should review and answer about your salon, such as:

- Have there been items placed in the way to impede traffic flow?

- Are the floors, desks, display stands, faucets, and drains all in good repair?

- Is the décor still fresh and does it reflect the brand?

- Are there any new services important to add to keep up with the trends?

- Are there any services that have never made enough money to justify their floor space?

Next, dive into the point-by-point design assessment and take a deeper look at the state of each area. Then, take the time to get your list of changes and improvements for your salon. Guess who will be happy when you are done freshening up your salon? That's right you, your staff, and your clients! Ready, set, go!

★ Five-Point Salon Design System ★
(Point-by-Point Reassessment)

POINT #1: **Doorway, Front Desk, & Waiting Area**	Designing your retail/reception area can lead to a more profitable salon. Many salons over- look this area when first designing their salon and then when reassessing they wish they had invested more money when they first opened. Here are some considerations for Point #1, including the doorway, the front desk, and the waiting area:
	• How is the approach?
	• Are the windows cluttered or obscuring the view into your salon?
	• How is the space being used? Are there people standing around waiting because there's not enough room at the counter when checking out? Then, consider expanding this area.
	• Do you have large counters that are mostly empty? Then, use this space could be used for retail.
	• Are your clients comfortable when waiting? Is there enough space for those who are waiting? Does the waiting area encourage conversation? Remember, the longer they are in the salon, the more likely they are to buy something. Make this space more comfortable with better chairs, rugs, music, etc. If the area is just too small or awkward, a redesign may pay off.
	• Is the floor holding up?
	• Are there nicks on the front desk?
	• Does the paint have permanent stains?
	• Is the furniture looking stained and worn?
	• Is there still good flow into and out of the salon or have displays and other mobile things encroached into the space?
POINT #2: **Retail Area**	Rethink the front-end of your salon to be consumer-friendly. Keep in mind retail is constant. You do not have to spend a fortune to change this area of your salon. It's not expensive to add things such as free standing retail cabinets or shuttles that can be placed and moved for an event or change of season. Here are some considerations for Point #2:
	• How are sales?
	• Are customers getting up and looking at the retail area?
	• Is the retail area visible and accessible?
	• Are you using lights, displays, etc., to get their attention?
	• Can you expand and add more retail displays or reconfigure to improve sales?

★ Five-Point Salon Design System ★ (Point-by-Point Reassessment)	
POINT #3: Service Area	Sometimes people invest in an area and it proves not to be lucrative. If a service is not pulling its weight in terms of profit per square foot, perhaps that area should be given over to increase the area of more profitable services. Here are some considerations for Point #3: • Do you have regular clients for all the services that your salon offers? • Are you using all the specialty areas? If not, consider swapping a manicure area to add another salon station. • Is there enough room to put in more stations or color bar or color consultation station? • Are there stains and chips on the chairs or countertops? • Are all the lights still shining and are they aimed where they need to be? • Does the flooring need to be replaced? • How about the smaller items such as curling irons, are the cords frayed? (Could be a safety hazard) • Does this area need paint or a good cleaning? • How are the ceiling tiles? Are they stained from age or do they have water stains? • Have you thought about LED lighting to better enhance color options for your clients?
POINT #4: Color/ Dispensary Area	The color area or dispensary area is hot in the beauty industry today. It has turned into another profit center in terms of selling services. Here are some considerations for Point #4: • Can you replace your old Formica sink units and sinks with new sleek backwash units. Do you have room to put in a small color dispensary area with stainless counter tops • Are you finding that the shampoo area does not accommodate larger clients and/or stylists? Maybe the shampoo area needs to be moved out into the salon to give the area more space? • Is the floor badly stained or peeling due to the heavy use of water? • Are the backwash units or sinks tired looking and need to be replaced? • Do you need more storage for towels or shampoo products? • Do your shampoo persons or stylists have enough room to rinse their clients' hair? • Does the walls around the shampoo area need paint? • Does the lighting need to be brighter for staff to perform their tasks?

★ Five-Point Salon Design System ★ (Point-by-Point Reassessment)	
POINT #5: Utility Area	When you opened the salon, maybe storage was not on your mind. Designing the front end of your salon business was the number one priority. Here are some considerations for Point #3: • Is the space being used well? Can you add cabinets or shelving for product storage? • Can you add a washer and dryer so you don't have to pay a linen service? • Is there room for a table for your staff to be used as a break room • Are there design problems you didn't anticipate? (Such as you can't open the door when the dryer is open). • Are all the faucets, sinks, and valves still working the way they should? • Are employees are using the rinsing sink for mop water because the utility sink isn't big enough?

When it comes to the salon business or any business for that matter, you have to look at is as rearing a child. Would you want your child to run around and look unkempt? No, of course not—your child is prodigy of you and your family. How they dress and act falls back on you and how you raised them. At each point in your child's life, they need new shoes, clothes, haircuts. They need attention and nourishment to flourish, grow, and stay alive. Your business needs all of these things: a new look, your attention, and nourishment. Only in this case, it's a fresh coat of paint, a refinished floor, new light fixtures, a new sign for your storefront, new salon furniture and equipment. All of this investment helps you to thrill your clients, keep your talented staff, and grow your salon into a sustainable, profitable business.

Ready, Set, Go! Expert Advice!

New paint makes everything look clean and bright again. And don't forget the ceiling. Paint the trim a contrasting color. Another option: Paint a wall three different shades of the same color. Measure equal sections and use painter's masking tape to mark off each area. Do the bottom of the wall first with the darkest shade. Once it dries, do the middle section with the next lightest shade and so on. Paint can transform a tired salon without spending a ton of money.

★ Five-Point Salon Design System ★
(Point-by-Point Reassessment)
What is your plan to freshen up each area?

POINT #1: The Entrance (Doorway/Front Desk/Waiting Area)

POINT #2: The Store Inside Your Salon (Retail Area)

POINT #3: Your Bread & Butter (Service Area)

POINT #4: Let Your Color Shine (Color & Dispensary Area)

POINT #5: Behind the Scenes (Utility Area)

CHAPTER 24

Time to Remodel

"The road to success is always under construction."

—Lily Tomlin

When you're in the retail salon business the question you always have to ask yourself is, "When is the right time to remodel?" Timing is everything, but picking the right time is not that easy. You may have had some things holding you back:

- Economic conditions.
- College expenses for your children
- SBA loan payments

On average, Internet retailers change their look one or more times every year. According to the WWD/DNR Specialty Stores newsletter referenced on retailers.com, "A good rule of thumb for specialty retailers, is a major facelift every five to seven years to keep your store brand fresh and distinctive." This is a good standard for fashion-focused businesses like salons.

The WWD/DNR Specialty Stores Newsletter also states that with remodels, "You can plan on spending $20–$50 a square foot, and a month's time, for a project that includes floor coverings, paint, and new fixtures."

Salon fixtures can take as long as eight to 14 weeks alone for delivery. "That can climb to $90 a square foot, and two-to-four months of construction for a complete, top-to-bottom redo," according to the WWD/DNR Specialty Stores Newsletter referenced at retailers.com. Here are two examples that will be quite easy to follow based on the numbers above:

Remodel (Construction, Paint, Furniture/Equipment)	Salon Square Footage	Price/Square Foot	Total Remodel Cost
Salon Remodel #1	1150	$20/Square Foot	1150 X $20 = $23,000
Salon Remodel #2	2300	$50/Square Foot	2300 X $50 = $115,000

Using your square footage (see your lease agreement), you should be able to get an overall price and budget based on the extent of your remodel.

The retailers.com article continues with some additional information that's important for the decision making and budgeting of a salon remodel. "The investment can pay off. The newsletter cites a Deloitte & Touche survey which found sales increases averaging 17 percent for a full remodel—with some stores reporting gains of 40 percent or more—and closer to 10 percent for partial remodels. In planning the job, it's suggested that you shoot for recouping your investment in two to three years' time."

While the thought of investing in a remodel can be overwhelming, don't let your fears get the best of you. If things are slow, use this time to focus on your salon remodel and a new image for your salon business. Perhaps you bought this book because you were already considering a remodel of your current salon. Or, you may revisit this chapter once your salon has been open for a few years and is in need of a new look, image, or décor.

Remodel Your Salon & Change Your Image

Over time everything deteriorates. The building you are in may need upgrades. The services you offer may need additions. Your décor choices from five years ago were hip and cool. Now, they are tired and out of fashion.

The marketing of your salon, the budgeting process, and how you manage customers and staff has to adapt for business survival. You can't expect your business to strive and do well without changing yourself.

The current appearance of your salon may look dated, maybe even dirty to your clients and your staff. You may cut and color hair according to the current styles and fashions. But, your salon is more than that. It's a "place" that should keep evolving too, just like the fashion and beauty industry. In fact, your salon must evolve or it will die a slow death as it becomes tired and outdated. You salon is about a lot more than just the hair. What does it say to you when a place of business is in shambles? Given the focus on image and appearance in the fashion and beauty industry, there is nothing worse than salon that looks like it is tired and falling apart. Chips or delamination on your front desk and styling stations are definite signs of wear that need to be fixed. Your walls and floors may have chips, dings, dents, scratches, and scuffs, making your salon appear run down and neglected. Even if you keep it clean, it will still look like it's in need of maintenance and repairs.

Showing wear is one thing; but, it's about style too. What's hot today is not hot tomorrow. Your choices in furniture, colors, lighting fixtures, finishes, etc. may not be "in" anymore. No one knows what the latest trends will be five years from now. Hair and fashion trends change quickly. In order to be successful, you must continually assess the salon's décor and ask yourself questions like the following:

• Is it time to move away from the style of furniture that you selected?

• What colors are gaining popularity in home décor magazines?

- Has your flooring stood up to the test of time? What's becoming the new flooring of choice?

- Are your lighting fixtures or their finishes becoming outdated?

Guess what happens when your clients and your staff aren't happy with the condition of your salon? That's right, they find someplace else to go or look for other employment opportunities. Once your salon reaches the point of no return, it may be too late for a quick, inexpensive rehab. The longer you wait to make changes, the more it will cost you in construction and improvements to catch up to your competition. So, ask yourself:

- What do you like most about your as it salon currently looks/functions?

- What do you dislike about your salon as it currently looks/functions?

- Are you happy with the flow?

- Are there areas that are cramped?

- Are there areas that are impeding service, sales, or revenue opportunities?

- Has your client demographic changed? Are you looking to change your style to better match your clientele and a niche that has developed since you first opened your business?

- Are you remodeling on a "tight" budget?

- Are you planning a "big" remodel?

As you know, there are different levels of "remodeling" that have differing budgets and might involve the following types of changes:

- **Design or layout/floor plan**—Look at your current salon. Does something in the original layout feel like it just isn't working? For example, the styling area or the color area may not be what you expected and the space may feel too closed off, the waiting area is too cramped, the shampoo area is too tight, etc.

- **Appearance/décor**—After a while, you'll start to notice the dings, scratches, and scuffs. You'll want to take care of these right away and bring your décor up to the current trends. If you can, switch up the color palette to go along with what you are seeing in future stores and home décor magazines. Changes might include painting, new accessories, new light fixtures, new towels, new pictures, adding molding, changing the ceiling tiles, etc. Or, the salon might just need a deep cleaning.

- **Functional**—When you discover that your current salon impedes workflow and is disruptive to providing services, then you definitely need to look at some changes. Sometimes some simple rearranging can do the trick, but sometimes you need to work in a "mini" construction project to get things working better for you and your staff. Take down a wall—opening a room you're not using dramatically changes the look of your salon. Open space is in. People want to see what is going on in your salon. Coloring behind closed doors is out.

- **Focus**—As trends change, you might need to change the focus of the salon. For example, a salon that is big on hair color services really should have a color bar or lab. If your color services are booming, explore whether it's time to showcase those services even more and think about the space and how to rearrange or rebuild to get the results that you want.

- **Rearrangement**—This can be as simple as moving things around to create a sense of interest. Retail displays that are on wheels can make it easy to do some simple rearranging. But, maybe it's a matter of changing shelves or moving some of your "more mobile" service stations to different areas.

- **Replacement**—Take a look at what needs to be replaced. Lighting, flooring, fixtures, furniture, equipment, etc. If it's looking worn out, then it's time to replace it.

- **Expansion**—When you want to add more services and increase your staff, you'll have to look at expanding your salon. Of course, the most affordable way to do this is to keep your existing space pretty much intact, but just add on. But, if this will put the integrity of the floor plan at risk for awkward flow or poor sightlines, then we would recommend a full remodel. If your existing furniture and equipment is in good shape, you might be able to just add on to what you already have. If it's worn out, then you should work with the furniture/equipment company on any buy back options or list your items on Craigslist or another online site to at least get something to go toward your new purchases.

Describe Your Remodel Project

What changes do you want to make and why are they important to the success of your business?

Changes	Specifically, this change involves . . .	This change will help the success of my business by . . .
Design or layout/floor plan		
Appearance/décor		
Functional		
Focus		
Rearrangement		

Changes	Specifically, this change involves . . .	This change will help the success of my business by . . .
Replacement		
Expansion		

Remodel Considerations

Now that you have described what you'd like to do for your remodel, take a moment to review these questions. This section lays out the foundation and factors that will influence how much to spend on your build-out, décor, and/or new salon furniture/equipment.

BUDGET	
• What is your budget? • What is the overall financial impact of the remodel? • How do you figure out what you want to spend? • How do you set an appropriate budget?	We all want the best of everything, but most of us have champagne tastes with a beer budget. Your list of needs and wants may exceed your ability to foot the bill. While the cost of the renovation will vary due to many different things, like how extensive the remodel is and what type of furniture and equipment you choose, you still have to establish a budget. Deciding on your budget is based on some critical information. Generally, it depends on your demographics, how much you charge for services, and what type of clients your salon attracts. You also need to know what you can afford as a monthly payment if financing is needed. You should factor in what you have put aside in cash for the project.
COST	
• How much will it cost? • How much will it cost to move a wall, rip out the old floor, and buy all new furniture and equipment? • What should you expect to spend?	Breaking it down to the simplest terms, the cost is a function of the materials you will need for your build-out, the duration (number of days) that the salon will be closed, the labor for the contractors to complete the work, and the new equipment you will be purchasing.

ROI (Return on Investment)	
• How long should you expect to take before all this pays you back? • How can you maximize your return on investment? • How do you know if your investment is going to pay off? • How long will it take to recoup your remodeling dollars? • Are there any tax benefits if I lease the new equipment?	There is a particular rule of thumb for return on investment in remodeling your salon business. Statistics show that normally you can expect an increase of business of about 20 percent in the first year of your remodel. This increase would come from new clients that have never visited your salon before the remodel. Your current staff and existing clients will have the benefit of working at and visiting the hottest salon in the area. The fact that you are keeping your current clientele and not losing staff to competitors down the street is a big factor that must weigh in when you calculate your overall return on investment.

What's Your Budget?

There are many ways to change a look of a salon. The cost does not have to be in the tens of thousands. Whether your budget is $1,000, $20,000, or $100,000, most changes will significantly increase business within the first year of the remodel. Keep in mind that the changes you make will keep your salon looking fresh and ahead of your competition. Your clients will appreciate it and so will your staff.

Next, we'll walk you through two different "remodel" scenarios:

- Remodeling Your Salon on a Tight Budget
- Renovating Your Salon – A "Big" Remodel

Remodeling Your Salon on a Tight Budget

If you are working on a tight budget, then most of your efforts will be around freshening up what you already have. It will involve some basic and easy tasks, such as cleaning, which you can do on your own and with your staff; or, you can hire a commercial cleaning service. Other changes that can still be done affordably involve replacing and/or painting ceiling tiles and repainting the walls and trim. Again, you can do this on your own to really save money or you can hire a commercial painting service to get the job done. Most of the work for these types of changes can be done before or after hours or on days when the salon is normally closed. Let's review the most affordable "remodeling" options for a tight budget that are a quick "fix me up" alternative or "makeover."

Remodeling Options for a Tight Budget

1. Mr. Clean

The best way to make your salon look fresh and give it a new look is with a deep clean. Roll up your sleeves and put on a fresh set of gloves and get down to business or hire a commercial cleaning service. We suggest that you periodically hire a commercial cleaning service—whether it's once or twice a year or even once a quarter. They will get into every corner of your business and wipe away years of grime. This will give your salon a fresh appearance that your customer will notice. Plus, a nice fresh floor waxing will make any salon look new.

- Check out your walls do they need paint?
- Check out your bathroom is your vanity tired and your toilet seat loose and lost its luster?
- Does your ceiling tiles have stains and do they need a cleaning
- Is your air conditioning vents dirty and stained
- Does your floor need to be re -grouted or a deep cleaning
- Do you lights need to be changed or replaced
- Does the chrome on your styling chairs need to be shined are they pitted?
- Does your front desk need an overhaul?
- Does your entrance door need a coat of paint?

2. It's a "Bright" Light

Replace every bulb in your salon. Light levels in bulbs and florescent bulbs tend to be less bright or give off a brownish glare after a couple of years. Changing your bulbs will brighten up the way everything in your salon looks. Light brings life! For more information, go to: A Bright Idea – Salon Lighting.

3. Bring in New Products

Changing your salon doesn't always have to be with a paint brush and a hammer. By bringing in new products, you are showing your customers you are committed to the beauty industry by introducing them to cutting-edge beauty products. You may have to add some new displays or shelving to showcase your new product line.

4. Look Up

If your ceiling is dirty or has water stains, either give it a coat of paint or change out the stained ceiling tiles. The worst thing in the salon business is when you are getting your hair shampooed and you look up and see a water-stained ceiling. This is a sign of true neglect in a salon. For more information, go to: Look Up Salon Ceilings.

5. Your "Door" to Success

The first and last thing your staff and clients see when walking into your salon is your front door. Your front door should always be clean. If it is wood, give it a fresh coat of paint. If it's full glass, you may want to put your name, logo, and hours on the door. This is an inexpensive way to make a noticeable change. For more information, go to: Point #1-The Entrance (Doorway/Front Desk/ Waiting Area).

Remodeling Options for a Tight Budget

6. Painting

What is the one thing that can instantly and affordably change the look and appearance of your salon once it is done? The answer is new, fresh paint. The best part about painting is that you don't always have to hire a professional to do the work. Most of us are capable of painting. It's usually easy to find family, friends, and maybe a few employees to assist with the project.

Consider changing the colors. Changing the color will give you and your clients the greatest sense of immediate change and satisfaction. For more information, go to: If the Walls Could Talk.

---

7. Re-Accessorize

Your theme when you opened may have been the beach look or the sleek South beach Miami look. Your salon can change without you doing and or spending a lot of money. Like a new dress or pair of shoes in your wardrobe it may be time to re-accessorize. Have some fun with this ask your staff, family, friends, and clients; and, with their help, come up with a new theme. You can find almost anything online or in a second hand furniture store. Why not roll out a new look with a few fun items.

Managing Your Budget-Friendly Project

Even smaller projects need to be managed to get the results that you expect and the return on your investment.

Step 1. Establish your budget and timeline (see chart that follows).

Step 2. Secure help from staff and/or contractors.

- If you will pay your staff an hourly rate for the project, let them know how much.

- Let staff and/or contractors know the hours when the project will be performed and the timeline for completing the project.

- Get contractor quotes (if applicable). For more information, go to: Working with Contractors.

Step 3. Manage your staff/contractors and results of the project.

Affordable Remodel Options	Description of what needs to be done . . .	Timeline (incl. which days of the week and specific hours)	Cost of Materials/ Supplies	Labor Costs/ Contractor Fees
Cleaning				
Lighting				
New Product Line				
Ceilings				
Walls				
Doorway/ Entrance				
Accessories				
		Totals		

Renovating Your Salon – A "Big" Remodel

A big remodel will mimic the original build out of your salon. Over the next several pages, you will find helpful guides for each of the steps (below) so that you can manage your remodel project. Running a project like this while your store is open for business can be tricky. We'll give you sample timelines that have minimal impact on your salon's operating hours and help you juggle permit requirements and the work of multiple contractors.

Step 1. Establish your budget and overall timeline (start/finish dates).

Step 2. Hire a designer/architect to draw up floor plan and blueprints.

Step 3. Get contractor quotes (if applicable).

Step 4. Inform your clients.

Step 5. Get permits (if applicable).

Step 6. Schedule the work.

Step 7. Clear the area to be remodeled.

Step 8. Complete the work.

Step 1. Establish your budget and overall timeline (start/finish dates).

Following is a spreadsheet with a sample of some of the types of costs you may incur for your remodel. By completing it, you'll get a full break down of the costs for what you want to do. It is a good guideline to start seeing how much money you can expect to spend and whether you can afford to do everything that you've identified in the remodeling project.

Remodel Budget Worksheet

Construction Break Down			Furniture/Equipment Break Down		
	Materials Cost	Labor/ Installation Costs		Furniture/ EquipmentCosts	Labor/ Installation Costs
Plumbing			Styling chairs		
Electrical			Dryer chairs		
Drywall			Shampoo units		
Painting			Shampoo cabinet		
Flooring			Pedicure chairs		
Construction demolition			Manicure stations		
Signage			Stools		
Telephone			Styling stations		
Computer			Color stations		
Window treatment			Color chairs		
Furniture installation			Dispensary		
Furniture demolition			Color lab		
Architect's plans			Makeup unit		
Permits			Reception desk		
Other			Reception furniture		
Other			Retail displays		
Totals			Totals		

Desired Start Date: _____

Desired Finish Date: _____

Contractors	Rates*	Installation Costs
Plumbers	$30–$75 per hour	Usually will give a quote on the entire project. They may work by the hour if it is a simple project.
Electricians	$65–$85 per hour	• Standard outlet (120 volt) = $100 each • Heavy-duty outlets (220-240 volts) = $100 each • Heavy-duty outlets (220-240 volts) = $100 each • Grounded outlets = $120 each • New circuit in electrical panel = $185 each • Upgrading electrical panel (adding circuit, running conduit, installing receptacle) = $650
Drywallers	$20–$30 per hour	Usually will give price on the entire sheetrock taping project. The contractor also should arrange this service
Painters	$15–$20 per hour	Painters usually will give you a price per job. They may work by the day price or by the hour if its not a big project.
General Contractors	$150–$300 per day	General contractors work by the entire project. Their pay per day can vary based on the magnitude of the project.
Flooring Installers	$15–$30 per hour	Flooring installers get paid by the job. It may be arranged through the place you by the floor or your contractor. They work on a price per square foot.

*Before/After Hours & Weekend Rates May Be Higher

Furniture / Equipment	Installation Time	Installation Rates*
Wall sink (cabinet installed by others)	1½ hours, including mounting the bracket	$100/unit
Freestanding backwash sink	4 hours on average with bolting the unit to the floor	$250/unit
Pedicure Unit	3 hours to install and assemble	$250/unit
Color lab sink or dispensary sink	1½ hours to install	$175/sink
Facial room sink installation	1½ hours to install	$150/sink
Bathroom fixture installation	Usually 1/2 day if it is a toilet and double vanity.	$400

*These prices do not reflect any changes in your plumbing, such as adding another sink or moving all the hot and cold water lines over to accommodate another sink unit.

Overall Timeline

A "big" remodel can be done over a four-to-five day period, closing either late Friday or Saturday afternoon and opening up on Thursday for business. All you need is good coordination and good subcontractors who are committed to getting your project done and your salon reopened in a timely manner.

Jon Lori Salon in Fair Haven, New Jersey did a complete facelift over a four-day period. The installation crew worked until 2:00 a.m. the day they reopened. A cleaning crew came in at 3:00 a.m. and they were finished and ready to reopen by 9:00 a.m. The secret was hard work and dedication from everyone involved.

STEP 2. Hire a designer/architect to draw up floor plan and blueprints.

To find out the costs of this endeavor, we recommend you bring in a specialist in the industry. Several companies specialize in salon layouts and salon furniture. They need to come to the salon, see what you want to change, and discuss the look you want to create. You will pay a design fee; but, if you are doing a complete makeover, we highly recommend it. They have the expertise and can give you advice on prioritizing your remodeling steps.

STEP 3. Get contractor quotes (if applicable).

For extensive changes/reconstruction, you will need to hire contractors. But, every situation is different and it depends on how much remodeling you want to do. If you are just replacing the salon furniture, your installation/labor costs should be minimal. You may only want to paint and change the floor. For this type of work, you may not need a general contractor, but just one or two contractors that you hire independently for the work. How do you know they are charging a fair price? We always recommend the following steps to assess costs:

1. Bring in a contractor and get a complete price on everything you want to do.

2. Bring in separate subcontractors: a plumber, electrician, floor specialist, and a drywall team to get separate prices on your projects. Our rule of thumb is to bring in two to three tradesmen from the same field and have them bid on the same work. Have a complete checklist to hand to them for the bid. Let them know that it might be weekend work or in the evenings, so that they price it accordingly. There may be a crew of two to three or just one. Get a complete price without the hourly breakdown. There are always some unforeseen situations and having a package deal is in your favor.

3. Compare bids. If you have three bids and two are about the same and one is considerably lower, you should be concerned. You may want to choose the lowest bidding contractor, but, be careful! They either did not include something or did not charge enough for labor. The contractor might be the type that is spread very thin so your remodel will not be finished in a timely fashion. We would also check their references and recent work. See if they finished on time and on budget.

For more information, go to: Working with Contractors.

Step 4. Inform your clients.

Put up a sign well in advance to let your clients know that you are closing for remodeling. It is also good to show the new design and some of the new furniture on a presentation board; this will excite the clients and staff. Several of your staff will give their opinion on the furniture, their likes and dislikes. Be diplomatic, but remember, this is your business and it's what YOU want to do. Book your last appointment early Saturday afternoon and have your staff ready.

Step 5. Get permits (if applicable).

If your salon is in operation, it is important to coordinate the remodel so you don't lose any business. If the job is large and permits are needed for the renovation, it is recommended that you do your remodel in stages.

For example, in changing your shampoo sinks, you need to pull out the old shampoo unit and cabinets, change the plumbing pipes, and install the new units. It is usually a two-day process. Once it's all done, then it's time to call the plumbing inspector in your city for inspection. Hopefully the inspector will pass the plumbing work. If not, you can't use the sinks and won't be able to open until it is satisfactory to the inspector and is compliant to all county or city codes. That is just one inspection! What if you are trying to coordinate several inspections? It is a very difficult task. In this case, you are hiring a general contractor and it's his responsibility to make sure everything is done on time. The key is to tell him your priorities and let him coordinate these tasks with his subcontractors. Timing is everything.

Step 6. Schedule the work.

Hopefully, you decided to consult a professional in the industry to help guide you with the layout and installation of any new furniture and equipment. Just before the work begins, we recommend a group meeting with all the subcontractors and your designer. Have all of the drawings and specifications on hand for all to review and ask questions. Coordinate a schedule so everyone is on the same path and understands. When possible, having the furniture and/or equipment on location is helpful so that everyone can see exactly what is involved. We've also included some sample schedules for projects that include plumbing and electrical. And, some tips for scheduling in projects that involve drywall work.

Plumbing Work – The Process	Schedule
Working on the shampoo area? Without shampoo sinks, your salon cannot function. You have to be efficient and work with a structured timeline for any makeovers or remodels to this area because without this department, your salon cannot reopen. For work in this area, it is important to have all of your furniture on-hand or have your equipment supplier deliver for Saturday evening or Sunday morning. You probably will pay a premium for this service. First, you must tear out the old cabinets and sink units. If you are remodeling the dispensary and any pedicure units, all of this must be taken out as well. Then, the installation begins. Use the schedule at the right to plan any plumbing work.	*(Close Saturday night, reopen Tuesday morning)* 1. On Friday, call for a plumbing inspection with the city or county for Monday afternoon. 2. On Friday, deliver all new furniture concerning plumbing. If you don't have the room, pay a premium to get it delivered on Sunday morning. It depends on your salon space. 3. On Saturday—early evening—demolish all plumbing needed for the change. 4. On Sunday morning, bring in your cabinet company to install all furniture concerning plumbing. 5. Mid-Sunday morning, have your plumber come in and start prep work on all plumbing fixtures. 6. By noon Monday, the plumber finishes and you should be ready for the inspector. 7. By Tuesday morning, you will have passed inspection and reopened.

Example installation times:

Three-sink shampoo cabinet	4 hours
Hook Up Sinks	1-3 hours/ each sink*

* A freestanding sink unit and chair usually takes the longest. They must be bolted to the floor securely, which is the responsibility of the plumber. If he is a "one-man band," it could take a day and a half to secure and install three units, so be prepared.

Electrical Work – The Process	Schedule
If you don't plan your electric properly, you will have circuit breakers tripping when stylists are in the middle of providing services to their clients. You can only run so many appliances on one circuit before it overloads and trips.	*(Close Saturday night, reopen Tuesday morning)*

Electrical Work – The Process

If you don't plan your electric properly, you will have circuit breakers tripping when stylists are in the middle of providing services to their clients. You can only run so many appliances on one circuit before it overloads and trips.

To avoid this problem, bring in an electrician and ask for advice. If you are changing the styling stations, show him the new design. In many cases, the electrical may be in the wrong spot and has to be moved.

Ask your salon design specialist to lay out your new stations with the current electrical setup in mind. You might not have to make any changes if you can work with what is already there and how it is currently wired.

Unless the salon owner is knowledgeable in electrical systems, the installation of outlets is not to be considered a "Do-it-Yourself" project. This is particularly true if new circuits need to be added to the fuse panel. Traditionally, installation is done by a professionally licensed electrician.

Schedule

(Close Saturday night, reopen Tuesday morning)

Note: We recommend you close on Saturday because of the unusual amount of electrical work and coordination for this process.

1. On Friday, call for inspection for Monday afternoon.
2. If possible, deliver all furniture that requires electrical work for inspection on Friday. If there is no room in the salon for this, have it delivered on Saturday.
3. Friday evening, demolish all old cabinets and furniture concerning electric.
4. Start installing furniture Saturday and finish either that day or Sunday.
5. Electrician comes in Saturday afternoon to start working and to make sure he has the right supplies to handle the job.
6. Electrician works on all new connections, moving whatever electrical is needed and reconnects all outlets.
7. Work is finished by noon Monday and inspector approves and signs off on permits.
8. Open on Tuesday.

Drywall Work – The Process

The work may get done after hours when the salon is closed or during a few hours every evening. It all depends on how extensive the work is. Two things you must be aware of concerning permits when working on partitions or building rooms:

1. The room or partition can only be built on one side and cannot be closed until you have approval from the framing inspector.
2. If there is any electrical or plumbing going in the wall, you will need a "rough" inspection before you close up the other side.

Once these inspections are approved, you can close up the wall and finish the room or partition. This just needs to be coordinated. You might be able to handle all of this while you are open—it all depends on the scope of the work. Discuss this with your contractor to strategize the best approach. Normally, the sheetrock crew comes in after all electric and plumbing is finished and the inspectors have approved their work. The contractor's sheetrock team usually operates around the schedule of all the other subcontractors. They move quickly, but tend to leave a mess behind them.

Timing is everything when you are moving walls. There really isn't a schedule to follow because each salon is different. Rely on your contractors to make sure that he organizers this type of work based on the days that you can rearrange schedules or close early. Sundays or Mondays usually are the best.

Step 7. Clear the area to be remodeled.

In order for the contractors to complete the project, they'll need the work area cleared. If you are replacing work stations, then the furniture will need to be emptied:

1. Have boxes for each staff member to clean out their station. Have them bring the box home or store it somewhere on the premises out of the way.

2. Have the front desk team do the same process and clean out the front desk. Also, mark the boxes for all your retail and try to keep it organized for restocking the shelves.

While your staff members pack up their stations, bring in your computer person to unhook and pack your credit card processor and computer system so they can reinstall it when ready and not misplace any cables or wires.

Step 8. Complete the project.

1. Tear out all unwanted furniture, cabinets, chairs, pedicure units—whatever you are remodeling—and have your salon furniture company or "buyers" pick it up.* Try to clear the space as much as possible so your installers or contractors are not tripping over each other.

2. For the tear-out, your electrician and plumber will need to be there to unhook the existing sinks and any existing electrical that may be attached to the old cabinets.

3. Your plumber and electrician will start modifying plumbing or electrical for the new equipment.

4. At the same time, bring in all of the new furniture for assembly/installation. Try to work on any assembly of furniture items in places that are not in the way of the plumber or electrician.

5. Coordinate with the subcontractors on hooking everything up.

6. Once everything is installed, call your staff to set up their stations or department.

7. Call your computer person to hook up your system and credit card terminal.

8. As everything is being set up, you can finish any light assembly work, such as building the styling chairs or dryer chairs. These items are very simple to put together.

9. Set up your retail, clean the salon, and get ready to open in the morning.

*See the pricing chart that follows for pricing your used furniture.

Selling Your Old Furniture & Equipment

Your old furniture and equipment may have some value. You may be able to work out a trade-in deal with the salon furniture and equipment company to help offset the cost of your new furniture. If not, try selling it yourself by putting ads on Craigslist.com or eBay classifieds. Get rid of it at any price. If you don't trade it in or sell it, you need to haul it away and that will cost hundreds of dollars.

Recommended Selling Prices for Used Furniture

The prices in the following chart are meant to be guidelines for you; prices for used furniture and equipment can vary widely. Remember, you are giving interested buyers a good price as long as they are willing to pick up the furniture on your schedule and timeline.

Item	Price Range
Styling chairs (depending on make, model, and condition)	$25–50
Dryer chair	$35–50
Reception desk - small (4 to 5 foot)	$50–100
Reception desk – large	$100–500
Shampoo sinks (plastic or fiberglass)	$25
Shampoo sinks (marble/porcelain)	$50–75
Shampoo chairs	$25
Freestanding sink units	$50–100
Freestanding sink units (European or were expensive when new)	$100–300
Styling stations (simple)	$10–25
Styling stations (freestanding/custom units)	$50–200
Nail tables	$25–50
Nail stools	$10
Pedicure unit (base model)	$50–100
Pedicure unit (motorized unit)	$250–500
Facial tables (standard style)	$25–75
Facial tables (hydraulic or electric style)	$100–500
Skin care unit	$100–300
Reception chairs	$10–50
Retail units	$25–300
Mirrors	$10–25
Dispensary cabinets	Anything!

Remodeling Project Checklist

Things to remember when starting your remodeling project:

○ Let customers know about what's going on and what to expect.

○ If you have a plan for a new design and layout, frame and display it for all to see.

○ Plan for delays. Murphy's Law may or may not strike your salon remodel project, but anticipate delays.

○ If money is needed from your banker, work out all details before you think about starting your remodel project.

○ Box all things that may be in the way of contractors and furniture/equipment installers.

○ Plan all of your clients' appointments around work schedules.

○ Plan that major construction or your new equipment install during the evening or when you are closed over the weekend.

Ready, Set, Go! Expert Advice!

General Remodeling Tips

• Be creative. There are often multiple solutions to accomplish a design objective, with some being more expensive than others. Discuss various options with your contractor and make clear what your budget is.

• If all the rooms in the salon really need a makeover, then make the most of changes with paint, as opposed to structural changes. Changing the color of a room can revitalize it. This is the easiest way to stay on budget and bring new life to a salon.

• Heavy or textured wallpaper can work wonders as well. You can save money by wallpapering a slightly damaged wall rather than replacing it. If the wall has grasscloth wallpaper on it, consider whitewashing it for a totally new look. Several layers of whitewash (in various shades of white) produce a clean, sophisticated look in any room.

• Faux finish painting or other textured decorative painting techniques can hide minor damage or irregularities that flat paint won't. If you're moving a wall or taking out a styling station no longer needed, try this approach.

Salon Owners Talk About . . .
the Good, the Bad, and the Ugly

"The best part of remodeling the salon I bought from my former employer was now having the ability to add what I felt would make the salon "me!" I wanted my customers to feel welcome and comfortable. I wanted a salon that I could call home and be proud of. When I was finished with my remodel, that's exactly how it was. My customers are happy and so am I. The worst part was realizing I had to get rid of nails. I needed the room for my hair business. The person I had to let go was a friend and colleague. I know a lot about hair and color, that is my passion. I knew nothing about nails. I had to let it go."

—Sue Gahr, Owner of Studio 2 Hair Salon, Point Pleasant, NJ

"The worst thing I did was not have a budget. What started as a small remodel turned into a three-month project. My budget was blown, and because I didn't plan well, it cost me a fortune with my contractor. Plan, budget, and put a timeline together. Without that, don't do it. Plus, I had no idea custom equipment could take as long as 10 to 12 weeks to get made. That killed me."

—Liz Howell, Get It Together Hair and Nail Salon, Houston, TX

PART V

APPENDICES

New Salon Checklist

◯ Define your business plan (Goal setting, clientele, demographics, etc.).

◯ Meet with your realtor.

◯ Site location with good visibility and easy access.

◯ Review preliminary lease. Is potential site zoned for a salon?

◯ Prepare estimated annual income projection.

◯ Preliminary budget plan.

◯ Preliminary design & floor plan with supplier of furnishings, architect, or designer.

◯ Design logo (designer or graphic artist).

◯ Write policies and employee manuals.

◯ Meet with your attorney to discuss setting up corporation and lease as well as items.

◯ Meet with your banker to discuss items.

◯ Meet with your accountant. Discuss purchase vs. leasing, bookkeeping vs. computer software, etc.

◯ Select furniture and color scheme.

◯ Set up delivery date for the equipment.

◯ Cash register, computer system or bookkeeping/software system.

◯ Intercom and/or music system.

◯ Finalize design and floor plan.

◯ Pick out flooring, wall coverings, lighting, accent pieces, etc.

◯ Meet with architect for complete set of plans that adhere to all city and state codes.

◯ Obtain bids for construction, usually with general contractor(s).

◯ Sign lease, order furnishings, and hire contractor(s).

◯ Arrange for electric, gas, water, phone service/internet provider and trash removal.

○ Plan opening date (make allowances for any delays).

○ Order dispensary and retail supplies and products.

○ Plan opening advertising (Yellow Pages, Internet listings, Facebook, local newspapers, direct mail, etc.).

○ Order magazines for customers.

○ Design and order outside sign in compliance with lease.

○ Order towels for shampoo area (special colors).

○ Price list on "Menu" of services.

○ Design customer sales tickets & service record files.

○ Order appointment cards, business cards, stamps and pads, stationary and envelopes.

○ Interview potential employees.

○ Set up payroll company.

○ Order plants or plant service and outside doormats if applicable.

○ Order washer and dryer and laundry supplies or arrange for towel service.

○ Arrange for credit card charge plate machine or Merchant Processing with your bank.

○ Arrange for vending machines if applicable.

○ Purchase bookkeeping record books, appointment book, pencils, pens, and stapler.

○ Purchase first aid kit, fire extinguisher, toilet paper, and paper towel dispenser for restroom.

○ Purchase file cabinet, file folders, vacuum cleaner, and brooms/dust pans.

○ Purchase coffee bar supplies or arrange for coffee service.

○ Purchase ashtrays, waste baskets, cleaning supplies, or arrange for cleaning service.

○ Plan Grand Opening; usually 30 days after opening.

○ Arrange for all inspections.

○ Ongoing advertising, promotions, and employee training.

Timeline

One Year (or more) Before Opening

- Look at the pros and cons of owning and operating your own salon
- Decide if you are ready
- Take the entrepreneurial self-test
- Will you buy an existing salon or start your own?
- Decide if you will rent booths

BUYING AN EXISTING SALON

- Remodeling an existing salon
- The first step
- Designer/Architect contractors
- Create a spreadsheet
- Budget
- Pick out furniture
- Ceiling tiles
- Permits
- Priorities—plumbing
- Hiring the subcontractors
- Permits—plumbing
- Priorities—electric
- Permits—electric
- Permits—drywall
- A transformation weekend

STARTING A NEW SALON

- Estimate the expenses, including one-time costs
- Decide on computers and software for your salon

- Choose a business phone system
- Choose a business structure
- Hire a lawyer
- Hire a bookkeeper or accountant
- Work on your new business checklists: business plan, incorporation, etc.
- Write a mission statement
- Write your employee manual (capture your codes)
- Decide if you will hire a commercial cleaning company or if you and your staff will clean the salon
- Name your salon
- Gather/apply for:
    - EIN (Employer Identification Number)
    - Articles of Incorporation
    - Resolution
    - Identification
    - Initial deposit
- Set up your business checking account
- Pick a credit card processor
- Pick a location for your new salon
- Negotiate your lease
- Obtain licenses and permits
    - Business operation license
    - Certificate of Occupancy
    - License to sell retail
    - Federal Employer Identification Number (EIN)
    - Fire department permit
    - Building permits
    - Cosmetology license
- Design and space-plan your salon
    - Price your salon furniture
    - Furnishing your retail area
    - Used furniture
- Choose beauty products to sell
- Obtain business insurance
- Choose a contractor and architect
- Choose the colors for your salon
- Plan your signage

- Decide about gift cards and online gift certificates
- Menu design, price point, and layout
  - Professional designers
  - Cover and logo
  - Shape, size, and color
  - Menus and real estate
  - Who designs the services?
  - Menu and Web site
  - Focus on your stars
  - Pricing
  - Costs and how much to print
- Web presence and social marketing: choose which social media outlets you will use, including blogs, and who will update them
- Complete the startup expense worksheet
- Fine-tune your plan
- Secure startup funds

WITHIN SIX MONTHS OF OPENING

- Plan salon promotions and loyalty programs
- Discreetly begin the hiring process

WITHIN THREE MONTHS OF OPENING

- Arrange for salon promotions and loyalty programs (negotiate with vendors, decide if you need loyalty cards, etc.)

WITHIN ONE MONTH OF OPENING

- Train staff on computer software and hardware

WITHIN TWO OR THREE WEEKS OF OPENING

- The controversial exit
- Preparing for the open house

AFTER OPENING

- Successful retail in year one
- Surviving the first year—what to expect and how to adjust
- Build your business to sell
- Moving your salon

Index

Works Cited

Bachner, John. "National Lighting Bureau." *National Lighting Bureau.* N.p., n.d. Web. 15 Jan. 2013. <http://nlb.org>.

Balle, Louise . "eHow | How to Videos, Articles & More - Discover the expert in you. | eHow.com." *eHow | How to Videos, Articles & More - Discover the expert in you. | eHow. com.* N.p., n.d. Web. 30 Jan. 2013. <http://ehow.com>.

"Backflow Prevention, Backflow Prevention, Watts." *Watts - Plumbing, Heating and Water Quality Products Manufacturer.* N.p., n.d. Web. 23 Feb. 2013. <http://www.watts.com/ backflowprevention>.

"Collins Manufacturing Company - Salon Equipment, Spa Equipment, Salon Furniture - Equipment for Salons, Spas, Barbers and Cosmetology Schools." *Collins Manufacturing Company - Salon Equipment, Spa Equipment, Salon Furniture - Equipment for Salons, Spas, Barbers and Cosmetology Schools.* N.p., n.d. Web. 30 Mar. 2013. <http://www. collinsmfgco.com>. Images used with permission.

"Freestyle Systems-Weightless Blow Drying System." *Freestyle Systems-Weightless Blow Drying System.* N.p., n.d. Web. 4 Dec. 2012. <http://www.freestylesystems.com/>.

"Feng Shui Wealth | The Red Lotus Letter | Kathryn Weber." *Feng Shui Wealth | The Red Lotus Letter | Kathryn Weber.* N.p., n.d. Web. 15 Dec. 2012. <http://redlotusletter.com>.

"Hawaii's Source for Renovation Tips | Hawaii Renovation." *Hawaii's Source for Renovation Tips | Hawaii Renovation.* N.p., n.d. Web. 8 Dec. 2013. <http://hawaiirenovation. staradvertiser.com/>.

"Michigan Retailers Association | Credit Card Processing | Insurance." *Michigan Retailers Association | Credit Card Processing | Insurance.* N.p., n.d. Web. 28 Jan. 2013. <http:// Retailers.com>.

"Peter Millard Salon Lighting | LED Beauty Salon Lighting." *Peter Millard Salon Lighting | LED Beauty Salon Lighting.* N.p., n.d. Web. 27 Mar. 2013. <http://www. beautysalonlighting.com/>.

"Salon Lighting | Minardi Color Perfect Lights | Eco Green Fixtures." *Salon Lighting | Minardi Color Perfect Lights | Eco Green Fixtures.* N.p., n.d. Web. 12 Jan. 2013. <http:// www.salonlights.com/>.

"Salon, Barber and Spa Equipment | Takara Belmont - Takara Belmont USA, Inc.." *Salon, Barber and Spa Equipment | Takara Belmont – Takara Belmont USA, Inc..* N.p., n.d. Web. 7 Apr. 2013. <http://beauty.takarabelmont.com>. Images used with permission.

"Small Business Advice | Business News & Articles | AllBusiness.com." *Small Business Advice | Business News & Articles | AllBusiness.com.* N.p., n.d. Web. 2 Mar. 2013. <http://allbusiness.com>.

"The RL Mace Universal Design Institute." *The RL Mace Universal Design Institute.* N.p., n.d. Web. 10 Mar. 2013. <http://udinstitute.org>.

"Welcome to SpaTrade by American Spa | SpaTrade." *Welcome to SpaTrade by American Spa | SpaTrade.* N.p., n.d. Web. 18 Jan. 2013. <http://www.spatrade.com/>.

Zheng, Kim. "Ezines.com - The Official Ezine Authority On All Things Email Newsletters/Ezines." *Ezines.com – The Official Ezine Authority On All Things Email Newsletters/Ezines.* N.p., n.d. Web. 5 Feb. 2013. <http://ezine.com>.

"architectualdepot.com." *architectualdepot.com.* N.p., n.d. Web. 22 Feb. 2013. <http://www.architectualdepot.com>. Images used with permission.

MLA formatting by BibMe.org.

Special Thanks

Jeff and Eric would like to especially thank and acknowledge Patrick Parenty, L'Oreal, and their divisions for supporting Ready, Set, Go! and helping to make this one-of-a-kind publication a reality!

Contributors

Salon Centric, Equipment Design Professionals, saloncentric.com

Kimber by Design, Kimber L. Atkinson, facebook.com/KimberbyDesign

Image Sources & Featured Products

Salon Centric, L'Oreal Equipment Design Professionals (Pete Hornig), saloncentric.com

Takara Belmont Equipment Design Professionals, takarabelmont.com

Kaemark Salon Furnishings, kaemark.com

Kimber by Design, Kimber L. Atkinson, facebook.com/KimberbyDesign

Special Mentions

Interiors by R.G. Shakour, interiorsbyrgshakour.com

Maletti, maletti.it

Continuum Footspas, salonpedicurespas.com

Editors & Page Layout

Kelly Cobane Condron, Content Editing

Robin Krauss, Page Layout

Facebook Fans

Thank you for providing your stories and allowing us to share The Good, The Bad, & The Ugly.*

Follow Jeff Grissler & Eric David Ryant on Facebook

*Quotes, provided via Facebook or direct emails, were offered freely by salon and barbershop owners and without obligation or compensation from Ready, Set, Go! Publishing, its authors, contributors, or endorsers. Quotes used in this book follow "fair

use" practices with proper attribution given to those who submitted comments. When content is offered via a public domain, such as Facebook, it means that those posting or commenting are allowing their posts or comments to be shared, used, or accessed by people on and off of Facebook.

Business Resources

- Salon Consulting
- Design Layout and Plans
- School-Class Education
- Equipment Procurement
- Business Education
- Consulting
- Location Procurement
- Lease Negotiations

Quest Resources, Beauty, Spa, Barber Equipment Finance Specialists
  Quest makes every salon owners dream possible through creative financing options.
  www.questrs.com

Jeff Grissler, jeffgrissler@gmail.com

Eric Ryant, ericryant@gmail.com

800-449-0777

www.readysetgobooks.com

Made in the USA
San Bernardino, CA
03 January 2014